Praise

LONG ROAD

"[One of the] Best Music Books of 2022"   —*Rolling Stone*

"[The] Best Rock Biography of the Year (2022)"

—*Corbin Reiff at SPIN*

"[A] Holiday Guide for the Rock and Roll Literate"   —*Aquarian*

⚡

"Steven Hyden is a brilliant rock chronicler, whether he's writing about great bands or terrible ones. But with *Long Road*, as Eddie Vedder would say, he's unleashed a lion."   —*Rolling Stone*

"[The] best rock biography [of 2022]...Steven Hyden has all the answers [to Pearl Jam] and delivers them with the kind of wittily insightful analysis you only get from an obsessed fan and expert critic."

—*Corbin Reiff, SPIN*

"One of the most entertaining summations of what a rock band can do to one's soul whether we like to admit it or not."   —*Aquarian*

"[*Long Road* is]...clear-eyed about Pearl Jam's strengths and weaknesses but also quite personal [with] the author infusing his own memories of coming of age at a time when *Vs.* and *Vitalogy* provided the soundtrack. The book wrestles with the question of why Pearl Jam mattered—and why, to some, they still very much do."   —*Inside Hook*

"In *Long Road*, [Steven] Hyden gives almost an autobiographical history of Pearl Jam from the fan's perspective, from the early albums, to their shying away from the spotlight, [and] through their embrace of playing unforgettable live shows in front of their increasingly fanatical fanbase."

—*AllMusic*

"A comprehensive look from the perspective of a devoted (if not sometimes concerned) fan, this book is organized like Hyden's favorite Pearl Jam mixtape; chapters correspond to a specific song and then elaborate from there, taking the reader to many fascinating, surprising places that aren't well-known about the Seattle icons."

—*SPIN*

"Through smart but accessible writing full of stories, asides, opinions, and analyses, Hyden makes a compelling case for why Pearl Jam's music matters....A joyous, thought-provoking and humane series of essays."

—*Pittsburgh Post-Gazette*

"A personal approach and valuable critical companion that does a great job of contextualizing the band's various life cycles."

—Wisconsin Public Radio

"Reading *Long Road* feels as if you're in an endlessly engrossing conversation about Pearl Jam with a fellow admirer."

—*Toronto Star*

"[Hyden has] penned a thoroughly compelling book about Pearl Jam."

—*Q101* Chicago alternative radio

"[A] must-read...There is no one writing about music with more passion and intellect than Steven Hyden."

—*The Film Stage*

"A critical consideration of one of rock's most durable and inscrutable acts...A music biography well suited to fans of both the band and 1990s pop culture."

—*Kirkus Reviews*

"Steven Hyden's *Long Road* takes us well beyond the Pearl Jam story that has been rehashed for decades. He argues that the most commercially successful band of the alt-rock era is fundamentally misunderstood, and then he backs up that assertion with chapter after chapter packed with insights and fresh context. In this rock bio-as-mixtape configuration, the prose is as much impressionistic as linear, a format that suits a band that has figured out how to reinvent and improvise its way to hard-earned longevity."

—Greg Kot, *Sound Opinions* co-host

"As a die-hard and nearly lifelong Pearl Jam fan, I cannot recommend *Long Road* enough. It is an essential perspective on one of the world's greatest bands with incredibly heartfelt insight from Steven Hyden."

—Brian Fallon of The Gaslight Anthem

LONG ROAD

Also by Steven Hyden:

*This Isn't Happening: Radiohead's "Kid A" and the
Beginning of the 21st Century*

*Hard to Handle: The Life and Death of the Black
Crowes—a Memoir* (with Steve Gorman)

Twilight of the Gods: A Journey to the End of Classic Rock

*Your Favorite Band Is Killing Me: What Pop Music
Rivalries Reveal About the Meaning of Life*

LONG ROAD

PEARL JAM

AND THE SOUNDTRACK OF A GENERATION

STEVEN HYDEN

hachette
BOOKS

New York

Hachette Books
Hachette Book Group
1290 Avenue of the Americas
New York, NY 10104
HachetteBooks.com
Twitter.com/HachetteBooks
Instagram.com/HachetteBooks

First Trade Paperback Edition: October 2023

Published by Hachette Books, an imprint of Hachette Book Group, Inc. The Hachette Books name and logo are trademarks of the Hachette Book Group.

The Hachette Speakers Bureau provides a wide range of authors for speaking events. To find out more, visit hachettespeakersbureau.com or email HachetteSpeakers@hbgusa.com.

The publisher is not responsible for websites (or their content) that are not owned by the publisher.

Print book interior design by Amy Quinn

Library of Congress Cataloging-in-Publication Data

Names: Hyden, Steven, author.
Title: Long road: Pearl Jam and the sound of a generation / Steven Hyden.
Description: First edition. | New York City: Hachette Books, 2022. | Includes index.
Identifiers: LCCN 2022019040 | ISBN 9780306826429 (hardcover) |
    ISBN 9780306826436 (paperback) | ISBN 9780306826443 (ebook)
Subjects: LCSH: Pearl Jam (Musical group) | Alternative rock
    Musicians—United States. | Grunge music—United States—History and criticism.
Classification: LCC ML421.P43 H93 2022 | DDC 782.42166092/2—dc23/eng/20220419

LC record available at https://lccn.loc.gov/2022019040

ISBNs: 9780306826429 (hardcover); 9780306826436 (trade paperback);
    9780306826443 (ebook)

Printed in the United States of America

LSC-C

Printing 1, 2023

For Val, Hen, Ro, Lu, Jer, and Sylvia—the grunge band of my dreams

CONTENTS

Side B

PREFACE

As a music critic, the subject that has always interested me most is career arcs. I am particularly fascinated by bands. How do bands start and why do they end? Why do some bands crash and burn after only a few years and why do others last for decades? What are the dynamics at play between the singer and the instrumentalists? The songwriters and the non-songwriters? How are friendships and business partnerships balanced? How do you reconcile the weight of history with the constant churn of the present?

If you pay close enough attention, patterns emerge. Bands tend to rise and fall for the same reasons. Every rock band that has ever broken up has, in some way, reenacted the story of the Beatles, a phenomenon gradually undone by deteriorating interpersonal relationships, bruised egos, and unrequited artistic ambitions. The particulars of their biography are now rock clichés—the conniving business managers, the creative and emotional split between the core duo, the talented underling with a backlog of songs that he can't get on the records, the hurt feelings left unexpressed, the girlfriends, the drugs. The Beatles not only profoundly influenced the idea of becoming a band but also the idea of *unbecoming* a band.

The Rolling Stones, meanwhile, are the model for bands who decide not to break up, ever. The value of knowing your role within the band, the power of conceding that your lead singer is the benevolent dictator, the ability to manage your disappointments and resentments for the greater good of grossing hundreds of millions of dollars on the road—these are the lessons of the Stones.

There are other role models. U2 invented the idea that you can remake a European post-punk band into a stadium-filling Americana act, and then remake yourself again into a post-modern dance-rock group. This mold was adopted by scores of would-be "biggest band in the world" candidates—Coldplay, the Killers, Arcade Fire, LCD Soundsystem—in the twenty-first century. There's also the Grateful Dead, who proved you could fill stadiums by cultivating an unpredictable live show and approaching albums with bemused indifference.

And then there's Pearl Jam. What is the Pearl Jam mold? You could define it as a combination of the aforementioned rock-band molds, though the specifics beyond that are jumbled and counterintuitive. Pearl Jam has committed to going the distance like the Stones, and their singer could be described as a kind of "benevolent dictator" within their inner power structure. But Pearl Jam is also a band in which every member writes songs—even the drummer!—which gives them a degree of parity that's uncommon for a band of their stature.

Since the turn of the century, Pearl Jam has been frequently compared to the Grateful Dead, due to the thriving community of devoted fans who collect bootleg recordings and pore over the band's every onstage utterance. But the Dead for years operated on the fringes of American culture without an omnipresent radio hit—they didn't become an actual pop success until the final decade of Jerry Garcia's life, with the 1987 single "Touch of Grey," which, to the chagrin of veteran Deadheads, made them exponentially more popular. Pearl Jam, however, had tremendous radio play at the *beginning* of their career. Over the course of their first three albums, they were more like U2, in terms of mainstream ubiquity. And *then* they turned into a cult band buoyed by a passionate counterculture.

Imagine Bono evolving into Jerry Garcia. You can't. It defies logic. And yet that approximates a rough sketch of Pearl Jam's development in their first decade.

The fact is that Pearl Jam is an anomaly. Most bands start small and achieve their greatest success by their third or fourth album, after which they slowly come to rely more and more on revisiting, repackaging, and reissuing their most beloved music. But Pearl Jam became the biggest band in America within two years of forming in 1990, propelled by the monumental sales and cultural impact of one of the best-selling debut albums in history, *Ten*. And then they slowly, and deliberately, reinvented themselves, all while maintaining their level of success. Only that success—commercial and artistic—would come to be measured primarily by live shows instead of record sales and hit singles.

The result is a strange, incomparable duality—a band that plays stadiums while having almost no media profile; a mega-selling act who, for most of their history, has ignored and even antagonized corporate rock radio; a group of superstars who function like an underground act; a famous institution hiding in plain sight. Like I said, an anomaly.

The Beatles are the sixties rock band most often associated with the baby boomer generation. While they subsequently appealed to *all* generations, the Beatles come with a lore that flatters the grandiosity of the boomers—they are the *greatest* band, we're told, and have been centered in media narratives about contemporary history (like so much of boomer culture) for the better part of sixty years. Pearl Jam, the band who willingly evaded the spotlight and now feels a little overlooked in discussions about the best American rock bands, is similarly definitional for Generation X, the "middle child" demographic that is *definitely* forgotten amid the endless conversations about boomers, millennials, and Zoomers. For the people who were in their teens and twenties when Pearl Jam first emerged in the nineties, they were a band that encompassed so many of our conflicting impulses—they sought attention but deplored overexposure; they craved community but also felt suffocated by it; they wanted the security of a career but suspected that it might be corrupting; they believed in the possibility of social change but wondered if such attempts were ultimately doomed.

I'm interested in all this: Pearl Jam's utterly unique path, their unlikely survival and evolution, and how this reflects—and is shaped by—their generation and the times they have lived in. I should add that this journey down the "long road" of this band's career is personal. I have not interviewed the band members for this book, mostly because a book composed of Pearl Jam's thoughts on Pearl Jam—it's called *Pearl Jam Twenty*, and it came out in 2011—has already been written. I am also, like I said, a music critic, which means I have the annoying (though hopefully endearing!) arrogance of a know-it-all who believes he can analyze and explain a band's legacy better than the band members themselves. At the very least, I suspect I will *enjoy* analyzing and explaining Pearl Jam's legacy more than they would.

Suiting the personal nature of this project, I've organized the book like a mixtape, with each chapter corresponding to a different song. The chapters are not *only* about those songs—they are simply an entry point for discussing an aspect of this band's history. In many cases, I've chosen to focus on bootleg recordings, as I believe that what Pearl Jam has achieved onstage remains the most essential part of their work, even more than their studio albums.

I hope the mixtape structure conveys how I see this book—as a homemade act of love. As is true for all Pearl Jam fans, their music has been woven into the fabric of my life. Understanding this band is a way of comprehending my own history and, I believe, *ourselves*.

SIDE A

"Don't let anyone call you Generation X, that's bullshit. They can call you Generation Y, because you're asking questions."

—Eddie Vedder, onstage in Milwaukee in 1995

CHAPTER 1
"FALLING DOWN"

(6/20/95, Morrison, Colorado)

A Beautiful Night at Red Rocks • Robert Plant's "Enjoy Cocaine" Pants Patch from 1972 • That *Rolling Stone* 1996 Hatchet Job of Eddie Vedder • Jordan Catalano • *Reality Bites* • Douglas Coupland's *Generation X* • A Hit Song That Never Was

Matt Chamberlain, their second of five drummers, once likened playing with Pearl Jam to boxing with Mike Tyson.

Such was their extreme physicality as a live act. On early tours, they raced wildly back and forth onstage, like convicts drunk on fleeting freedom in the midst of a prison riot. Meanwhile their singer, Eddie Vedder, tempted permanent paralysis by hanging from the rafters dozens of feet above the stage, a hyperactive problem child acting out against parents powerless to stop him.

Mike Tyson's strategy was based upon intimidation; he was the baddest man in the game, and this reputation defeated his opponents before the match even began. Once in the ring, he charged quickly and with tremendous aggression, a "shock and awe" tactic design to score an early knockout. Pearl Jam in the early nineties had a similar MO, but they also had endurance. If they somehow didn't immediately overwhelm an audience, they would eventually wear them out.

But *that* Pearl Jam is no longer the band that is performing on this night at Red Rocks Amphitheater. Oh yes, Red Rocks. One of rock's great cathedrals. It's been said that the Ute tribe used to hold spiritual rituals there, decades before the theater was built in June 1941. It's long had a draw for rock bands and rock fans in search of a mind-blowing musical experience. You're in the mountains, closer to the clouds than the ground. You're already high before a note has been played or any substances— some of which are now legal in Colorado—are consumed. A special place indeed. For many, a pilgrimage to Red Rocks is a rite of passage. For a rock band, playing there is a sign that you have reached an exalted status.

But for Pearl Jam on this night, playing at Red Rocks seems like a burden. Instead of bounding out in front of the nine thousand fans standing at attention as late afternoon turns to dusk, the band members stroll out lackadaisically, one by one, each at a different pace, as if in a daze. The audience roars anyway; they are prepared to throw the hammer down. (This is signified by someone literally waving a large inflatable hammer around near the stage for some reason.)

Each member carries out a metal folding chair and places it next to the others in a semicircle near the stage's edge. Jeff Ament—the jockish bassist—sits first, holding a stand-up bass. Mike McCready—the brilliant and (for now) troubled lead guitarist—saunters up soon after, lighting a cigarette while readying his ax. Across the semicircle is the other guitarist, the band's self-appointed devil's advocate Stone Gossard, dressed in shorts that make him resemble a college RA. Behind them is Jack Irons, the band's fourth drummer, a few months shy of lodging his first full year inside the Pearl Jam circus.

Finally, there's the singer, Eddie, who is now also playing guitar. The purpose of this, presumably, is to make him seem more like "one of the guys." Which is a strange thing for the most magnetic front man of his generation to be. Being "one of the guys" does not come naturally to Eddie Vedder.

When he sits down, he actually forgets his guitar. After fetching it from a stand in front of the drum kit, he is ready to address the assembled grunge congregation.

"Get comfortable," he says, not quite invitingly. "We're going to be here for a while."

$$\bf{\it{f}}$$

Pearl Jam at this very moment is touring in support of their third consecutive multiplatinum album, *Vitalogy*. But this isn't a moment of triumph. Because Pearl Jam doesn't resemble a world-conquering rock band. Instead, they're set up onstage—to quote a song from their current hit LP—like "victims in demand for public show."

Given the setting, it is hard not to contrast this scene with U2's iconic *Under a Blood Red Sky* concert from a dozen years prior, in which Bono embraced the messianic theatrics of the rock singer handbook in a manner not dissimilar to Eddie Vedder back when Pearl Jam's 1991 debut, *Ten*, was just starting to sell. When people think of Red Rocks, they typically pull up mental images from the music video for the live version of "Sunday Bloody Sunday" included on *Under a Blood Red Sky*. The rain-soaked audience, the shadowy mountains on the horizon, those incredible flaming torches that ring the theater high above the audience. In truth, Red Rocks doesn't look *exactly* like that all the time. How many bands, upon finally having an opportunity to headline Red Rocks, have been disappointed by the absence of those *Game of Thrones*–like flaming torches?

Under a Blood Red Sky is also on Vedder's mind. During the previous night's show at Red Rocks, he introduced a prickly new song, "Habit," with a jokey nod to U2, deadpanning, "This is not a rebel song."

Other ghosts linger. Almost exactly twenty-three years earlier—on June 21, 1972—Led Zeppelin had stormed Colorado, playing about twenty miles away from Red Rocks at a sold-out Denver Coliseum. In the mid-nineties, drawing a line connecting Zeppelin to Pearl Jam would have earned scorn from boomers and Gen Xers alike—scandalizing the former on the grounds of protecting the sanctity of their precious classic-rock heroes and the latter based on the younger generation's resentment of those same inescapable FM radio warhorses.

But there are some crucial parallels between Pearl Jam and Zeppelin, starting with the incredible popularity of both bands. Going strictly by sales statistics, Pearl Jam in 1995 was actually *more* popular than Led Zeppelin in 1972. No rock band had ever sold nearly one million copies of an album in one week before Pearl Jam did it with *Vs.* in 1993. The following year, their third record, *Vitalogy*, moved nearly nine hundred thousand units in its opening week.

Ten still ranks among the best-selling albums of the era; in fact, it is one of the last mega-selling rock LPs *ever*, moving more than thirteen million units, a staggering number that seems even more astronomical the further we get from it. Popular music culture now is several decades removed from a time when it was even possible for a band like Pearl Jam to have a hit as enormous as *Ten*, an album that in the nineties went beyond being a mere phenomenon with scores of radio singles to becoming its own genre of music. *Ten* inadvertently invented dozens of other bands who also went platinum, only because people loved what Pearl Jam was doing that much.

In those years, Pearl Jam's music and influence were everywhere. Their biggest songs define the era—"Alive," "Even Flow," "Jeremy," "Daughter," "Rearviewmirror," "Better Man," "Corduroy," "Not for You." And then there's Eddie Vedder, whose fame as the most emulated rock singer in the world dwarfed his band. Vedder's decidedly unglamorous sartorial sense—brown shirt, brown corduroy jacket, dark shorts, Dr. Martens boots—inspired a fashion fad. His darkly handsome features and enigmatic personality spawned hunky antiheroes on television (like Jared Leto's Jordan Catalano on *My So-Called Life*) and film (Ethan Hawke's character in *Reality Bites*). His confrontational persona—against the music industry, vapid consumerist culture, and even his own stardom—eventually landed him on the cover of *Time* magazine, a stamp of institutional approval in the waning days of pre-internet media.

Pearl Jam responded to their unprecedented success by shutting out the media and staying off television, a policy also followed by Zeppelin in their prime. But in Zeppelin's case, this media blackout created an indelible mystique. People *liked* that they were inaccessible. They appreciated how the band members didn't seem like regular people. Zeppelin was an enigmatic canvas on to which the audience projected their fantasies. An X-rated *Lord of the Rings*.

For instance, here's an excerpt from a review of Zeppelin's Denver '72 gig, printed in a local alt-weekly:

> Lead vocalist Robert Plant, tall, built like an Olympic swimmer, with a voice like a siren is Led Zeppelin's sex symbol. Wearing blue jeans, with a jet plane patch on his arse, an "Enjoy Cocaine" patch sewed to his inner thigh, and a white crescent across his fly, he sped from one end of the stage to the other, like a wild stud in heat bucking, whirling yet with the styling grace of a professional dancer.

When Pearl Jam first broke, they also had mystique. But nobody called them bucking wild studs because rock culture had moved beyond all that overripe "sex god" stuff. In fact, rock culture had been building toward a band like Pearl Jam for some time. They were the perfect bridge act, the one group capable of marrying rock's otherwise incompatible halves—the old-world dinosaur rock deities from the sixties and seventies like Zeppelin and the Who, and the eighties indie-rock underclass that stood in opposition to Zeppelin and their brethren. They aspired to what Matt Cameron, their fifth drummer, later dubbed "punk-rock arena rock," more approachable than the typical punk band and more human than the classic-rock behemoths. A band that could be "alternative" and also sell as many records as the top pop acts. In retrospect, it was a phenomenon that could have only existed in the nineties, a decade in which the twentieth century both culminated and began to fade away.

The ways in which Pearl Jam succeeded and failed at being that bridge band defines their career, in the nineties and beyond. In the early part of the decade, they had perfect timing, turning out the kinds of songs—larger-than-life chest beaters that felt like intensely personal missives from a very relatable yet also extremely good-looking man—at the precise moment when the rock audience craved exactly that. And not only did they want Pearl Jam, they also wanted lots of bands that did the same thing Pearl Jam did except in a dumber, less insightful way.[1]

By 1995, however, fate had seemingly turned against them. Three years earlier, Pearl Jam had been the right band for the moment. But the winds had shifted. Now, they were facing a backlash fueled by the hang-ups of two different generations.

From baby boomers came the inevitable accusations that Pearl Jam was simply rehashing what *their* bands had done twenty years earlier, which meant they could never be authentic. "He is supposed to stand for being the antistar, the one who is against all this privileged treatment," *Rolling Stone* publisher Jann Wenner once said of Eddie Vedder. "Well, in my view he is just a very, very wealthy, very spoiled guy."

In 1996, Wenner's magazine published a notorious hatchet piece against Vedder, right when the band's commercial fortunes started to slip upon the release of their fourth album, *No Code*. The article was what journalists refer to as a "write-around," which is a magazine profile written without the participation of the subject. In this case, the magazine fixated on that very noninvolvement—the hostility over Vedder's anti-media hostility was palpable in every word of their cover story. *Rolling Stone* alleged that Eddie Vedder *actually* wasn't the tortured spokesman of a generation, but rather an opportunist and huckster who in high school was a popular and happy-go-lucky (here's the worst sin of all) theater kid.[2]

---

1 I'm obviously referring to "post-grunge" bands like Creed, Nickelback, and Fuel, who are mostly terrible. But this could also apply to Stone Temple Pilots, a very good and unfairly maligned band that will be discussed later in this book.

2 The most interesting takeaway from the *Rolling Stone* piece is that Vedder grew up worshipping Dustin Hoffman. Eddie once subtly acknowledged this during a 2016 concert at

The implication of the *Rolling Stone* article couldn't be clearer: *This guy isn't for real*. Never mind that Wenner had made his magazine's fortune on the backs of other "frauds" from his own generation. Free-spirited Woody Guthrie acolyte Bob Dylan was really just a nice Jewish boy from Minnesota named Robert Zimmerman. Blues-rock sex god Mick Jagger was a former economics student. Working-class hero John Lennon had a relatively well-to-do childhood. Outlaw penis-waver Jim Morrison was the son of a navy admiral. Neil Young complained often about his own success, but he always dutifully returned to CSNY for another payday. Similarly, Pete Townshend, Roger Waters, and Bruce Springsteen foregrounded their own misgivings about mainstream popularity in their songs, all while continuing to rake in millions.

Yes, Eddie Vedder had his contradictions, but those contradictions were nothing new for a person in his position. They were inherent to rock superstardom long before Pearl Jam.[3]

But as bad as the boomers could be, Pearl Jam had an even harder time with their own people, the Gen Xers. Pearl Jam is the ultimate Generation X band precisely because so many Gen Xers have had problems with them.[4] From the beginning, Pearl Jam was pilloried by Gen X music critics as sellouts, bandwagon jumpers, overheated arena rockers, and hopelessly middle-of-the-road poseurs. Even when they were undoubtedly the most popular band in the world, they were dismissed as shallow and irrelevant, a flash-in-the-pan fad.

Madison Square Garden, when he dedicated the song "Rats" to Enrico Salvatore Rizzo, the name of Hoffman's character in 1969's *Midnight Cowboy*.

3 Jann Wenner of course is a man rife with his own inconsistencies. The assertion that he rejected Vedder's request to pick his own writer, among other calls for preferential treatment, for the *Rolling Stone* piece is fascinating coming from the man who wrote the most infamous review in the magazine's history, the ridiculous five-star write-up for 2001's *Goddess in the Doorway* by his buddy Mick Jagger.

4 Technically, Vedder, b. 1964, and Ament, b. 1963, are classified as boomers. But nobody in the Beach Boys, save Dennis Wilson, actually surfed, either. The iconography is what matters. Those guys are Gen Xers.

Most generations are highly parochial; they tend to believe that their culture—the music, the movies, the terrible kiddie TV shows—is the best. But many Gen Xers seemed to believe that their culture was *worse*, along with everything else about their lot in life. Some of this was conditioning from boomers, who never failed to reiterate that their kids had missed the boat on rock 'n' roll, free love, fun drugs, and all the other earthly delights of their youth. But the profound media saturation that permeated the lives of Gen Xers from the cradle onward made them prone to extreme reflexiveness about pretty much everything. They—*we*—are people who constantly second-guess ourselves. Is this impulse healthy? Is my *analyzing* of this impulse healthy? If I am *aware* that I am *analyzing* what is *supposed to be* a natural feeling, can it really be natural? Can *anything* be natural? Is all of this fake? These mind games were endless in the nineties.

Douglas Coupland's landmark 1991 novel *Generation X: Tales for an Accelerated Culture*—from which the name for the people born in the mid-sixties up through 1980 derives—is loaded with pithy, semi-jokey terms that all describe the same thing: *historical underdosing, successphobia, underdogging, terminal wanderlust*. This was a generation for which "success" as a concept was met with skepticism about whether it really equated with true happiness. And yet, at the same time, Gen Xers craved the security and status of boomers. It was a mindset engineered to guarantee dissatisfaction and anxiety.

They—*we*—instinctually identified with the underdog while also recognizing that willful loserdom was a pose that only the idle rich could afford. Gen Xers wanted it all, and also distrusted those desires, prompting us to lash out at those who managed to achieve anything. This point of view, at least in the press, doomed Pearl Jam. But it also pit at least one person inside Pearl Jam *against* Pearl Jam since he was wired the same way as his peers.

Eddie Vedder was doubly cursed with both the contradictions of a rock star and the contradictions of his generation. In the spring of 1995—perhaps as an act of penance, and certainly as a way to "hide" while making a show of "hiding"—he toured with Mike Watt, formerly of unimpeachable eighties indie band, the Minutemen.[5] Each night, Vedder would sing "Against the 70's," a warning about the dangers of dead-end nostalgia and a pep talk for young people dragged down by the "you shoulda been there!" hectoring of their parents: "Baby boomers selling you rumors of their history," Eddie sang. "Forcing youth away from the truth of what's real today."

But many in Watt's audience did not see Vedder as "real." This made the tour, at times, a painful experience for him. "It was really great until the middle, and then I think I couldn't handle it," he reflected years later. "There were people throwing coins in Chicago—Minutemen fans who didn't want to see a corporate-rock-band guy on the same stage as Watt. And I was frustrated. I was thinking, 'I'm supporting your guy; he's my hero too.' Goddamn."

Yes, he was frustrated, but Vedder couldn't resist adding a typically self-defeating Gen Xer–style addendum. "I understand where they're coming from. I might have been one to throw the coin myself."

$$\notin$$

By the time of the Red Rocks concerts, Pearl Jam had reached a breaking point. Their life as a band had grown increasingly chaotic and incomprehensible, with triumphs commingling with tragedies. In 1994, they visited the White House the day after Kurt Cobain's body was found. Later that year, they put out one of their best and most popular albums, *Vitalogy*, and nearly ripped themselves apart in the process. Dave Abbruzzese, their third drummer, was fired that August; Stone Gossard delivered the news, though Abbruzzese's tensions were mainly with Vedder. He apparently hated that Abbruzzese agreed to appear on the cover of *Modern Drummer* during a media blackout he had imposed on the band, the most Spinal Tap–like detail to this most Spinal Tap–like subplot of the Pearl Jam story.

---

5 This tour also included another rock star "hiding out" in the middle of an intense period of personal and professional turmoil, Dave Grohl.

The other main conflict in the band was between Gossard, whose original demos had formed the basis of Pearl Jam's debut *Ten* and basically invented their career, and Vedder, the irreplaceable singer and leading man. The power balance in Pearl Jam inevitably, irrevocably shifted in a bloodless coup. Stone had to give up control to Eddie so that the band could survive. That McCready was deep enough into booze and cocaine to require rehab somehow was among their lesser problems.

Unbeknownst to the band, there were also unseen forces that would eventually conspire against them. One month before *Vitalogy* came out, a band of Adidas-wearing funk-metal mooks named Korn released their self-titled debut. It took more than two years to go platinum—as opposed to two weeks for *Vitalogy*—but by then the nü-metal movement Korn spearheaded had completely taken over rock music, kicking grunge and post-grunge and anyone else sporting soul-patches and flannel to the curb. Also around the time of *Vitalogy*'s release, a sleazy Ponzi-scheme artist named Lou Pearlman rustled his young male musical protégés in the Backstreet Boys into a recording studio for the first time, beginning work on what would become their blockbuster 1996 self-titled debut. That album launched the teen pop craze that assisted in alternative rock's unceremonious death in the late nineties.

And then there was the debacle with Ticketmaster. Pearl Jam had put themselves in the impossible position in 1995 of essentially proving that Ticketmaster was a monopoly by attempting to wage a tour without them. They made their point about the impossibility of doing business as a big-time act—the *biggest* act—without the massive ticketing agency, but in the process they severely sandbagged their career when they should have been at their commercial zenith. Two mammoth shows in San Diego scheduled for June 26 and 27 were canceled due to safety concerns by the local sheriff's department over the non-Ticketmaster-affiliated backwater venue they were forced to use. Pearl Jam fans did not appreciate the band's financial sacrifices for their benefit. Rather, they grew increasingly exasperated with their heroes.

Meanwhile Vedder was traveling by van to all the gigs that summer while the rest of Pearl Jam traveled by plane. *This will keep me grounded,* he reasoned. But what it did instead was make him feel exhausted while cutting him off from the rest of his band.

Whenever journalists and critics talk about Pearl Jam in the summer of 1995, they tend to focus on the disastrous June 24 show in San Francisco, when Vedder fell ill and was forced to leave the stage after just seven songs. Neil Young replaced him, and the rest of the band previewed material from the not-yet-released Neil Young/Pearl Jam collaboration *Mirror Ball* and a selection of Young oldies, including two separate renditions of "Rockin' in the Free World." They were rewarded with a chorus of ugly boos from fifty thousand pissed-off onlookers.

The following day, after a lengthy meeting, they decided to cancel the next seven shows. At the time, McCready wondered if their singer was embarrassed to be in Pearl Jam. Vedder was acting like he wanted to be in Fugazi; the guys in Pearl Jam liked and respected the Washington DC indie band, but come on, Pearl Jam was never going to be Fugazi, the paragons of indie virtue famous for not selling merch and charging only $5 per show. That fact was clear to everyone in the world except Pearl Jam's front man. The way he was acting, it wasn't clear if he actually wanted to still be in the biggest band in the world.

Rolling Stone subsequently zeroed in on the canceled shows as it twisted the knife, estimating that Pearl Jam lost $30 million by refusing to play ball in the summer of '95, as if that mattered to anybody not in the band. Later, the gossipy 1998 biography *Five Against One* by *Rolling Stone* writer Kim Neely used the San Francisco concert as a framing device. In a sense, rock journalists were already writing Pearl Jam's obituary by the end of the nineties and contextualizing San Francisco as the beginning of the end.

But, as we now know, Pearl Jam is the one band that *didn't* die. As contemporaries like Nirvana, Soundgarden, and Alice in Chains imploded under tragic circumstances, Pearl Jam found a way to persevere. So, because this is a story not about premature death but rather long-term survival, San Francisco is merely an interesting footnote, not a bellwether. What matters more is that second show at Red Rocks from June 20.

⚡

Kim Gordon once astutely explained the allure of rock stardom like this: "People pay money to see others believe in themselves." That was certainly the appeal of seeing Led Zeppelin in 1972. But even as Pearl Jam assumed a Zeppelin-size place in nineties rock, they didn't yet have Zeppelin-size confidence. In 1995, they hadn't yet figured out who they really were.

Things had happened too fast. As soon as Gossard, Ament, and McCready met Vedder in the fall of 1990, they were writing songs together. As soon as they had songs they had a record deal. As soon as they had a record deal they had a debut album. As soon as they had a debut album they were on the road. As soon as they were on the road they swiftly built a loyal audience. Several drummers, of course, entered and exited the band along the way. But Pearl Jam never moved slower than light speed in the first half of the nineties.

They had come remarkably far in a remarkably short period of time, fueled by the boundless energy each person brought to the operation: Gossard's magnetic riffs, McCready's relentless leads, Ament's muscular bass, Abbruzzese's machinelike rhythms, and Vedder's uncanny knack for cutting straight to the heart of the matter for millions of teenagers with his voice and lyrics.

But if you don't know who you are—are we Fugazi or Aerosmith or Fugazi *in the body* of Aerosmith?—then you will lose yourself. And that's what happened to Pearl Jam.

The thrill of listening to the 6/20/95 bootleg recording is witnessing Pearl Jam's attempt to finally figure out the "who the hell are we?" question once and for all in real time. They begin with a song they debuted live just four days earlier, on June 16, in Casper, Wyoming: "Long Road." Vedder introduced it at the end of the *Mirror Ball* sessions in early 1995, a period when he was otherwise making himself scarce due to ongoing problems with a stalker. The song was inspired by the death of Clayton Liggett, his high school drama teacher and a surrogate father figure when Vedder's family was falling apart in the midst of his parents' bitter divorce.

This bruising but formative stage of his life was eventually mythologized in Pearl Jam's early songs and closely parsed by journalists, to Vedder's profound discomfort.

"Long Road" not only is unfamiliar to the audience at Red Rocks, but the song's pensive, spiritually questing introspection is the opposite of what the ready-to-party people in the crowd want. But Pearl Jam doubles down with the next song, a radical reinvention of their biggest MTV hit, "Jeremy," that downplays the song's anthemic qualities and removes the chorus altogether.

If the audience is getting restless, the feeling is carrying over to the band. Gossard gets up from his chair briefly during "Long Road," and he does it again during this Jeremy-less version of "Jeremy." The song builds and builds, gathering steam from the initial exhausted tempo. But Eddie keeps cutting the song's legs out from under it. The cathartic "try to forget this / try to erase this" section is also excised. He does muster a climactic "*whoaaaaaa!*" in the closing section but again the point is to subvert the melodrama, taking it out of high school and bringing it to a weary and ravaged present.

"So, obviously we're making this up as we go along tonight," Vedder says. "We got all fucking night, this will be like the Grateful Dead or something."

Only this isn't like the Grateful Dead, a band that improvised within the parameters of well-known and familiar songs in a manner that was understood and accepted by their fans. Dead shows were unpredictable, but there was usually some semblance of a plan. The Dead knew who they were. Pearl Jam on this night, however, is throwing *anything* against the wall, in the hopes that whatever sticks will constitute an identity.

This is, in a way, as thrilling as listening to prime-era Zeppelin, who signified sexy and swaggering danger without ever putting themselves *in* danger onstage, like Pearl Jam is doing right now. The next song, a cover of Nick Cave's "The Ship Song," is aborted after about ninety seconds, because the band doesn't know how to play it. "We need to work that one out a little better," Vedder says sheepishly. "Sounded great backstage . . ."

"Footsteps" follows. By most band's standards, this is an obscurity, a B-side recorded during a 1992 radio interview, the final piece of the mythical "Momma-Son" trilogy (with "Alive" and "Once") that was left off *Ten.* But the hordes greet it like a long-lost friend after the confounding trio of songs that opened the concert.

After that, there's another new song, but this immediately sounds like the most welcoming music of the night so far. It's called "Falling Down," and this is the only time it will ever be performed publicly. Vedder's words are a jumble of moans and half-formed sentences, but this is not one of the spur-of-the moment "improv" live numbers that dot their voluminous bootlegs. The arrangement is rough, but the lilting melody is undeniably beautiful, evoking the classic *Ten*-era power ballad "Black" with a dash of the *Vitalogy* stunner "Immortality."

When the lyrics can be made out, they sound like a farewell from a person unsure if he wants anyone to notice that he's gone. "Oh something to remember me by / oh something to place in your hand," Vedder (I think) is singing. "Oh something so you will feel all grown up when you call my name." There is none of Vedder's trademark grunge-dude bellowing here; his voice is soft and sounds unspeakably sad. "Can't feel the heat / of something fresh coming," he sings. "Can somebody hide me?"

The song peaks during the guitar solo, taken by Gossard, who once again stands up and plays some finely wrought lines. After that, the song doesn't so much end as slowly come to a stop. Vedder sounds like a man stepping back from the light so that the darkness can slowly envelop him. "I cannot apologize," he croons, and the lyric hangs briefly in the air until the song's heartbeat suddenly ceases.

⚡

After that incredible opening, 6/20/95 downshifts to a very good "normal" Pearl Jam show. Which is why, as good as the rest of the bootleg is, I tend to stop listening after "Falling Down." You can hear something change, or even die, inside this band during that song. Every time I hear it, I'm convinced that it is the hit song that Pearl Jam's next album, *No Code*, not necessarily *needed*, but certainly could have benefited from as it struggled to sell upon release in the late summer of 1996.

But "Falling Down" didn't show up on *No Code*, or any other Pearl Jam album. After nearly crashing and burning during the San Francisco debacle, Pearl Jam rallied for some excellent shows in Milwaukee and Chicago that July. Feeling suddenly revitalized, they entered a Chicago recording studio the day after playing for forty-seven thousand fans at Soldier Field to begin working up songs for their fourth album.

"Falling Down" subsequently resurfaced in two unlikely places—first as the musical basis of the song "Distress" from the self-titled 1999 debut by Mike McCready's side project the Rockfords, and then as a fan club single (along with the 6/20/95 non-Jeremy "Jeremy") in 2010. Other than that, "Falling Down" came and went onstage that night at Red Rocks. It's the potential Pearl Jam classic that never came to be.

That Pearl Jam opted to make "Falling Down" a one-off treasured by fans, rather than transform it into the smash power ballad it could have been, might strike some as a lost opportunity, another instance of generational self-sabotage. But if something died that night, there was also an aspect of Pearl Jam that was reborn.

This is, after all, a survival story, and "Falling Down" sounds to me like a path that was considered and ultimately abandoned in favor of a different destiny that has carried this band further than they could have possibly imagined during the dregs of their troubled summer in 1995.

The future would not be about hit songs, it would be about living in the now and creating moments that were special *because* they were fleeting. Maybe Eddie Vedder didn't have to play-act as a struggling indie rocker by touring in a van. But Pearl Jam also didn't have to be Led Zeppelin. They could be a band that played the biggest stages in the world and never acted like the other bands who played those stages. They could step outside the grandly plotted machinations and orchestrations that keep arena-rock bands locked into predictable and stifling patterns. Above all, they could harness the power of "no," where you create something and then walk away from it to create something else the next night in a different city. When you do that, people will follow you to that next city to find out what you do next.

Here was an identity. A *Pearl Jam* identity. On that night at Red Rocks, they started to figure out how to just *be*.

CHAPTER 2
"FOOTSTEPS"

(5/11/92, *Rockline*)

Incest • Murder • B-sides • Surfing • The Who • FM Radio Talk Shows • *Straight Time*

How do you mark a band's birthday? Is it the anniversary of the debut album? Does it memorialize the first show? Or do you have to go all the way back to the earliest rehearsal, if anyone involved can even remember when it happened?

For Pearl Jam, I propose that the band's birth took place on November 21, 1989. Actually, if we're being technical, this is more like the moment of conception. But it's nevertheless an important moment that catalyzed everything that came afterward.

As is the case for so many things with Eddie Vedder, it begins with Joe Strummer.

Eddie was a twenty-four-year-old gas station attendant living in San Diego. But more important, he worked at a gas station so he could also work for free at a local rock club. Situated unceremoniously inside a strip mall on Clairemont Mesa Boulevard, the Bacchanal was not, as the name suggests, a beacon of decadence and self-indulgence fit for the opulent ruling class. It was a hole in the wall known for low ceilings and loud music, the kind of venue, as Vedder later recalled, that either hosted young bands on their way up or veteran acts that had plateaued and were now trending downward.

The Bacchanal's management apparently didn't have the money to pay their stage crew. But Eddie didn't mind. He worked the graveyard shift at the gas station so he could hump gear and schlep backstage amenities for the future stars and present-day has-beens who played the club without being destitute. He relished the opportunity to be around musicians and soak up the atmosphere peripheral to the rock show experience. He romanticized all of it, even sound checks. *Especially* sound checks. Sometimes, the sound check was even better than the actual gig. It was the relative calm before the audience stormed in. The period reserved just for the band and the crew who worked to make the shows happen. Even then, it seems, Eddie could be wary of crowds.

A lover of the Clash, Eddie was excited to see Strummer—then touring in support of his first proper solo album, *Earthquake Weather*, released two months prior—that night. Strummer was neither an up-and-comer or a has-been. He was the spark plug of the Clash, the godfather of punk rock arena rock, a genuine hero. Movie-star handsome, he could've starred in film noir classics had he been born in a different time. As it was, he came along at the precise right moment for Eddie Vedder, who gravitated to the Clash's politically charged anthems as a teenager and would come to emulate Strummer's deeply moral and intractable humanism.

Strummer was a no-show to his sound check, as was most of his band. Only his drummer, Jack Irons, appeared. Eddie nevertheless pounced. The drummer was another hero of his. Irons had recently exited his previous band, the Red Hot Chili Peppers, upon the drug-related death of Hillel Slovak, the band's effervescent but star-crossed guitarist. Slovak was only twenty-six years old when he retreated from the group after a troubled European tour, and subsequently died alone in his LA apartment of a heroin overdose. Irons was so devastated by Slovak's death that he couldn't bear to play with the Chili Peppers any longer. As the band carried on in 1989 with their first album made with new guitarist John Frusciante and drummer Chad Smith, *Mother's Milk*, Irons toured and recorded with Strummer.

Now here was a roadie who wanted Irons to confirm whether he played drums on the live Chili Peppers bootleg tape stuck in his car stereo, or if it was his predecessor, Cliff Martinez.[1] Irons agreed to follow this guy to his Toyota Corolla for an impromptu listening party, so long as he fetched him some bananas.

From there, a friendship formed. Not long after the Joe Strummer gig, Jack would slip Eddie a cassette tape. It was a demo made by some guys from Seattle who were looking for a singer. Jack wanted to know if Eddie was interested.

He was. He considered the tape an art project. But it was, of course, more than that. Here was a life-changing moment. For Eddie. For Jack. For the guys who recorded the demo. For millions of people who would finally hear that music. It was the beginning of Pearl Jam.

$$\lightning$$

The "Momma-Son"[2] tape is to Pearl Jam what Bruce Wayne's dead parents are to Batman. It's the origin story, the source of the larger overall mythology, the core of their smash debut *Ten*, a tale as old as time that gets retold time and again.

---

1 Actually, in the tangled timeline of the Chili Peppers, Irons preceded Martinez, as he was a founding member. But he didn't actually play on a Chili Peppers record until their third album, 1987's *The Uplift Mofo Party Plan*. It would be the only Chili Peppers record to include Irons.

2 For years this was known among Pearl Jam fans as "Mamasan," but subsequent official missives from the band, including *Pearl Jam Twenty*, have highlighted the "correct" spelling.

If you are a Pearl Jam fan, you have doubtless heard it before. However, anytime there is a new iteration of Batman, they have to once again show Bruce Wayne's parents being murdered in an alley. So here we are.

The story begins in the spring of 1990—almost four months after Eddie Vedder meets Jack Irons—with the death of Andrew Wood and the end of Mother Love Bone, the preposterous and often thrilling band that Stone Gossard and Jeff Ament played in before Pearl Jam. Wood died on March 19, 1990, three days after he overdosed on heroin. Mother Love Bone's lone album, *Apple*, was released exactly four months later. But the band by then was long gone.

Suddenly adrift after seemingly being on the brink of fame and fortune, Gossard immediately gets to work on writing new songs. Within six months, he writes the music for what will become some of Pearl Jam's most iconic songs. He also recruits two guys to play with him: his partner from Mother Love Bone, Jeff Ament, and a former hair-metal guitarist turned blues acolyte named Mike McCready.[3] Matt Cameron, presently of Soundgarden, is recruited to play drums on the demo. All they need now is a vocalist.

Let's skip ahead to the part where a tape containing several of these demos ends up in the hands of the gas station attendant from San Diego. Eddie plays the tape and is drawn to three pieces: "Dollar Short," which sounds like Ian MacKaye attempting to write "Free Bird"; "Agyptian Cave," which resembles Jane's Addiction without the junk habit; and "Times of Trouble," which reimagines the music of the Mississippi Delta as if it emerged from the shores of Elliott Bay.

At this point, the story takes its mythic turn: Eddie goes surfing and hears some melodies and lyrics in his head playing against the white noise of the waves. He then returns home, and with the sand still in his

---

3 In Pearl Jam's early videos, Mike McCready dresses like Stevie Ray Vaughan, who died on August 27, 1990, exactly one year before the release of *Ten*.

toes he commences recording. It's all very spiritual. (I picture him as Patrick Swayze in *Point Break* at this moment.) Eddie lays down these songs—now known as "Alive," "Once," "Footsteps"—over a repurposed promo cassette of a Merle Haggard 1980s greatest hits album.[4] He titles the tape "Momma-Son," for reasons that aren't immediately apparent but will eventually be dutifully explained once Pearl Jam becomes famous.

That starts to happen around the middle of 1992, about two years after Stone and Jeff and Mike get the tape back from Eddie and subsequently invite the sage surfer to Seattle, at which point they immediately start writing more songs and forming into a highly efficient live unit. By mid-'92, Pearl Jam is blowing up in America and Europe. And the "Momma-Son" mythology is beginning to entrench in band lore.

While on tour in Europe that June, Pearl Jam performs the "Momma-Son" songs in order for the first time, during four consecutive shows in Milan, Zurich, Vienna, and Paris. In Zurich on June 18, Vedder tells the audience that the songs are linked by a larger narrative, which he claims to have never divulged publicly. "I don't wanna ruin any interpretations of the songs that you have," he says, "but it's about incest and it's about murder and all those good things."

To the Swiss people in the audience—or the fans around the world who will eventually hear this on a bootleg tape—this must have been at least mildly surprising, given that these songs weren't previously presented in this specific sequence. "Alive" was the first song from Pearl Jam's debut *Ten* released to radio and MTV, about seven weeks before the LP came out on August 27, 1991. On the album, it's the third track, situated after "Once," even though it's placed *before* "Once" in the "Momma-Son" sequence. And then there is "Footsteps," which didn't even make *Ten* and was most familiar to fans as the basis of a Temple of the Dog

---

4 One of the songs on that Merle tape, "A Place to Fall Apart," sums up the emotional tenor of Eddie's lyrics.

track, "Times of Trouble," which has a different vocal melody and set of lyrics.

The "Momma-Son" narrative was eventually explained in greater detail for a much larger audience more than a year later, in an article written by Cameron Crowe for *Rolling Stone* in the fall of 1993. Vedder—apparently no longer concerned with ruining personal fan interpretations—spoke at length about how the songs are connected. "Alive" is about a mother who pursues an incestuous relationship with her son after the boy's father dies. "Once" is about how that kid is scarred for life by the sexual abuse and subsequently becomes a serial killer. And "Footsteps" is about how the killer ends up on death row and is finally executed.

Not long after the *Rolling Stone* profile was published, Pearl Jam played "Momma-Son" for the first time in America, during an especially surly hometown show in Seattle on December 8, 1993. At the Zurich show, Vedder talked about the trilogy's story to the point of overexplaining. In Seattle, however, he was more sheepish, mockingly referring to the song cycle as Pearl Jam's version of *The Nutcracker*. He also used a decidedly un–punk rock term that he had previously applied to "Momma-Son" in Europe: mini-opera.

Right then and there, in case it wasn't already obvious, Eddie Vedder made plain his allegiance to his most profound rock 'n' roll influence: the Who.

$$\frac{}{}$$

It's plain to see how Pearl Jam's "mini-opera" was inspired by the band most associated with rock operas. The sexual abuse element of "Alive" is borrowed from *Tommy*; the mental illness aspect of "Once" harkens to *Quadrophenia*. And Vedder's impassioned growl—caricatured by the end of the nineties as the "yarl" of post-grunge, as coined by Seattle indie-rock musician and producer Jack Endino—derives significantly from Roger Daltrey's hyper-macho post-*Tommy* era.[5]

---

5 There's also a less significant but certainly not *insignificant* dash of the Doors, both from the Oedipal melodrama of "The End" and Jim Morrison's own lusty, *yarl-y* yarl.

Vedder has done little to conceal any of this. On the contrary, he talks about the Who with the kind of awe and adoration that drove him nuts when it was directed at him from Pearl Jam fans in the nineties. He credited a babysitter with introducing him to *Who's Next* when he was nine. "The parents were gone. The windows shook. The shelves were rattling," he recalled in 2016. "That began an exploration into music that had soul, rebellion, aggression, affection."

More than that, the Who offered a blueprint for the "punk rock arena rock" aesthetic that Vedder and his bandmates would pursue in Pearl Jam. "They were an incredible band whose main songwriter happened to be on a quest for reason and harmony in his life," Vedder said of the Who and their leader, Pete Townshend. "He shared that journey with the listener, becoming an inspiration for others to seek out their own path. They did all this while also being in the *Guinness Book of World Records* as the world's loudest band."

When Eddie Vedder talks about the Who it often sounds like he could be talking about his own band. Surely, Pearl Jam's arc over the course of several decades could be described as Vedder's own quest for "reason and harmony in his life."

Unlike their contemporaries in the seventies—Led Zeppelin, the Rolling Stones, Queen, Black Sabbath—the Who meshed a bombastic musical attack with a sensitive and singular point of view. While those other bands indulged in pure arena-rock spectacle, the Who functioned as the world's loudest singer-songwriter act. You could conceptualize the Who as a four-headed entity in which each member had a decisive role to play, but ultimately it was all in service of songs written by a guy expressing thoughts, concerns, passions, and hang-ups specific to him and only him. Pete Townshend selfishly hoarded his band's pet themes; it did not matter to him whether John Entwistle also found Meher Baba transcendent, only that the Ox's fluid octopus basslines properly conveyed the punishing tumult of a life devoid of spiritual satisfaction. That was the dynamic of the Who, and it would become how Pearl Jam operated as well. Both bands were made up of equals, but one guy was always a little more equal than the others.

The tension in the Who is that Townshend most of the time did not sing his lyrics; it was up to Daltrey to sell lines like "Goodbye all you punks / stay young and stay high / hand me my checkbook / and I'll crawl off to die." It didn't matter that this particular song, "They Are All in Love" from 1975's *The Who by Numbers*, didn't line up with his own point of view. Daltrey was always more comfortable in his own skin than Townshend; he couldn't care less about the emerging punk generation and he surely wasn't one to slink off in self-pitying defeat. He was, unapologetically, a rock god. But it was that very self-assurance that allowed him to put his own feelings aside and communicate the emotional truth of Pete Townshend's confessionals.

Pearl Jam, especially early on, had an inverse tension—Stone Gossard wrote the grabby, AOR-inspired rock riffs that Vedder used as vehicles for expressing his innermost neuroses. What Townshend and Vedder share as songwriters is their preference for writing about characters who may or may not be stand-ins for themselves. Townshend had *Tommy*, and Vedder had "Jeremy," which is not actually sung from the perspective of the title character but rather a person who bullied the title character.[6]

Even without the "Momma-Son" concept, it's apparent that Vedder isn't really writing about himself in "Alive" or "Once" any more than he is in "Jeremy," the jokey serial killer B-side "Dirty Frank," "Why Go" (one of the earliest Pearl Jam songs sung from a female perspective, a trend that became more prominent on the second record, *Vs.*), or the drug addict character study "Deep." Elements of Vedder's childhood might be exaggerated in those songs, but he did not actually have sex with his mother and he certainly never murdered anyone.

---

6 In that way, "Jeremy" resembles Townshend's own villain POV song from *Who's Next*, "Behind Blue Eyes." Perhaps nine-year-old Eddie was already taking mental notes.

Using Daltrey as a front for even his most scathing and self-lacerating songs gave Townshend a degree of cover that Vedder would not have upon the onset of *Ten*-mania. Years later, when he was floundering in the glare of his initial fame in the early nineties, Vedder turned to Townshend for advice on how to survive. "I gave him my philosophy," Townshend writes in his churlish 2012 memoir, *Who I Am*. "We don't make the choice; the public does. We are elected by them, even if we never stood for office. Accept it."

But Townshend was less glib in the early seventies, when he was in the exact position in which Eddie Vedder found himself in the early nineties. Back then, Townshend was similarly obsessed with his own childhood and the identity crisis prompted by the Who's tremendous success in the wake of *Tommy*. In his next batch of songs, he wrote exclusively about his desire to bridge the growing expanse between his band and his audience. He envisioned rock 'n' roll not as show business, but as an avenue for demolishing social hierarchies and, to use extremely sixties terminology, enabling all people "to live as one." He envisioned an absurdly ambitious sci-fi concept album called *Lifehouse* that nobody other than Pete Townshend understood, based on likening the shared feelings of elation that exists during a fantastic rock show to an embryonic version of the internet. In the early seventies, it was an imaginary form of technology connecting millions of people like never before.

Part of the *Lifehouse* concept involved playing experimental rock shows during the making of the album. Townshend envisioned two thousand people gathering at the Young Vic Theatre in London, and then living there with the band for as long as six months. "The group would play and characters would emerge from them, and eventually the group would play a very minor role," he theorized. "Maybe about five hundred of the two thousand people would stay during the six months, and we would have filmed all that happened."

Now, this plainly crazy idea didn't actually work, to the surprise of no one not named Pete Townshend. The Who played a handful of shows at the Young Vic in February and April 1971 and became frustrated that the audience just wanted them to play "My Generation" and smash up their instruments. But Townshend wasn't interested in business as usual. He pushed the Who to play spiritually questing songs that openly expressed his alienation from rock stardom.

The titles of Townshend's new songs—which received mixed reactions from an audience unfamiliar with them—tell the story: "Getting in Tune," "Too Much of Anything," "I Don't Even Know Myself," "Won't Get Fooled Again." Eventually, Townshend grew disenchanted, canceled the remaining Young Vic concerts. Smarting from this failure, he teetered on the brink of a nervous breakdown. Daltrey thought they were going to break up. But the Who didn't implode. They survived. They took the *Lifehouse* songs and reshaped them into *Who's Next*, an album with no concept other than "here are the most perfect stadium rock songs ever made." It was the record that ended up blowing young Eddie Vedder's mind.

Those Young Vic Who shows are a more extreme version of that Pearl Jam concert at Red Rocks in 1995, in which a band strains to reimagine a new relationship with their fans, only to find that many of them only want to hear the familiar hits. Though that's not true of *all* Who fans—some of them are like Vedder, who will forever be drawn to the Who because they embody an impossible contradiction at the heart of precious few rock bands, the one about seeking the community that can only exist at a rock show to achieve an inner peace so private that you "can't explain" it outside a larger-than-life anthem.

Vedder has singled out *Quadrophenia* as an album that "saved my life" when he was around thirteen or fourteen and in the thick of his family falling apart. Around that time, he saw the Who play live for the first time, at the San Diego Sports Arena on June 18, 1980. This was not an especially good time for Vedder's favorite band—they had just returned to the road for the first time since Keith Moon's death in 1978 in support of their worst album, *Who Are You*. In December 1979, eleven fans were crushed to death at a Who show in Cincinnati. Three years later, they would limp along on their "farewell" 1982 tour, a group of middle-aged men dressed like England's trendy wave of "New Romantics" bands who were half their age, lamely playing out the string to cash in on beer company sponsorship money.

But Eddie did not view the Who cynically as past-their-prime poseurs. "For the first half of the show, I couldn't get around the fact that those four guys were standing in the same room in San Diego," he later recalled. "And that's where the rock gods came down and blessed us. Really, the excitement of that, seeing them for the first time."

Years later, in an interview for *The Believer*, Vedder was asked by Carrie Brownstein of Sleater-Kinney if he was involved in the SoCal punk scene that was thriving during his teen years in the early eighties, when iconic bands like Black Flag, Circle Jerks, and Fear played frequently throughout the region. Black Flag, for instance, played San Diego at least four times in 1980 alone, at venues like the Roxy and the North Park Lions Club.

But Eddie didn't know about these local punk bands. "I was just in some kind of suburb, and the waves didn't reach that far or something. And I think the other thing is that my parents split up when I was a teenager and I had a job. So I couldn't have a mohawk," he said. Vedder then added ruefully, "You know, I wish I was part of that. It would have been great, and it probably would have changed for me musically a little bit."

What's left unsaid is that young Eddie's imagination in 1980 was tied up with the opposite of Black Flag. He wasn't seeking out brash, mile-a-minute punks playing in VFW halls. He yearned instead for arena rock played by British men who were pushing forty. Even a band like the Clash, a foundational influence for all punk groups, was closer to the Who—for whom they opened on that 1982 "farewell" tour—than Black Flag.

As he would frequently do as a young man throughout the eighties, Vedder snuck a tape recorder into the San Diego Sports Arena to procure an excessively fuzzy and barely audible bootleg of his favorite gods performing in concert. He later claimed that he listened to the tape at least 350 times, blasting it on headphones and filling in the gaping sonic holes of the poor recording with his memories of the gig and what he imagined it all signified.

I've searched high and low online for a recording of the specific Who show attended by teenaged Eddie Vedder in 1980, to no avail. But I have several bootlegs of concerts from the same tour. Like Eddie, I listen to these tapes on headphones and turn up the volume as high as it can go, because that's how music always sounds and feels the best, and also because the recordings are so bad that you can't really make out the songs much of the time.

I do this because I love the Who, and also because those tapes conceal just enough to force me to project my own dreams and desires onto them. I hear a brilliant band that I have in a sense re-created in my mind, a mix of reality and fantasy, as I'm sure Eddie Vedder did, as this is what all rock fans do with their old, faded heroes. In those moments, Eddie must have also been imagining *his* band, as it might exist one day.

⚡

My favorite part of the "Momma-Son" trilogy—and a song that moves as much as any by Pearl Jam—is the one track from that tape that did not make it on *Ten*. The most logical explanation for why the concluding piece, "Footsteps," was left off is that *Ten* was preceded by "Times of Trouble," from the self-titled Temple of the Dog record, by about five months. But I also believe that "Footsteps" would have changed the emotional arc of *Ten*, particularly if you think of that album (as I do) as its own kind of narrative piece.

In the "Momma-Son" story, "Footsteps" is the downer seventies movie ending, the part when the protagonist—who has been victimized and abused by his parents—drifts into a pitch-black abyss without any possibility of redemption. The song is hopeless from the start: "Don't even think about reaching me / I won't be home." It's suggested that he's already fully lost his mind, which means the execution of his body is merely an anticlimactic epilogue to a more profound spiritual and mental death. The abuse of the physical self isn't really felt here; it only marks the ways in which the soul has been damaged: "I got scratches all over my arms / one for each day since I fell apart."

Ten, however, does not have the arc of "Momma-Son." It's not a downer, it's cathartic and uplifting, and that has a lot to do with how the songs are sequenced. On the album, the killing spree track "Once" is placed before the less overtly violent "Alive," subtly but decisively altering how those songs progress from one to the other. In the context of *Ten*, the characters slowly drift from damnation to redemption, as opposed to the opposite trajectory of "Momma-Son." It's this very arc that helped to make *Ten* an era-defining phenomenon.

The killer of "Once" becomes the victim of "Alive," who becomes the captive of "Why Go" and then the lovesick loner pining for a lost relationship in "Black." After we meet the teen martyr portrayed in "Jeremy," there is a triumphant, Springsteen-esque escape from childhood circumstances in "Porch," prompting a confrontation of adult realities like death ("Garden") and the ultimate rejection of youthful nihilism ("Deep"). By the time *Ten* climaxes with "Release," it's in a place entirely removed from the bleakness of "Momma-Son." It's more like the end of *Quadrophenia*, in which the mentally ill protagonist Jimmy hears the rain crash against the waves of the sea in "Love Reign o'er Me" and imagines his sins and fears being cleansed. Meanwhile, Eddie Vedder, the surfer, finds solace in riding "the wave where it takes me" in "Release."

There's no place for "Footsteps" in that story. It's a song that must stand alone, in its own haunted and poisoned atmosphere.

By the way, I want to make it clear that any reference I make to "Footsteps" pertains to the version on the "Jeremy" single released in 1992. I am *not* referring to the bastardized take on the 2003 "odds and sods" *Lost Dogs* compilation, in which a corny harmonica lick is overdubbed throughout. The *real* "Footsteps" derives from a radio session on the syndicated rock 'n' roll talk show *Rockline* that took place on May 11, 1992, not long before the European tour where they finally premiered the "Momma-Son" suite in concert.

After hearing "Footsteps" so many times on its own outside the context of the *Rockline* radio interview, it was deeply weird to hear it *in* that context. On its own, "Footsteps" is so stark and emotionally ravaged that it verges on blues—I don't mean the white-boy bar-band stuff, I mean music that conveys a feeling of loneliness so deep and unsparing that death seems preferable. It makes me think about the protagonist of one of my favorite films with a great downer seventies ending, the 1978 crime thriller *Straight Time*, in which Vedder's boyhood hero Dustin Hoffman plays an ex-con named Max Dembo.

In the film, Hoffman's character tries and fails to escape the criminal life. At the end of the movie, he botches a jewelry heist that leaves his best friend dead and causes him to personally kill another of his close buddies out of revenge. He then goes on the lam with his girlfriend (Theresa Russell) but eventually sends her off on a bus back home.

"Why can't I go with you?" she asks.

"Because I wanna get caught," Max replies blankly.

That's the guy in "Footsteps," and Vedder captures him perfectly. And this, again, is *weird* when you hear the whole interview, which is otherwise loose and funny and not at all on the razor's edge of life and death, the way that "Footsteps" feels. This is a *performance*, just like Dustin Hoffman's tough, unsentimental portrayal of Max Dembo.

Rockline was a nationally syndicated radio show launched in 1981 that broadcasted from legendary Sunset Sound studio in Hollywood. For thirty-three years and 1,650 episodes, it aired twice a week and was hosted most of the time by Bob Coburn, an ingratiating fixture of LA rock radio who appeared on KLOS 95.5 from 1980 until his death in 2016. In the days back when it was still rare to hear your favorite rock musicians speak at length about their craft, *Rockline* was appointment listening for rock nerds. It was also in a state of flux in 1992, like the rest of the rock world.

The myth of this era is that as soon as "Smells Like Teen Spirit" entered regular rotation on MTV, the hair metal bands and rock dinosaurs who reigned supreme before then were instantly vanquished. But the slate of *Rockline* guests in 1992 dispels this idea. It's a fascinating snapshot of the mainstream rock world as it existed then. Yes, things were changing with the rise of a new generation of bands. But it's not as if the old bands just spontaneously disappeared.

Pearl Jam wasn't even the headliner of their episode; it was Gary Moore, the former Thin Lizzy guitarist and current blues rock star who appeared on the show to promote his ninth album, *After Hours*. Geddy Lee of Rush guested the following week. A special episode on June 1 about the Seattle music scene featured seventies-arena-rock-stars-turned-eighties-power-balladeers Heart and the progressive metal band Queensrÿche alongside Nirvana and Alice in Chains. In the following months the occasional episodes starring alt-rock bands like R.E.M. and the Red Hot Chili Peppers were far outnumbered by episodes featuring groups like Def Leppard, Slaughter, and Great White.

By the second quarter of 1992, Pearl Jam had already won over MTV and a growing army of teenagers. But they were still regarded as outsiders by the scores of mainstream rock radio stations that carried *Rockline*. The program directors who worked at those stations and determined what millions of listeners heard every day in a Precambrian, pre-internet media landscape really were inclined to initially view a band like Queensrÿche as the true paradigm-shifting rock act.

A product of Bellevue, a Seattle suburb, Queensrÿche's career trajectory was more level than Pearl Jam's, finally peaking in 1990 with their fourth studio album, *Empire*, and the extremely Pink Floyd–esque hit power ballad, "Silent Lucidity," which helped the LP go triple platinum. Queensrÿche would come to be viewed as passé pompous bombast in light of the grunge revolution by the time of their next album, 1994's *Promised Land*. But in that small early-nineties window that predates the ascendance of Pearl Jam, an album like *Empire* really did offer an "alternative" to Mötley Crüe, the paragon of hedonistic hair metal whose only common ground with the self-serious likes of Queensrÿche was a weakness for umlauts. I would even make a case for Queensrÿche being a bridge band from the makeup and spandex era of the eighties to the jeans and T-shirts standard set in the nineties. A song like "Black" might not seem all that similar to "Silent Lucidity" upon first listen, but the big ballad from *Ten* is closer in spirit to Queensrÿche's signature hit than it is to Mötley Crüe's defining power ballad, "Home Sweet Home."

Even though his band was still novelty in this context, Eddie Vedder was one of those rock nerds who listened to *Rockline* each week. At the start of the interview, he reminisces about hearing two of his heroes, Pete Townshend and Joe Strummer, on the show. Now it was his turn on *Rockline*. You can tell this isn't just another interview for him. He has reason to make it special by pulling off a transcendent performance of a "lost" song.

Ten became a phenomenon because it had a feral energy and anger that made it seem new and exciting, and a grasp of rock 'n' roll songwriting fundamentals that it made also feel familiar and comfortable. It was both intimate and grandiose, adversarial and inviting, youthful and traditional. "Footsteps" doesn't fit in that paradigm. *Ten* is a mainstream rock record in the guise of an underground statement, but "Footsteps" is *actually* on the outside, a portrait of an enigmatic loner that nobody can ever truly know. The song's placement in Pearl Jam's mini-opera notwithstanding, there's nothing grand about it.

What connects the listener to "Footsteps"—in the same way I'm sure it connected Stone, Jeff, and Mike when they first heard the "Momma-Son" tape—is Eddie Vedder's voice. After *Ten*, there was a bumper crop of fake Vedders in alt-rock who copied and exaggerated the throatiest and most masculine aspects of his voice, culminating with the post-grunge bozos in Creed and Nickelback.

But these pretenders, who caricatured Eddie Vedder as a barrel-chested He-Man, could never crack what made him such an evocative and emotional vocalist. It's a cliché to praise Vedder as the type of singer who sounds like he's only singing to you. In the case of "Footsteps," I don't even think that's true—it's more like he's allowing you to hear him sing as he would only for himself, at the absolute worst moment of his life. Like when a kid loses his parents in an instant. Or murders them.

CHAPTER 3
"PORCH"

(3/16/92, New York, New York)

The *Singles* Soundtrack • "Hunger Strike" • Lollapalooza • Bruce
Springsteen • Yarling • The Greatest "Heyyyyyyyyy!" in Rock History

When Eddie Vedder was fifteen, he dreamt about being part of a world-famous music scene. Like so many Gen X rock fans, he read about his favorite boomer-era bands and wished he *could have just been there*. He imagined being in London in 1967 and seeing the Who or Hendrix onstage at the Marquee, all while rubbing shoulders with McCartney and Jagger and Keith Richards. And he would curse his parents for somehow not having him twenty years earlier.

But in the early nineties, he actually *was* a part of a world-famous music scene, possibly the last truly iconic rock 'n' roll scene ever. Only now that he was inside it, Vedder found that he didn't enjoy being the subject of so many aspirational fantasies by the latest generation of fifteen-year-old rock misfits.

When you listen to bootlegs from Pearl Jam's spring European tour in 1992—a period when the band had not yet attained superstardom but was rapidly ascending to that status—you hear Vedder already complaining about his band being lumped into a larger hype about the so-called "Seattle sound." Sometimes, he could be funny about it. At a gig from early February in Paris, Eddie stopped the show after "Alive" to address "this big rumor" currently circulating about the band: "We're not from Seattle," he deadpanned. "I just had to say it because if someone else asks me about the Seattle scene one more time, I think I'm gonna puke, piss, and shit all at the same time."

But as Pearl Jam's fame grew, so did Vedder's discomfort with the exploding Seattle sensation. One month later at a concert in Berlin, he declared from the stage, "We are not *the* sound of Seattle. There are many sounds of Seattle."

I wonder to what degree Vedder—the devoted classic rock fan who achieved his boyhood dreams, though in a cursed, Monkey's Paw kind of way—was influenced by the sniping from some of the hippest (and far less successful) members of the Seattle music community. From the moment that Seattle entered the mainstream of rock conversation in the early nineties, there was a vocal contingent from that music scene who insisted on calling this cultural phenomenon a fraud. There was no honeymoon period for Seattle in the national spotlight, no singular moment when the city encouraged young people to flock to this rain-soaked mecca like there was in the sixties with San Francisco, when the Scott McKenzie oldie "San Francisco" implored young people to move there with flowers in their hair. Hype about the Seattle scene arrived with the cynicism about the Seattle scene baked in.

This was informed by the politics of punk purity that reigned at the time, of course. But it also reflected the isolation of Seattle—geographically, culturally, and even meteorologically, given the city's famously rainy climate that kept residents indoors about one-third of the year. This was not a place to which one would normally migrate to become a rock star. Not before the early nineties, anyway. Before grunge happened, Seattle was either a place to which you returned, with your tail between your legs, after failing to establish a career in Los Angeles (as Mike McCready did), or a regional magnet that attracted rural kids who couldn't conceive of (or afford) living in New York or LA (which describes Jeff Ament). Either way living in Seattle meant—by design or resignation—accepting that you would not (and more important *could* not) become famous. So it was naturally an unwelcome surprise to some in the local music community that you really could, in fact, stay in Seattle and also take over the world. Pearl Jam's success could now also be construed as the failure of their local contemporaries.

From all the oral histories I've read about grunge, a quote from Robert Roth of the band Truly has remained burned into my brain: "I don't want to sound snobby, but I *was* a snob back then, so why not—it wasn't punk rock, it wasn't underground, it wasn't rebellious to me. I saw it as being very mainstream. Now had I been living in the Midwest and was bored with everything on MTV, and didn't realize there was all this cool stuff going on, maybe I would have been charged by it, too."

Roth was talking specifically about Pearl Jam. And I'm sure his feelings were representative of how a lot of local scenesters felt as they watched *Ten* go platinum many times over. But the reason this quote stuck with me is that Roth is basically describing my experience at the time, in terms I find extremely irritating but ultimately irrefutable.

Yes, I was a teenager living in the Midwest in 1992. And, of course, I was bored with everything on MTV. And, sorry, but I did not realize there was all this cool stuff going on. The arrival of Nirvana, and then Pearl Jam, pretty much exploded my world in the early nineties. The alt-rock bands were like gateways to a whole other way of experiencing life and culture. I had lived in the dark and those bands were a light. I apologize if I sound like a talking head in a documentary about the nineties, but just because a sentiment has been repeated so many times that it's become a cliché does not make it any less genuine or true. It, in fact, means the opposite—it's a cliché precisely because it's *universal*. Alt-rock mattered to millions of kids who lived in towns without cool college radio stations or independent record stores, which in a pre-internet world meant they had no ability to hear music that slotted even a fraction to the left or right of the most oppressive and corporate-controlled culture.

The absolute *narrowness* of the media then is almost impossible to convey now. But it amplified the impact of *Ten, Nevermind, Badmotorfinger*, and dozens of other albums that suddenly showed up in contexts where they absolutely were not previously welcome. Generation X has one foot in this prehistoric past and another foot in our present world of omnipresent interconnectedness. But even Gen Xers forget what it was really like to live back then. Things could actually surprise you. You might discover this whole new corner of civilization that existed for years or even decades without you knowing about it. And now it was available to you to join and feel transformed by.

The perception of Pearl Jam in the early nineties as a paradigm shifter—or as a callow facsimile of genuinely subversive bands still lurking in the underground—was shaped by more than just the media or the age of the beholder. It was also influenced by class. As Roth suggests, Pearl Jam connected most profoundly with kids "living in the Midwest" who previously had little or no knowledge of indie music scenes. This was not a cool, in-the-know audience. They were, from the perspective of people like Roth, middle-of-the-road hayseeds with bad taste. And that association condemned Pearl Jam by association. In the view of indie aesthetes, Pearl Jam simply appealed to the wrong crowd.

That this slur wasn't *completely* inaccurate—one suspects Pearl Jam did not go down as well at private colleges as they did at public universities—doesn't make it any less insulting or pernicious. It certainly hurt Pearl Jam's standing with music critics, particularly New York City writers already inclined to look askance at bands who dared to build music scenes beyond the east coast. The self-proclaimed "dean" of American rock critics, Robert Christgau, used his bully pulpit at the nation's most prestigious alt-weekly, *The Village Voice*, to dismiss the defining American indie act of the eighties, the proudly southern and nonurban R.E.M., as a "talented minor band" who "valorize the past by definition." In a column published in 1991, he compared the Athens quartet unfavorably to a similarly jangly group from nearby New Jersey, the Feelies, calling out R.E.M.'s supposed "corn quotient" while praising the Feelies' "Passaic County fastness" and "spare downtown cool." As Christgau finally declared, "There was no question which aesthetic was more suitable, more satisfying, more powerful."

There was no question for *him*, anyway. But Christgau was nothing if not consistent in his provincialism. From his Manhattan vantage, Seattle was merely another distant hick town, an Athens for the nineties. In the *Voice*, he broadly dismissed the emerging generation of rock bands coming out of the city, from "scag-dragged Alice In Chains" to "straight-heavy Temple Of The Dog" to "psychedelic stooges Mudhoney," protesting that he risked "deja entendu" from hearing "all these white male longhairs play their guitars too long but not too well." In a "B-minus" review of *Ten*, compiled in his "Turkey Shoot" column of "objectionable-to-awful records," he attacked Pearl Jam on the same grounds that he had once criticized R.E.M.—as "hippie" music lacking in big-city cool and sophistication. And then he went further, likening them to sixties boogie bands like Blue Cheer and Quicksilver Messenger Service that several generations prior had appealed to bleary-eyed, pot-smoking teenagers.

Pearl Jam's actual roots lie with the seventies arena-rock bands who came after the Woodstock-era groups Christgau referenced—Led Zeppelin, Kiss, Cheap Trick, Aerosmith, Van Halen, Iron Maiden—all of whom had also been dismissed over the years by Christgau as (to quote his capsule review of *Led Zeppelin II*) "wah-wah mannerist groups, so dirty they drool on demand." In other words, he thought Pearl Jam—and the groups who influenced them—were stupid. He concluded his pan of *Ten* by characterizing Pearl Jam's demographic as "wasted," in which the "right drugs" are required "to find time to note distinguishing characteristics."[1]

It's easy to be cynical about this in retrospect. I could affect an ironic distance from the small-town kid I used to be, and mock my own ignorance, and pretend that I was more like Robert Christgau or the cool indie-rock singer from the big city who all along despised grunge for not being punk enough. But that would be a lie. I prefer the much tougher path through memory and experience that leads back to innocence, to a time when I was more open to change and more willing to admit what I didn't know. I aspire to recovering my lost naivety, if only for a moment or two.

When I do that, I feel the kind of pure, uncut rage that only a teenager can feel while reading a condescending review of an album you love. Those guys were wrong then, and they're wrong now.

⚡

Alt-rock exploded when I was fourteen, about the same age as Eddie Vedder when he was fantasizing about seeing the Who in a club. Like Vedder, I was also obsessed with classic rock and the sixties, and I'm sure I also harbored my own resentments about not being born during that era. But in 1992, I came to believe that the nineties could be *my* sixties.

If you put the nineties on a continuum, it really is a journey from idealism to nihilism. There was a sense of nihilism certainly in the early nineties—you don't end up with Kurt Cobain taking his own life without some underlying feeling of hopelessness. But there was also a real sense for a few years that things might get better. The Reagan-Bush years—a period that had taken up the majority of every early-nineties teenager's life at that point—had just ended. You had a new, more progressive president in the White House. In pop culture, you had rock stars standing up for feminism, anti-racism, abortion rights, and other progressive principles. There

---

1 To be fair, Christgau later gave an "A-minus" to *Vitalogy* and *Yield*.

was this idea that rock and hip-hop could destroy or at least upend the stranglehold that corporations had on culture. There was a real political consciousness that motivated people to get involved because they thought it would actually make a difference.

Looking back, you can see how and when disillusionment eventually set in. This new insurgent subculture that took over pop culture was commodified and corporatized. Suddenly the market was flooded with lots of lame rip-off bands that inevitability diminished the original innovators. What was cool and revolutionary now seemed tired. Then, in April 1994, Kurt Cobain died, which sucked the air out of grunge. And Pearl Jam spent the next several years wandering in a different wilderness, figuring out a way to survive in a more hostile time.

But before *all that* happened, there really was hope, and Seattle was a symbol of that hope, with Pearl Jam positioned as the figurehead of the scene. This might not have been *technically* true in terms of the people who actually lived in Seattle. Certainly Pearl Jam didn't have the indie cred of Mudhoney or Nirvana. But Pearl Jam was a lot more famous than Mudhoney, and they also were more suited to the role than Nirvana.

I'm just stating plainly what was subliminally communicated to suburban kids like myself via what they saw on MTV in 1992. Nirvana was the outsider band, the group for stubborn nonjoiners, the trio of long-haired weirdos playing the demonic pep rally at the hellish gymnasium and inciting tattooed high schoolers to burn down the school. That had its own power, but it was predestined to burn out quickly. What Pearl Jam offered instead was community. They invited you in, no matter Eddie's occasional protestations to the contrary.

When I entered the eighth grade in the fall of 1992, it felt like Pearl Jam was the biggest band in the world. *Ten* already went platinum in May, peaking at no. 2 on the *Billboard* chart and remaining parked in the Top 10 for months. But Pearl Jam's fame extended beyond just one album. Their reach exploded that summer due to a confluence of three separate phenomena that collectively grounded Pearl Jam's identity in a larger community: Lollapalooza, the Temple of the Dog song "Hunger Strike," and the *Singles* soundtrack.

Released at the end of that June, the *Singles* soundtrack accompanied a Cameron Crowe rom-com about a group of twenty-somethings who actually look thirty-five trying to find love and happiness in Seattle.[2] But, really, the soundtrack is all anybody cared about. *Singles* was a primer for some of the best and most important hard rock bands from Seattle at the time, including Soundgarden, Alice in Chains, Mudhoney, and of course Pearl Jam, which was afforded two songs on the album, "Breath" and "State of Love and Trust," the latter of which quickly became one of their most-loved early songs.

Around this time, the video for "Hunger Strike" entered heavy rotation on MTV, more than a year after its initial release. When Temple of the Dog's self-titled album originally came out in March 1991, *Ten* was still five months away from release. For the original video, the members of Pearl Jam lobbied against Chris Cornell's wishes to shoot an arty clip with minimal footage of the musicians. They wanted (and needed) the exposure an MTV video would provide. This also extended to the rest of the modest Temple of the Dog publicity rollout. The members of Pearl Jam looked for face time wherever they could get it. This prompted a publicist for A&M Records to allegedly remark upon seeing the Temple of the Dog PR photos, "Who the fuck is Eddie Vedder and why is he in my picture?"

By the time most people finally saw "Hunger Strike" in the summer of 1992, it had been re-edited to include even more footage of Vedder. Seattle was also prominently featured—the setting for the shoot was Discovery Park, a rural enclave in the city that offered an array of rustic and wet-looking scenic vistas. In the video, Seattle is portrayed as a dark-hued,

---

2 Eddie Vedder, Jeff Ament, and Stone Gossard appear briefly in the film as the backing musicians for Matt Dillon's grunge band Citizen Dick. Weirdly, they play characters named "Eddie Vedder," "Jeff Ament," and "Stone Gossard," though in this universe Pearl Jam doesn't exist and Eddie is a drummer in spite of being more handsome and charismatic than Dillon's character.

nature-oriented backwater dotted with man-size weeds and shadowy forests populated by brooding guys who wear long underwear beneath their baggy shorts and Dr. Martens.

When "Hunger Strike" was released in early '91, Cornell was the star of the video, a smoldering leading man expressing sorrow over the loss of his friend, Mother Love Bone singer Andrew Wood. But Pearl Jam's subsequent fame decisively shifted the video's perspective. Watching it in the summer of '92, what stood out was Eddie's Vedder's dramatic entrance at the seventy-second mark. There he is, surrounded by the weeds, black leather set against brown flannel, his cheek bones looking so sharp they cut through the screen.

Eddie was not trying to upstage Cornell—the fact that he's *not* trying to draw you in is what draws you in. He's like Jack Nicholson in *Easy Rider*, the bit player who suddenly takes over and captivates the audience because that's simply what was meant to be. It's star power in its purest form. To say Vedder's look in "Hunger Strike" was *instantly* iconic would be an exaggeration, but it rapidly burned itself into the minds of MTV viewers during weeks of constant rotation that summer.

It wasn't just how Eddie Vedder looked, of course, but also the emotional resonance of his voice. He already sounds so much like *him*. That *I'm goin' hungrrrrrry*—as much as even the biggest hits from *Ten*—became the source material for all the bad Eddie impersonations that would eventually subsume alt-rock. A less charitable listener might even cite it as an example of "yarling," the derogatory term coined by Jack Endino for "an annoying, exaggerated vocal affectation" in which a rock vocalist sings, as Endino put it, "melodramatically with a sort of barely suppressed letter 'r' sound lurking beneath every other syllable."

Endino for his part did not single out Vedder as an egregious yarler, insisting that he "hardly did it after *Ten*." But *Ten* certainly is a watershed moment in yarling history, an unwitting blueprint for countless shitty nineties rock bands.

Endino traces yarling back to the arena rock singers of the seventies, but in Eddie Vedder's case his clearest vocal antecedent is Bruce Springsteen.

I refer specifically to the albums *Born to Run* and *Darkness on the Edge of Town*, in which Springsteen wrote heightened and bombastic songs rooted in the struggle to reconcile youthful energy with the pressures of the adult world. (Springsteen and Vedder are also linked by their rage at the dysfunctional father figures that loom large in their early songs.) Springsteen at this time was apt to move beyond lyrics and express the inarticulate speech of his wounded heart with operatic wails. You hear this at the climax of "Backstreets" from *Born to Run*, and during crucial make-or-break moments in "Something in the Night" and "Adam Raised a Cain" from *Darkness on the Edge of Town*. A guttural, pained howl that can easily descend into petulant yarling when executed less artfully.

In the book *Pearl Jam Twenty*, Springsteen offers the most insightful summation of Vedder's potency as a vocalist that I've ever read. "Eddie had an unusual voice for a hard rock singer," Springsteen remarked upon hearing early Pearl Jam songs like "Alive" and "Jeremy." He describes Vedder's voice as a "folk-like tremolo" that "created an intimacy in the midst of what could be a violent sound that reached your heart."

Listening to "Hunger Strike" with Springsteen's ears, you can almost hear it as a folk song, with Vedder operating in the lineage of big-voiced sixties revival belters like Odetta and the Clancy Brothers. These singers specialized in tremulous, impassioned ballads delivered with the conviction of one who believes that this song might very well be the last that they ever sing.

That's the level of intense intimacy to which Springsteen himself aspired, and it's what enabled him to recognize it in Eddie Vedder.

⚡

Not everyone was wrapped up in grunge mania in the summer of 1992. Even as Pearl Jam flourished across multiple high-charting albums, the top LP for months was Billy Ray Cyrus's country-himbo quasi-classic *Some Gave All*. For millions of people, "Achy Breaky Heart" defines that year. But if you were young, and you loved rock 'n' roll, and you lived in the middle of the country, and you watched MTV constantly, your world was dominated by Pearl Jam.

The degree to which the *Singles* soundtrack and *Temple of the Dog* and the hits from *Ten* were coordinated with the Lollapalooza tour—which included Pearl Jam and Soundgarden, bringing the community that you saw regularly on MTV to your town—is difficult to quantify. But when the tour commenced in July, right as all three of those albums were peaking, it underscored the novel way that Pearl Jam was marketed.

Not only were they positioned as the Seattle scene figurehead, but there was also special emphasis put on their potency as a live act. Their first two music videos, for "Alive" and "Even Flow," were relatively raw depictions of a typical Pearl Jam gig, in which the audience is given nearly as much prominence as the band. Onstage, you see the musicians eschew the slickness that was endemic to big-time rock right before the rise of alternative— there are no pyrotechnics or spandex, just five guys dressed down in tank tops and cargo shorts. (With the exception of Mike McCready's Stevie Ray Vaughan homages, of course.)

The band looks identical to the audience, which resembles a typical group of teens and twenty-somethings from the early nineties, only much *freer*. Anyone stuck at home watching Pearl Jam videos saw their peers achieving a catharsis on-screen that was not available to them at school, at home, or any place else in their cloistered and stifling communities. At a Pearl Jam show, you could scream, jump, crowd-surf, or do anything else that finally (*finally!*) expressed what was going on inside you. Those music videos sold Pearl Jam as one of the great live acts of their generation. But they also marketed a feeling of togetherness that was very hard to find any place else in mainstream culture.

Anyone unable to see Pearl Jam on the Lollapalooza tour had to settle for watching their *MTV Unplugged* episode, which aired on the channel that summer almost as often as "Hunger Strike." In the hierarchy of *MTV Unplugged* installments, Pearl Jam isn't mentioned as often as Nirvana. This makes sense, given that Nirvana's *MTV Unplugged* was released as an album in the aftermath of Kurt Cobain's death, and was commonly perceived to be a comment *on* his death. Pearl Jam's *MTV Unplugged* meanwhile didn't come out as an official album until 2019—though it was widely bootlegged long before that—and it lacked the psycho-drama subtext of the Nirvana record, which unfolds like a man hosting his own wake.

The power of Pearl Jam's *MTV Unplugged* is that it occurred at the beginning of their career, not the end, and ultimately functioned as an advertisement for life rather than a dirge about death. This is communicated subtly by the staging of each performance. When you watch the Nirvana *MTV Unplugged*, Cobain seems to grow smaller and more distant as the performance unfolds, which makes his screams at the end of the concluding song, the Lead Belly cover "Where Did You Sleep Last Night," hit that much harder. But in the Pearl Jam *MTV Unplugged*, Eddie Vedder grows in stature, as all great rock singers must, even when it's only an optical illusion.[3]

When the show opens with "Oceans," Vedder is wearing a hat and keeping his arms close to his body. He's crouching into himself while seated on a stool, emphasizing his diminutive stature. (This is his Clark Kent pose.) For the next tune, "State of Love and Trust"—at the time not yet released on the *Singles* soundtrack—he sings louder and furiously pumps his right leg. Then comes "Alive," the first "hit" of the performance, and the hat comes off, exposing that distinctive early-nineties Eddie Vedder mane that adds several inches to his stature. At the end of the song, he picks up his mic stand and mock-slams it into Dave Abbruzzese's cymbals. Then comes "Black" and "Jeremy," at this point still album cuts. Vedder howls them with all his characteristic mannerisms—eyes bulging, cheekbones protruding, long hair waving. (This is his rock Superman guise.)

---

3 At 5-foot-7, Eddie is 1 inch taller than Bono and 3 inches shorter than Mick Jagger.

The most memorable part of Pearl Jam's *MTV Unplugged* is the final song, "Porch." On *Ten*, "Porch" is the sound of escape—from your town, your circumstances, and your own fears and hang-ups. I imagine it taking place on the same porch where Mary dances like a vision while the radio plays in Bruce Springsteen's "Thunder Road." Like Mary, the protagonist of the Pearl Jam song is implored to leave the porch by a companion who is determined to transcend all constraints, be they physical or spiritual: "This could be the day / Hold my hand, walk beside me."

During a typical Pearl Jam concert in 1992, "Porch" came at the end of the proper set, right before the encore. But it was really the night's major set piece, with an extended instrumental jam in the middle spotlighted by McCready's excellent soloing, in which he frequently quoted the riff from Jimi Hendrix's "Voodoo Child (Slight Return)." Meanwhile Vedder would climb the scaffolding above the stage or traverse balconies and show boxes hanging over the audience, before actually hurling himself down dozens of feet *into* the audience. For Vedder, these theatrical and extremely dangerous stage moves were a way to act out the meaning of "Porch," a "seize the day" maneuver that extrapolated his life-or-death vocal delivery into an actual life-or-death gesture.

When you listen to bootlegs from this period, it's amazing how coherent these "Porch" jams are compared with how anarchic they look when you revisit them on video. Not only because of Vedder's antics, but also due to the pandemonium among the musicians he temporarily leaves behind onstage. Pearl Jam's historic performance in June at the Pinkpop Festival in the Netherlands is probably the most notorious example of Ament, Gossard, and McCready stomping recklessly from stage left to stage right and back again and nearly braining one another with their instruments. And yet when you listen to the tape, they manage to hit pretty much every note. (The most *important* notes, at any rate.)

On *MTV Unplugged*, "Porch" is put at the end of the episode, right after their current hit at the time, "Even Flow." Though in reality they played "Porch" *before* "Even Flow" at the taping, which you can tell if you watch the performance closely. For instance, the most famous part of the *MTV Unplugged* "Porch" occurs when Vedder—after he falls off his stool and then rides it like a surf board—grabs a marker and writes "PRO-CHOICE !!!" on his left arm. If you look at Vedder's left hand during the "Even Flow" performance as it was broadcast, you can see the exclamation marks that *he has not actually drawn yet in the edited version of the show.*

This *very* minor continuity issue aside, MTV's decision to re-edit the *Unplugged* performance to put "Porch" last was a wise one. For any purist who feels that it should have been left as it actually is, I offer this retort: "HEYYYYYYYYYYYYYYYYY HEYYYYYYYYYYYYYYY HEYYYYYYYYYYYYY YEAHHHH YEAHHH YEAH YEAH YEAH YEAH WOW!"

I refer to one of the most glorious utterances in Pearl Jam history, which occurs at the end of the *MTV Unplugged* "Porch" jam. It goes on for an incredible twenty-five seconds. Eddie goes and goes and *goes* and *GOES* until every single hair on every single neck in the immediate vicinity is standing up. It's an expression of total exhilaration, a musical manifestation of a car careening off a cliff at top speed and somehow, against all odds, never hitting the ground. An incredible feat of strength that achieves the death-defying majesty of Vedder's onstage Evel Knievel stunts solely with the go-for-broke power of his voice. It transforms "Thunder Road" into "Born to Run."

You don't need anything else after that. Another song would have felt redundant. This was the ultimate closing statement for a band making its case for eternal greatness to a national TV audience. It's not just a rock singer successfully rousing an audience. It is a *Braveheart*-level "follow me into the depths of hell" exhortation. For countless viewers, seeing *MTV Unplugged* was an invitation to join the Pearl Jam bandwagon and ride it wherever it might go.

CHAPTER 4
"JEREMY"

(From *Ten*)

John Entwistle vs. Gene Simmons • Rastacaps • Tom Petersson's
Twelve-String Bass • How Music Videos Ruin Songs (but Not Really)
• *Detention: The Siege at Johnson High*

Before we examine "Jeremy"—unquestionably one of Pearl Jam's most
famous and iconic songs—as a piece of music, a music video, and a signi-
fier of social problems, we must first discuss it as a metaphor for shifting
power dynamics inside Pearl Jam in the early nineties.

Naturally, we'll begin by discussing Jeff Ament's collection of floppy
hats.

When Pearl Jam's bassist started playing the instrument in 1981, the
year he turned eighteen, his musical role models were the Who's John
Entwistle and Kiss's Gene Simmons. At first glance, it's hard to imagine
two musicians—one quiet and stoic onstage, the other bombastic and
blood-spitting—who are more different. Entwistle, for one, is perhaps the

most technically gifted bass player in rock history; Gene Simmons, on the other hand, is not.

But upon closer examination, there is one essential attribute linking Simmons and Entwistle to Ament—they were all players who demanded the audience's attention, in a manner that isn't typical for bass players. Simmons did it with his loud, brash sartorial choices, and Entwistle did it with his loud, brash bass tones. Ament in the early nineties decided to take *both* approaches.

Following Simmons's example, Ament took to wearing tams—also known as rastacaps—onstage. Coupled with his excitable, athletic stage presence, these hats made Ament impossible to ignore in Pearl Jam's early music videos, immediately distinguishing him from at least 90 percent of bass players in rock history. Eddie Vedder was the obvious focus, but Ament was the second most recognizable member of Pearl Jam in those days. In essence, he forcefully assumed a "second in command" role usually fulfilled by the lead guitarist, and he did it by dressing like Gary Oldman's character in *True Romance*.

But Ament also emulated Entwistle by pushing his bass to the front of Pearl Jam's music. And he did this on *Ten* by using instruments that were unusual for a rock bassist at the time—fretless and twelve-string basses. This guaranteed that Ament's tones would stand out in a way that bass didn't in most alternative rock bands.

Ament first utilized twelve-string bass on the Mother Love Bone songs "Star Dog Champion" and "Holy Roller," from their only full-length album, 1990's *Apple*. He borrowed the instrument from Cheap Trick's Tom Petersson, a pioneer of the twelve-string bass whose metallic and melodic playing on songs like "Gonna Raise Hell" and "Need Your Love" had caught Ament's ear as a teenager.

Back then, Ament would often describe songs he loved by Kiss, Cheap Trick, or Aerosmith by humming the bass line instead of the guitar riff or vocal melody. When he wrote his earliest songs for Pearl Jam, he was determined to put his bass at the center of the music. It was, in a sense, a power move. But it also genuinely reflected how he heard music.

You can hear Ament's twelve-string bass most prominently on two *Ten* tracks, "Why Go" and "Jeremy." On the latter song, especially, the bass is the most prominent part of the music. Not only is the central riff played by Ament, but you barely hear the guitars at all. (The second most audible instrument is cello.) Anyone who attempts to hum the music *has* to perform the bass line. It was as if Ament's teenaged self had scored a victory for bass-obsessed kids everywhere.

On subsequent Pearl Jam records, however, Ament found that he had to temper his use of the twelve-string bass out of musical necessity. By the time of their third LP, *Vitalogy*, Vedder was playing guitar, which meant there were now three guitar players competing for space in the upper ranges of the music. Given that the tactile clanging of the twelve-string also lurked in that same sonic space, Ament realized "there was already a lot happening on that frequency," as he put it in a later interview, and pulled back to a more conventional supporting role.

But this retreat didn't only stem from musical concerns. It also reflects power struggles over creative control and a shift in the hierarchy within the band. When Pearl Jam began, Ament and Stone Gossard were the acknowledged leaders—they were the most experienced musicians, they put the band together, and they wrote most of the songs. But by the time of *Vitalogy*, Vedder had assumed the leadership position.

Ironically, this process began with the video for Ament's song, "Jeremy." When the video exploded into the public consciousness in late summer 1992, nobody was talking about Ament's bass playing. The focus was almost entirely on the singer.

⚡

It was "Jeremy"—more than *Singles*, "Hunger Strike," or any other song on *Ten*—that elevated Pearl Jam from popular rock band to genuine cultural phenomenon, and Vedder from budding rock star to generational spokesman. This was compounded by the relative slowness of pre-internet culture—"Jeremy" hung around for a *long* time, finally winning a Video of the Year trophy at the MTV Video Music Awards a full thirteen months after it first aired in August 1992.

You don't have to be a Pearl Jam fan to recall images from the "Jeremy" video, especially if you happened to be young and watching MTV regularly in the early nineties. Jeremy wanders a forest alone, drawing his childlike pictures. At school, he is taunted by classmates whose faces are frozen into teasing rictus grins. At home, his parents similarly freeze him out. So he's sent back to the woods to vent his demons. And then there's that shocking ending . . . which was widely misinterpreted due to MTV's censorship.

More than any other music video made by a commercially successful alt-rock band at the time, "Jeremy" was a scathing critique of conformist mainstream American culture. Not only is the American flag surrounded by flames—though not quite set on fire—but a classroom of students doing the Pledge of Allegiance is equated with them performing a Nazi salute. There's also a reference to Genesis 3:6, a Bible verse about how the arrogance of humans led to the destruction of the Garden of Eden.

The "Jeremy" video was not subtle. But despite all these highly charged visual provocations, which were devised by director Mark Pellington, the video is undoubtedly centered on Vedder. Amid the clips of the video's "A" story starring fourteen-year-old actor Trevor Wilson, we see Vedder seated on a stool and relating the lyrics with extreme intensity. This image of Vedder rhymed with the recent *MTV Unplugged*, which was still playing constantly on the channel. He looks in the video almost exactly like he did performing "Jeremy" on *Unplugged* three months earlier, effectively burnishing his emerging icon status. This version of Vedder—a furrowed brow clad in various shades of brown corduroy and denim—is still embedded deep in the collective cultural memory of Pearl Jam.

When I interviewed Pellington in 2017, he said his decision to spin his camera around Vedder—the video literally revolves around him—was intended to draw in the audience by creating the illusion of "an electronic campfire." Thanks to Pellington's directorial nudging, we are made to feel as though we are sitting in a circle around Vedder, pulling us deeper into his fatalistic and riveting storytelling.

As a story song, "Jeremy" combined a real-life incident with Vedder's own bad childhood memories and imagination. The inspiration came from the tragic story of Jeremy Wade Delle, a fifteen-year-old boy from Richardson, Texas, who took his own life in front of his classmates on January 8, 1991. In the video, a shirtless Jeremy tosses his teacher an apple before pulling the trigger. In reality, Delle briefly left class after his teacher told him to get an attendance slip because he arrived late that morning. He returned instead with a .357 Magnum and declared, "Miss, I got what I really went for." And then he shot himself.

After the video created a sensation—and transformed Delle into a folk hero—his parents protested over the song's depiction of them as uncaring and inattentive. In real life, they had sought out counseling for their son after he was diagnosed with depression. The song's dramatic embellishment likely derived from Vedder's own troubled relationship with his parents as a teenager, as well as the preoccupations with murder and mental illness as evinced in the "Momma-Son" songs. Ultimately, the anti-parent sentiment made "Jeremy" feel more universal as a teen angst anthem than a brooding character study about a troubled Texas teenager might otherwise be.

For the video, Vedder's interpretation of Delle's story was further extrapolated by Pellington, who was grappling with his own difficult memories from childhood. His father was ill with Alzheimer's at the time, which dredged up "feelings of alienation and loneliness and child abandonment and all those really primal feelings that speak to kids," he told me. Pellington was also guided by Vedder, who related Delle's story as Pellington scribbled visual ideas on index cards. He then wrote a treatment on his computer, which crashed. Forced to rewrite the treatment, what "poured out of me and was probably a little more stream of consciousness and a little more writing on emotion rather than logic," he recalled.

When it came time to shoot Vedder's sequences, Pellington found Pearl Jam's singer to be a natural actor, and he knocked it out in three takes. "What really pushes it though, and makes it transcend into something artistic that lasts, is Eddie's performance," he said.

What Vedder does in the "Jeremy" video quickly became another source text for anyone who wanted to caricature him—the theatrical hand signals that act out lyrics, the exaggerated facial contortions that emphasize those cheekbones, the sudden explosions of neck-bursting rage. But during the first, say, hundred times I saw the "Jeremy" video, I found Vedder to be an electrifying manifestation of all the horribly relatable feelings he was singing about. It was as if he took what was lurking inside your guts, put it inside his own body, and then proceeded to purge it in a spectacular body-quaking spasm. As Pellington put it, "It was an internal thing that he was then unleashing in a very contained space."

Perhaps if I had been five years older, this would have read as corny or ham-fisted because Vedder dared to not allow himself any ironic distance from what he was conjuring. Most adult rock stars in his position would protect themselves by being at least a little patronizing to their teenaged audience. But Vedder earnestly channeled the tangible rage, fear, and loneliness felt by all young adults without apology or arched eyebrows. There is nothing ironic about the "Jeremy" video. The result is a historic work of teen-centered art.

If Vedder was a natural at expressing the essence of his songs in the music video format, "Jeremy" would ultimately become a symbol of how Pearl Jam didn't want to conduct its career. This narrative began in earnest the same month that "Jeremy" became the toast of the VMAs in September 1993, via Cameron Crowe's *Rolling Stone* cover story. Crowe includes an anecdote related by Ament about Mark Eitzel of American Music Club complimenting him on "Jeremy" but adding, "But the video sucked. It ruined my vision of the song."

"Ten years from now," Ament says, "I don't want people to remember our songs as videos." Vedder immediately agrees, promising that the next Pearl Jam record won't have any videos, a vow that would hold true for the next five years.

"I don't even have MTV," Vedder adds.

The idea that the "Jeremy" video somehow ruined the song has been subsequently taken as gospel in conversations about Pearl Jam's career.

Which doesn't make any sense to me. Yes, the video is a little heavy-handed and it was certainly overplayed by MTV throughout late 1992 and early '93. But it stuck with people because the filmmaking is compelling and Vedder's performance is magnetic. For the majority of viewers, the video *enhanced* their enjoyment of "Jeremy." If the video had truly "ruined" the song, it's unlikely that Pearl Jam would have continued playing "Jeremy" regularly on every tour they've ever done since.

When I spoke with Pellington, he forwarded a different, less parroted theory about how the band—and Vedder specifically—reacted to the fallout from "Jeremy." It was related to a common misunderstanding caused by MTV's censorship of the video.

In Pellington's original edit—which is now commonly available on YouTube—Jeremy is clearly seen putting the gun barrel in his mouth. While you don't see him literally commit suicide, the implication is obvious. MTV, however, insisted on cutting these crucial frames. This made it unclear whether the frozen, blood-splattered faces of his classmates we see at the video's end signify their horror over Jeremy's death or *their own deaths* at Jeremy's hand. MTV's prohibition inadvertently changed "Jeremy" from a video about suicide to a video about a school shooting.

This perception unwittingly was aided by Vedder's lyrics, which could now be interpreted differently in light of the edit. The most underrated aspect of "Jeremy" is the cleverness of Vedder's storytelling, which for the most part does not come from Jeremy's point of view. Rather, he speaks on behalf of the classmates who abused him. In their eyes, Jeremy appeared to be a "harmless little fuck" until their teasing "unleashed a lion," causing him to lash out and bite "the recess lady's breast." (This detail suggests that the fictional Jeremy had already been an outcast for years, since his grade-school days.)

"Jeremy" is really a song about everybody *around* Jeremy. This narrative construction puts the listener in the place of the villains rather than the hero, an approach no doubt inspired by a multitude of Pete Townshend songs about marginalized loner freaks, from "Happy Jack" to *Tommy*. The exception is the first verse, in which Vedder writes from an omniscient perspective that paints Jeremy in a more sinister light—the pictures he draws by himself allude to fantasies of revenge and dominance, with Jeremy's "arms raised in a V / as the dead lay in pools of maroon below."

In the video, this is muddled further by the casting of Wilson, a darkly handsome young man whose rich brown hair and high cheekbones bear more than a passing resemblance to a teenaged Eddie Vedder. This puts the idea in the viewer's mind that Jeremy *is* Vedder, who presumably eluded authorities all these years ago in order to relate his story. Again, this is only possible because viewers originally couldn't see the gun go in Jeremy's mouth at the end of the video.

Editing out the "offensive" content actually made "Jeremy" more dangerous and even irresponsible. "For 98 percent of people, it's 'Oh, he shot them.' And that's just wrong. It's just that the censorship made the meaning different than the real meaning," Pellington maintained. "Later, real kids shot people and said, 'I was inspired by 'Jeremy.'"

In Pellington's view, that's the real reason Pearl Jam turned so hard against music videos. "I'd also be like, 'See? Videos are fucked up, man.'"

$$\lightning$$

On February 2, 1996, a fourteen-year-old boy named Barry Loukaitis entered Frontier Middle School in Moses Lake, Washington—a community about 180 miles east of Seattle—carrying a hunting rifle, two handguns, and dozens of rounds of ammunition. Walking into his fifth period algebra class, he shot and killed two fellow students and his teacher.

At the trial, Loukaitis's attorneys claimed that the boy was inspired by two pieces of media: the Stephen King novel *Rage*, about a disturbed teenager who takes his algebra class hostage, and the "Jeremy" video. "This boy *is* Jeremy," one of the lawyers argued. But this defense failed—Loukaitis was subsequently found guilty and sentenced to two life sentences plus an additional 205 years without the possibility of parole.

Nineteen years later, in an article for the *New Yorker*, Malcolm Gladwell seized upon the Loukaitis story as the beginning of the "modern phenomenon" of school shootings. "There were scattered instances of gunmen or bombers attacking schools in the years before Barry Loukaitis, but they were lower profile," Gladwell writes.

According to a 2018 study conducted by criminology professor James Alan Fox of Northeastern University, there were actually *more* school shootings in the early nineties than in the years afterward. The difference now is that each school shooting is taken more seriously. They seem more impactful because the media and general public dwells on them more.

For instance, the week before *Ten* was certified platinum in May 1992, a twenty-year-old man named Eric Houston returned to his former high school in Olivehurst, California, and shot and killed three students and one teacher and injured ten more people. Five years later, this tragedy was turned into a made-for-TV thriller called *Detention: The Siege at Johnson High*.[1] In the film, former *Silver Spoons* star Rick Schroeder plays a character based on Houston while Henry "The Fonz" Winkler portrays a police officer who tries to coax the shooter into surrendering.

It's unlikely that a contemporary school shooting would ever be turned into fodder for a crass, low-rent thriller. But the existence of *Detention: The Siege at Johnson High* speaks to how dysfunctional nineties culture was. Throughout the decade, there was a toxic strain of entertainment that catered to the rage and entitlement of disaffected young white men, ranging from nü-metal acts like Limp Bizkit and Kid Rock to the lecherous likes of the *Girls Gone Wild* and *American Pie* franchises. This aspect of the nineties remains fraught for the people who came of age during the decade, particularly given the harsh judgments of younger generations. There's a part of me that appreciates growing up at a time when pushing the envelope was encouraged and often rewarded. At that time, the cool kids were fighting *against* political correctness because it was usually aligned with right-wing, repressive movements. An edgy indifference toward moral and ethical consequences defines a lot of the culture I grew

---

1 It's also known as *Hostage High* or *Target for Rage*.

up with during my formative years, and if I'm honest, that conditioning hasn't totally left me.

But pondering cultural detritus like *Detention: The Siege at Johnson High* causes me to believe that a certain kind of numbness had set in among my generation by the end of the decade. Cool indifference gave way to spiritual impotence, where people watched and listened to terrible, vacuous entertainment because it was the only way to feel anything. A collective belief in the meaningless of modern existence had inevitability led to self-destruction.

The degree to which any of this influenced Pearl Jam is unclear. What is apparent, however, is that Vedder would never again write songs that expressed sympathy for disaffected and potentially violent white guys. Instead, Vedder began criticizing those people in his lyrics.

On the next Pearl Jam album, *Vs.*, he wrote often about female protagonists bristling against the control of the men in their lives, a theme that spoke even more directly to the reality of Vedder's childhood—and the hostility he harbored toward his stepfather well into adulthood—than the heightened melodrama of "Jeremy." And then there's "W.M.A.," in which Vedder wrote directly about his own white privilege.

It was inspired by an incident in which Vedder and his friend, a Black man, were accosted by two police officers one morning outside a rehearsal studio. "Compared to me, this guy looks as respectable as fuck. But they started hassling him, and that just blew me the fuck away," he recalled. "I was just really wound up by it. I had all this fucking energy rushing through me. I was mad. Really fucking angry. I got back to the studio and the guys had been working on this thing and I just went straight in and did the vocals, and that was the song."

Intentional or not, "W.M.A." plays like the anti-"Jeremy." Once again, Vedder takes an outsider's perspective, only this time he looks upon the protagonist with disdain. Whereas Jeremy *bit* the recess lady's breast as an expression of his inner turmoil, the "white male American" *takes* "his mother's white breast to his tongue," a sign of his privilege and indulgence. He's not the cursed victim of "Jeremy" but rather a spoiled kid gifted by the circumstance of his race and gender, having "won the lottery by being born."

Nevertheless, the "Jeremy" video continued to link Pearl Jam to the nineties white male rage entertainment complex long after the decade ended. In a 2016 *New Yorker* article by Daniel Wenger, the video is cited as part of the "intractable cultural script" of school shooters. Wegner highlights the scene that visualizes the "arms raised in a V" lyric, showing Jeremy in apparent triumph as a forest fire rages around him. This same pose has been re-created in photos and videos posted by numerous school shooters, including Seung-Hui Cho, who killed thirty-two people and then himself in 2007 at Virginia Tech.

Pellington, who later filmed a PSA about gun violence in 2014, was asked by Wegner what he would do differently if he could make the video today. "I'd pull focus right up to the gun," he replied. "That's the proper shot."

As for Pearl Jam, "Jeremy" marked a turning point in their engagement with the popular culture of the nineties. The video put them at the center's public attention, which made them—particularly Vedder—extremely uncomfortable. It wasn't *just* the attention, but rather the culture itself, that proved incompatible with the band. Pearl Jam was part of a wave of artists in the early nineties—many of whom were musicians, though it was also expanding to film and literature—who were against the mainstream status quo. But the anger and rebellion that fueled their rise quickly metastasized into something altogether gross and untenable.

Pearl Jam had helped to rapidly remake the culture. But the revolution no longer was theirs. Soon, they would look for a way out.

CHAPTER 5

"ANIMAL" > "ROCKIN' IN THE FREE WORLD"

(1993 MTV Video Music Awards)

Stone Temple Pilots • Ripping Off Boston • The Mall of America • Why Bonding with Pete Townshend and Neil Young Is Better Than Shooting Heroin

When "poseur"—a French word for "an insincere or affected person"—emerged as an English language term in the mid-nineteenth century, it was used to describe a vaguely sinister individual who aspired to a higher status in society without earning it. A poseur was viewed as calculating and mercenary, constantly angling to put himself in the best light in order to impress others and gain influence. He pretended, with dramatic flair and considerable charm, to be rich or cultured. But in his own mind he was constantly worried about being outed as a phony.

This fear drove the poseur to extreme means of obfuscation. The poseur might even take on a criminal edge, like the character of Tom Ripley, created by author Patricia Highsmith for a series of novels and later played in movies by Matt Damon (*The Talented Mr. Ripley*), Dennis Hopper (*The American Friend*), Alain Delon (*Purple Noon*), and John Malkovich (*Ripley's Game*). Ripley is a genuine villain, a con man who eventually takes to theft and murder. A poseur with a very real dangerous side. Though, in his defense, at least he never formed a post-grunge band.

In modern times, "poseur" usually has a musical connotation. Particularly in the worlds of indie rock, punk, and hip-hop, it describes a kind of charlatan, an artist only in the sense of being a rip-off artist. This person steals ideas, of course, but no artist is wholly original and everyone has obvious antecedents. But the poseur's most offensive act is jacking the essence of a perceived superior artist. The idea is that a poseur can fool the public into believing that he has achieved parity with the person he's robbing from. He might even *supplant* his superior. The only way to prevent this is for self-appointed authenticity arbiters—known officially as music critics, though amateur authenticity arbiters abound—to step in and call out the poseurs before they do any lasting damage.

Music culture in the twenty-first century has mostly moved on from the poseur phenomenon. Policing the intentions of strangers—which requires peering into their very souls to determine whether they're "authentic"—is tedious and pointless work. There's also an unspoken, culture-wide recognition that in the age of social media, everybody is a poseur. We all carefully curate an online persona that presents an attractive, effortlessly cool, and entirely phony portrait of ourselves for public consumption. What keeps the scam going is our collective agreement to not acknowledge this mass charade; calling out one person, even a celebrity, could bring the whole system to its knees.

There are rare exceptions. For instance, in December 2015, *GQ* magazine published a tribute to Scott Weiland called "Rock's Greatest Poseur." The headline was a winking acknowledgment of a moment in American pop culture when we hit peak "poseur," back in the nineties. At that time, "poseur" accusations were prevalent in hip-hop, with rappers literally murdering one another to underline the realness of their lyrics and music videos. In alternative rock, the results were less violent but no less pervasive and destructive.

For Pearl Jam, their meteoric rise, intense MTV exposure, and MOR classic-rock evangelism made them susceptible to poseur charges. In the early nineties, everyone from Kurt Cobain to *Entertainment Weekly*[1] sniffed that they weren't alternative or underground enough. Another person who viewed them as frauds initially was Scott Weiland. "I was on the pro-Nirvana, anti–Pearl Jam bandwagon," he told *Rolling Stone*'s David Fricke in 1997. "I didn't get to the point where I respected Pearl Jam as a band until I saw them on Lollapalooza [in 1992], when they played in the middle of the day. Before that I was, 'Pearl Jam? Fakes.' "

The irony of this was not lost on Weiland. His band, Stone Temple Pilots, were viewed in the nineties as the biggest alt-rock poseurs of all. And unlike Pearl Jam, the band they were most often accused of ripping off, STP never was able to shed that reputation. Which is why, twenty-three years after the release of his band's debut album, *Core*, Scott Weiland was still being labeled a poseur by a major men's fashion magazine.

I'm leaving out one crucial bit of context: The *GQ* article ran the day after Weiland died. He was only forty-eight years old. His body was discovered lying inside a tour bus parked near the Mall of America in Bloomington, Minnesota. In the months before his death, Weiland had been hit by a tsunami of personal problems: his mother and father were diagnosed with cancer, he was estranged from his two children, he was bipolar and had contracted Hepatitis C, he was nearly broke, and he had a nasty drinking problem. Weiland's current band the Wildabouts—he had been fired years earlier from Stone Temple Pilots—was embarrassed after

---

1 *Entertainment Weekly* published dismissive reviews of *Ten* and *Vs.*, concluding in the former that Pearl Jam is "another mainstream, he-man rock band." Only in the nineties would a publication like *Entertainment Weekly*—which was otherwise as reverent and nonskeptical of mainstream culture as any magazine of the time—take it upon themselves to affect a "more alternative than thou" posture.

a video featuring a lethargic performance of the STP hit "Vasoline" went viral. After decades of drug addiction and mental illness driving him into scrapes with the law and his bandmates in STP and Velvet Revolver, Scott Weiland was at the very bottom of his personal and professional fortunes.

The local county medical examiner's office later ruled that he died of mixed-drug toxicity from cocaine, ethanol, and amphetamine MDA. He also had cardiovascular disease, asthma, and multiple-substance dependence, plus a medicine-cabinet's worth of prescriptions in his system: Lunesta, Klonopin, Viagra, Dalmane, Buprenex, and Geodon.

Even after all *that*, Scott Weiland was still called a poseur. He died a broken man, lying alone in a parking lot while subarctic winds slammed against his lonely bus, *and even then* he couldn't quite convince people that he was a legitimately troubled guy.

How could this be? Was something "fake" about his death? Did *GQ* expect him to leap out of the coffin and perform a song that kind of sounded like "Even Flow"? He was dead. I think that means he wins the alt-rock authenticity sweepstakes.

⚡

The story of Scott Weiland and Stone Temple Pilots fascinates me in the context of Pearl Jam because STP is like the bizarro world version of Pearl Jam. STP represents an alternate timeline for how things might have turned out for them if their circumstances were less favorable and infinitely unluckier. Scott Weiland is the answer to the question, "What if Eddie Vedder had dealt with the pressures of fame by trying heroin?"

STP's first album, *Core*, was released on September 29, 1992. That same week, "Jeremy" was officially released as a single, though by then the song had already been massively exposed by MTV. "Jeremy" becoming a such a big hit essentially ended *Ten*'s album cycle; the record company's desire to release the already popular power ballad "Black" as a single was rebuffed by Vedder, who concluded (probably wisely) that Pearl Jam had already achieved maximum exposure. (Though the song became a radio hit anyway.) This created a space for *Core* to move in and provide a Pearl Jam–hungry public with similarly grungy rock songs.

While the timing of *Core* was fortuitous in the short run, over time it cast a pall on Stone Temple Pilots that they were never able to overcome. Through no real fault of their own, the release of their debut made them seem like opportunists eager to cash in on the latest alt-rock craze by following closely in the footsteps of the scene's most popular band.

Truth be told, I don't think Stone Temple Pilots actually sounds all that much like Pearl Jam, especially on the albums after *Core*. When I interviewed Dean and Robert DeLeo—STP's Stone and Jeff figures—in 2016, they spoke enthusiastically about playing Rush and King Crimson covers back in New Jersey in their pre-fame band, Tyrus. There was little trace of punk or indie rock in their musical upbringing; they were proud products of seventies arena rock, an influence you hear loud and clear in their music. When they embraced glitter rock and AM pop influences on subsequent albums like 1994's *Purple* and 1996's *Tiny Music . . . Songs from the Vatican Gift Shop*, they moved even further from the DIY evangelism that Pearl Jam was foregrounding on their records. As STP evolved, they sounded more and more like the sort of self-aware and unapologetically bombastic pop-metal band that Andrew Wood would have wanted to be the singer for.

At the center was Weiland, one of the era's most gifted rock vocalists, who would come to demonstrate a chameleon-like ability to sing in different styles. On *Core*, he could affect an Eddie Vedder–esque growl because that's what was required to get STP's songs on rock radio and MTV with maximum efficiency during a Pearl Jam–obsessed era. But on the band's later albums, he could slip just as easily into a David Bowie–style croon or a John Lennon–esque whine to better serve STP's music as it moved in a more melodic direction.

After Weiland's death, Robert DeLeo suggested that his former bandmate did not have a secure sense of self. "He was always searching for something that wasn't really him," he said. "I don't think he was genuinely happy with himself." While this anxiety ultimately crippled him in his personal life, it might also explain why he was such a multifaceted singer. His vocals would never be as distinctive as Vedder's, but he was more versatile and malleable. Whatever STP's songs required, he could deliver.

What linked Stone Temple Pilots to Pearl Jam were two key collaborators—producer Brendan O'Brien and video director Josh Taft. Both men had only recently come to prominence in the early nineties. Back in the eighties, O'Brien was only famous in Atlanta, where he was known locally as a hotshot guitarist and successful record engineer who could get good sounds quickly and cheaply. His first national exposure was engineering *Shake Your Money Maker*, the hit multiplatinum 1990 debut by Atlanta trad rockers the Black Crowes. (He also played the guitar solo on the album's breakout single, a hard-rock cover of Otis Redding's "Hard to Handle.") The Black Crowes' label was Def American, the imprint founded by former hip-hop impresario-turned-rock producer Rick Rubin, who eventually brought O'Brien in to engineer one of the most popular alt-rock albums of the early nineties, *Blood Sugar Sex Magik* by the Red Hot Chili Peppers.

Core signaled O'Brien's transition from sought-after engineer to successful record producer, setting him on a course to become a key sonic architect of nineties rock. Just six months after *Core* was released, he was in the studio with Pearl Jam for the first time, assisting with the making of their second album, *Vs.* About seven months after *Vs.* was released, he was back with Stone Temple Pilots for the making of their second record, *Purple.* The back-and-forth between both bands continued through the rest of the decade, with the albums *Vitalogy, No Code,* and *Yield* for Pearl Jam and *Tiny Music . . . Songs from the Vatican Gift Shop* and *No. 4* for Stone Temple Pilots.

Taft meanwhile directed the first two Stone Temple Pilots videos, for the songs "Sex Type Thing" and "Plush," just as he had directed the first two Pearl Jam videos, for the songs "Alive" and "Even Flow." Taft's rise was fairly meteoric—he had only graduated from NYU film school in 1989, at which point he returned home to Seattle and reconnected with his local musician friends, including members of Soundgarden and Mother Love Bone. While he eventually branched out to working with rap acts such as Nas and a Tribe Called Quest, his grunge-related clips had the greatest cultural impact.

In the cases of Pearl Jam and Stone Temple Pilots, Taft's visual representations formed indelible impressions that resonated for decades afterward. Only in the instance of STP would I argue that the effect was negative. For "Sex Type Thing," which came out as a single in January 1993, Taft chose to put the band in what appeared to be a sweaty and foreboding S&M sex dungeon. In the video, Scott Weiland is shirtless and beefy, glowering at the camera. We see him at an upward angle from the ground, which maximizes his powerful menace.

It's a strange visual choice that totally muddled the song's anti–date rape message, eradicating the irony of Weiland's lyric by presenting him as a weird and frightening brute. Comparing "Sex Type Thing" to "Jeremy" underscores Taft's failure—even though Vedder (like Weiland) writes from the point of the view of an abuser, the "Jeremy" video leaves no doubt that the audience's sympathy should be with the titular victim. (Even those who misinterpreted the video as a depiction of a school shooting were still inclined to see Jeremy as a tragic figure pushed to the brink by a cruel world.) The "Sex Type Thing" video, however, seems to present the lyric where Weiland drawls "I know you want what's on my mind" at face value.[2]

But the video for "Plush" was even worse. While Taft's camera lingers below Weiland in the "Sex Type Thing" clip, it hovers above him in the "Plush" video. Factoring in the way the scene is lit, which accentuates Weiland's cheekbones and deranged facial expressions, it seems like the idea is to remind the audience as much as possible of Eddie Vedder. The song itself is the closest that STP ever came to sounding like *Ten*-era Pearl Jam—the growly delivery of the "to find it, to find it, to find it" hook

2 The utter wrongness of the "Sex Type Thing" video was compounded years later when Weiland revealed in his memoir *Not Dead & Not for Sale* that he himself had been raped at the age of twelve.

is pure yarling while the line about "when the dogs begin to smell her" instantly evokes "Hunger Strike."

The "Plush" video is what put the "Pearl Jam rip-off" tag on Stone Temple Pilots as *Core* became one of the most popular rock albums of 1993. Even Pearl Jam commented on it in that year's Cameron Crowe–penned *Rolling Stone* cover story. After taking their lumps in the previous year for supposedly being inferior to Nirvana, they were in a unique position to lend STP a lifeline. They chose not to do that. Vedder instead was unsparing in his dismissal:

> Ament tells Vedder about the "Plush" video, with the singer's uncanny appropriation of Vedder's mannerisms. Vedder's heard it before. In fact, he hears it daily. From fans, from friends, even from a French musician who complimented him on the song and his new short orange hair. (Vedder's hair is still longish and brown.)
>
> "Apparently, it's something that the guy is dealing with, too," Vedder suggests. "It's like, am I supposed to feel sympathy? Get your own trip, man. I don't think I was copping anybody's trip. I wasn't copping Andy Wood's trip. I wasn't copping Kurt Cobain's trip, even though Kurt Cobain's one of the best trips I could ever cop. But Beth and I were part of the San Diego scene. We knew everything that was going on, and it was small enough to know. Those guys came from there? I never heard of 'em."

No young Pearl Jam fan in 1993 was going to cut Stone Temple Pilots a break after reading that. I know I didn't. But years later, after I let go of the alt-rock politics of the time and listened to STP with fresh ears, I felt that Eddie was being unjust.

I truly believe that if the "Plush" video hadn't come out—or if it had been a performance clip in the vein of "Alive" and "Even Flow"—Stone Temple Pilots' career would have turned out differently. Musically, the resemblance of "Plush" to *Ten* seems less a case of deliberate imitation than shared influences. Robert DeLeo wrote the music in 1989, well before Pearl Jam was even a band. Weiland originally disliked it, complaining that it sounded too much like Boston. Fortunately, the STP guys realized that sounding too much like Boston is a good thing.

At first, STP had a sense of humor about the Pearl Jam comparisons. For instance, before they played "Plush" at a concert in Seattle, Weiland said, "This is the song Pearl Jam wrote for us." But a devastating media narrative had now set in: *Stone Temple Pilots are poseurs.* And no amount of self-deprecation could remedy this.

When *Spin* put Scott Weiland on the cover in September 1993, writer Jonathan Gold immediately snarked about STP's status as musical thieves: "When you first heard Stone Temple Pilots on MTV—admit it—you probably thought it was a Pearl Jam song you'd forgotten about, unless you thought it was Kurt Cobain singing, except that the chorus sounded a little bit more like Soundgarden." Venerable rock critic Greil Marcus was even meaner, calling them "a national joke" for "their shameless impersonations of Pearl Jam and Nirvana." But, again, it wasn't just STP's supposed imitations of other bands that so troubled music critics. It was the suspicion that these guys *didn't really mean it, man.* Cobain and Vedder were *authentically* troubled, but Scott Weiland? What a poseur. "With Kurt Cobain dead," Marcus concluded, "to hear his misery and his intelligence transformed so blithely into someone else's kitsch commodity is sickening."

When Greil Marcus wrote that in 1994, Scott Weiland's life was likely already falling apart, though nobody outside Stone Temple Pilots knew that yet. The first signs of trouble came in 1995, when he was convicted of buying crack cocaine and sentenced to one year's probation. Three years later, he was convicted again, this time for heroin possession. In 1999, he finally served prison time after violating his probation. In his final years, he would have periods of sobriety but couldn't fully evade his addictions.

As for his band, Stone Temple Pilots became prisoners of context, forever defined by the first album coming out in the midst of Pearl Jam's early wave of success, and then their second video hewing a little too close to Pearl Jam's iconography. No matter what Scott Weiland did, there was no escape. Even in death, he was a poseur.

$$\lightning$$

Clearly, Pearl Jam was not like Stone Temple Pilots in the areas that counted most. Their singer did not have a serious drug problem. They had a stronger support network. And, most important, they are a better and more resilient band.

But when I think about Pearl Jam's story, the crucial question for me is this: How did they survive and thrive well into middle age when so many of their peers crashed and burned? Time and again, this is the mystery to which I return. Comparing them with Stone Temple Pilots, and contrasting Eddie Vedder's ultimately triumphant path with Scott Weiland's tragic one, offers some insight into this question.

Zeroing in on the late summer months of 1993, one of the most intense periods for both bands, I think there are two inflection points that sent them off to their respective fates. The first inflection point occurs in August 1993, when Scott Weiland tries heroin for the first time at the Royalton Hotel in New York City after the last date of their tour with the Butthole Surfers.[3]

"It made me feel safe. It was like the womb," Weiland later recalled in an interview with *Esquire* in 2005. "I felt completely sure of myself. It took away all the fears."

Eddie Vedder, meanwhile, does not try heroin that August. Instead, he meets his hero, Pete Townshend, for the first time, at a concert in Berkeley, California. Like Weiland, Vedder does not feel sure of himself at this time. "I was in a terrible space. I enjoyed the show incredibly, but I was ready to fall apart mentally," Vedder said later.

But rather than ingest a highly addictive narcotic, Vedder is able to feel safe in Townshend's presence, not merely as a fan but as a *friend*. This

---

3 In a Pearl Jam–esque move, STP turned down an offer to play arenas as an opener for Aerosmith in order to tour with a respected eighties indie act.

is the kind of company that puts Eddie Vedder at ease—he's constantly seeking out father figures. Pete is perhaps the most crucial.

It's similar to an encounter that Pearl Jam had about one year prior with Neil Young, who entered the band's orbit at the Bob Dylan thirtieth anniversary concert at Madison Square Garden in October 1992. This led to an invitation to play Young's annual Bridge School benefit concert for the first time that December and an eventual slot opening for Young during a tour of Europe and North America in the summer of 1993.

Young also dispensed some advice to Vedder, as Eddie recalled in a 2020 Howard Stern interview. "He said, 'Hey, just so you know, there might be some people that'll try to pull you away from this group but you guys, the sum is greater than the parts. Remember that. I'm sure that's probably already happened to you.' I thought no, I'm good with these guys."

This leads to the second inflection point, in September 1993. The same week that the *Spin* cover story skewering Stone Temple Pilots—dampening what should have been a moment of career triumph—hits newsstands, Pearl Jam wins four Moonman trophies at the MTV Video Music Awards, including Video of the Year for "Jeremy." But the part everyone will remember is the band's performance of "Animal," followed by a duet with Neil Young on "Rockin' in the Free World."

If I had been fifteen years old when the Beatles performed on *The Ed Sullivan Show*, I would surely remember it as the most momentous TV performance by a rock band of my lifetime. But I wasn't alive then. I was, however, fifteen years old when Pearl Jam and Neil Young played on the 1993 MTV Video Music Awards, and it remains the single greatest live rock 'n' roll performance I've ever witnessed on television.

When contextualizing this, remember that many Pearl Jam fans had still not seen them in concert, or even all that much on television. As good as they were on *MTV Unplugged*, the 1993 VMAs presented them in full-on *berserker* mode, with the amps cranked and Jeff Ament violently slapping his bass guitar as Mike McCready attacked his amp like it owed him money.

As a preview of *Vs.*, the performance of "Animal" promised that it would be a brawnier and more physical record. The song itself was drawn from the same well as the earliest *Ten* songs, originating as a demo called "Weird A" in Stone Gossard's batch of song ideas from 1990. Like many of those tracks, "Animal" ranks among Gossard's riffiest compositions, a funk-metal hybrid that hits like a punk-rock redux of *Houses of the Holy*.

Vedder's lyrics, in characteristic fashion, can be read a couple of ways. The "five against one" chant seems like a straightforward taunt from Pearl Jam's five members toward the singular, unseen monster that is the corporate rock industry. "Animal" also could be interpreted as a song about sexual assault sung from the perspective of the victim—a person "abducted from the street" who quickly dissociates from her abusers. In that light, it's a better, more thoughtful rewrite of "Sex Type Thing."

After "Animal," Neil Young came out. I wish I could convey the magnitude of this with a better phrase than "came out." Is "descended from heaven in order to unleash a musical apocalypse" too dramatic? Alas, it will have to do. In 1993, Pearl Jam was a fit and muscular live unit, whipped into tiptop shape from many months of touring. They were extremely tight, but "tight" isn't always what the job requires. For Neil, Pearl Jam needed to be loosened up, and they needed to be loosened *by* Neil, so they could play the song like a garage band.

Neil's gift to Pearl Jam at the VMAs was teaching them how to not give a fuck—even on national TV, even at the height of their career or *any* career in rock history. That's what I see whenever I rewatch the "Rockin' in the Free World" performance. I appreciate the effortless power of the band and how it's expressed via the interplay of Stone Gossard's slashing rhythm guitar and McCready's reckless solos, along with the hammering foundation held down by Dave Abbruzzese's tectonic drums and Jeff Ament's bopping bass. But what comes through most is *fun*. Even under the uncomfortable glare of attention from a music network they had come to despise, Neil Young gave Pearl Jam enough cover to finally lose themselves in simply performing the task of being an excellent rock 'n' roll band.

Pearl Jam had already been playing "Rockin' in the Free World" for eighteen months by then, premiering the song in Berlin on March 9, 1992. A week later, they played the song at the *MTV Unplugged* taping, though the performance was edited out of the telecast. From there, it entered the rotation of reliable concert closers, rivaling "Yellow Ledbetter" and "Baba O'Riley" as a constant in encores for decades afterward.

Appearing originally on Neil Young's 1989 comeback record, *Freedom*, "Rockin' in the Free World" was actually debuted onstage in Seattle, during a concert at the Paramount Theater on February 21, 1989. When it showed up as the first and last track on *Freedom*—the dueling acoustic and electric versions that harkened to "My, My, Hey, Hey (Out of the Blue)" and "Hey, Hey, My, My (Into the Black)" from *Rust Never Sleeps*—"Rockin' in the Free World" swiftly became Young's most celebrated song of the eighties, an otherwise commercially and artistically fallow period for him.

For Pearl Jam, "Rockin' in the Free World" felt like a contemporary rock hit, no matter Young's boomer rocker status. Jeff Ament subsequently recalled seeing Neil Young play it on *Saturday Night Live* in 1989, one of the most iconic TV performances by a rock artist ever, and feeling like it was a rare instance when the power of a live rock show fully translated on TV. A bitter rebuke of the Reagan–Bush years, "Rockin' in the Free World" entered Pearl Jam's set lists at the very end of that political era. And yet the song's relevance for the band has never faded because Pearl Jam has always been aligned more with Neil Young's world than the continuum of nineties alt-rock bands.

Vedder and his bandmates could not have possibly known this at the time, but alternative rock was wired with a self-destruct device. By the middle of the decade, it killed the genre and nearly all the bands associated with it. Neil Young, however, signified a more enduring life in rock 'n' roll. Neil always followed his gut, damn the consequences, and this all but ensured a bumpy career. If you followed his example, there would be incredible highs and unfathomable lows. But at least there would always be forward motion. You would always live an interesting life, and that's what matters.

In September 1993, one month before the release of their second album, *Vs.*, Pearl Jam would take their first step outside the context of nineties rock—the very prison that stifled and then crippled Scott Weiland and Stone Temple Pilots. Performing with Neil Young was that step. It said to the MTV audience, "We're no longer with you, we're with him and what he represents now. This is our new paradigm."

When Eddie Vedder needed a friend, he bonded with Pete Townshend and Neil Young. When Scott Weiland needed a friend, he was offered heroin. These are the breaks that separate a so-called poseur from a survivor.

CHAPTER 6

"GLORIFIED G"

(From *Vs.*)

Poochie the Rockin' Dog • Rock Star Cars • Gun Control • Alternative vs. Indie • The Pre-Internet vs. Post-Internet Worlds • David Letterman • The Most "Alternative" Alternative Album of All Time

I will never be able to pronounce "Abbruzzese" correctly.

I won't be able to spell it, either. For instance, the sentence above has nine words, and it took me ten minutes to type. My problem is that I'm always overconfident that *this* time I will know how many b's and z's there are. And then I proceed to be wrong, every single time. Oh, and there's also an "s" for some reason? Why is this name written in a 7/8 time signature?

It's a shame, because I've long had a soft spot for Pearl Jam's third drummer, the black sheep of the band's story, Mr. Dave Abbruzzese. I admire his soul patch and his absurdly long hair. I appreciate that he was the most

Tesla-looking guy in a band that at the time desperately wanted to be like Fugazi. And I enjoy occasionally cueing up on YouTube his endearingly goofy acceptance speeches at the 1993 American Music Awards, when he was the only member of Pearl Jam who bothered to show up.[1]

In the Pearl Jam story, Abbruzzese is the human version of my favorite *Simpsons* joke—he's Poochie the Rockin' Dog, the surfing canine who shows suddenly up on *Itchy & Scratchy* at a crucial moment to revitalize the operation and then just as mysteriously disappears. Abbruzzese was in the band for almost exactly three years, joining right before the release of *Ten* in August 1991 and exiting involuntarily in August 1994. To this day, I think of him as the "real" Pearl Jam drummer, which doesn't seem logical, given his relatively brief tenure in the band. But those three years feel more like twenty in Pearl Jam years, whereas the decades that Matt Cameron has spent behind the kit aren't as momentous. Abbruzzese was there during Pearl Jam's imperial period, which coincides with my teen years, and this is extremely powerful. Right or wrong, Abbruzzese's goofy mug always shows up in my immediate mental picture when I think about this band.

I suspect this is true of other people who got into Pearl Jam early on, back in the early nineties. But it's likely less true to the fans who got on board later, given that the band has largely written Abbruzzese out of their narrative. I understand why this has happened, but it still makes me sad. After all this time, I have love for Pearl Jam's Poochie.

The fact is that Dave Abbruzzese is a divisive figure among Pearl Jam fans, and that is due almost entirely to Kim Neely's 1998 biography, *Five Against One*. Abbruzzese was the only band member interviewed for the book, and his axe-grinding against Eddie Vedder provides much of the bio's dishiest dirt. There are embarrassing stories about Vedder that come explicitly from Abbruzzese, like the one from the 1993

---

1 The band won for Favorite New Pop-Rock Artist and, weirdly, Best New Heavy Metal Artist. The latter award was presented by three members of Firehouse, the previous year's winner.

MTV Video Music Awards where Dave alleges that Eddie pretended to be drunk in a misguided attempt to emulate Jim Morrison. And then there are stories that are *implied* to have come from Abbruzzese without stating it outright, like the bizarre claim that Vedder secretly tape-recorded his bandmates' backstage conversations while on tour in Europe in 1992.

And then there's my favorite anecdote from *Five Against One*, in which Abbruzzese eagerly drives up to the luxurious studio in Northern California where Pearl Jam is making *Vs.* in order to show off the new jet-black Infiniti he's just purchased.

"Check it out," he said, beaming. "What do you think?"

The others stood in a huddle, silent.

"Huh," Jeff said finally.

"Well," said Stone. "That's *rock*."

Nobody got in, nobody wanted to see the interior or peek under the hood. Eddie, who'd parted with some of his *Ten* royalties to pay off the same beat-up truck he'd been driving when he first arrived in Seattle, stood with his arms crossed, eyes flickering distastefully over the Infiniti's shiny black paint job and chrome wheels.

Whatever, Dave thought. He sat in his new car as they walked away, absent-mindedly jiggling the keys that hung from the ignition with one aimless finger. He sat there for a long time after the others had gone home.

Truly the most tragic story of all time about a rock star buying a sports car.

For Neely and other Vedder skeptics, stories like this prove that Pearl Jam's leader is a joyless scold who made being in America's most popular rock band of the early nineties a miserable experience. This makes Abbruzzese, by proxy, the antagonist of *Five Against One*, the fun-loving anti-Vedder who was crucified for the sin of wanting to enjoy his good fortune.

Now, I think that's reductive and unfair. But it's proven to be a durable trope when it comes to how Pearl Jam is discussed and contextualized. And it's not *entirely* wrong, either. There really was something about Abbruzzese that stuck in Vedder's craw, even when his drummer acted in ways that might otherwise seem endearing to most people. (Vedder, for one, supposedly hated Abbruzzese's speeches at the American Music Awards, claiming that Abbruzzese "embarrassed the shit out of me." The source for this, of course, is *Five Against One*, so we know that this is how Abbruzzese remembers it.)

Abbruzzese wasn't fired until after the next Pearl Jam album, *Vitalogy*, was recorded. (The news was delivered by Stone Gossard, Vedder's other primary antagonist who also happened to be far more essential to the band.) But the trouble between Abbruzzese and Vedder really flared up during the making of *Vs.* Vedder's discomfort with the circumstances of the album's recording are well documented—he didn't like that Pearl Jam decamped to a studio in Marin County that seemed better suited for Eric Clapton or Guns N' Roses than . . . well, actually, Pearl Jam belonged in exactly that company after selling so many copies of *Ten*. Like a millionaire method actor desperate to contrive some grittiness for an upcoming role, Vedder took to sleeping in his truck for several nights for lyrical inspiration. Reflecting on the experience years later, he called *Vs.* "the album I enjoyed making the least."

Vedder's problem was not unique for a person in his position: He suddenly wasn't a normal guy anymore, and he wouldn't be one ever again. Like any musician whose dreams come true, he no longer had anything standing in his way. On the contrary, the world was laid at Eddie Vedder's feet after *Ten*. But how can you sing about *that* and not have your audience turn on you? On *Vs.*, he had to manufacture some hardship and strife for songwriting material.

Enter Dave Abbruzzese. Here was a guy in his own band who signified many of the things that Eddie Vedder did not want to be. This eventually developed into a problem that could only be solved by firing Abbruzzese.

But at the time of *Vs.* it was a *useful* problem. Abbruzzese could function, in a way, as Vedder's muse.

This was literally the case for "Glorified G," the big anti-gun anthem on *Vs.* This song is not subtle in its messaging. In the lyrics, Vedder mocks gun owners as insecure hypocrites who use firearms to compensate for their compromised masculinity: "Got a gun, fact I got two / That's OK, man, 'cause I love God / Glorified version of a pellet gun / Feels so manly, when armed."

What's less remarked-upon with "Glorified G" is that Vedder is specifically mocking his drummer. The song was inspired by an in-studio conversation during the *Vs.* sessions in which Vedder reacted in horror to Abbruzzese casually mentioning that he just bought a gun.

"You bought a gun?" Vedder asked incredulously.

"In fact, I bought two," Abbruzzese replied.

And the rest is Pearl Jam history.

The inspiration for "Glorified G" was also likely topical. Gun control measures, never an easy policy to implement on the federal level, had real momentum at the time. One month before work on *Vs.* began, in February 1993, the Brady Handgun Violence Prevention Act was introduced in Congress. Named after James Brady, a former White House Press Secretary who was wounded during an assassination attempt on Ronald Reagan in 1981, the proposed legislation—signed into law by President Bill Clinton that November—mandated federal background checks for gun buyers and implemented a mandatory five-day waiting period for purchases.

Ironically, "Glorified G" has since become the easiest track from *Vs.* to mock. In an otherwise positive review of the *Vs.* reissue from 2011, *Pitchfork* singled out the "cringe-inducing" song for derision, snickering at Vedder's "hokey fake-jingo accent" and the "corn-pone Skynyrd guitar lick" and ultimately dismissing the entire package as a "mess."

Personally, I have warmer feelings for "Glorified G." Yes, the lyrics are a little obvious. But the music is so straightforward and immediate that it almost plays like a parody of arena rock. (I would liken it more to *Rocks*-era Aerosmith than Skynyrd. "Alive" is Pearl Jam's Skynyrd homage.) The core of "Glorified G" is the excellent guitar interplay between Gossard and McCready, which is buoyed by Ament's meaty bass line. It all comes together during the gorgeous bridge, in which the song opens up like one of the effortlessly fluid, extemporaneous jams that Pearl Jam could easily slip into onstage. (Even *Pitchfork* conceded that the "Glorified G" bridge is great.)

You know who else sounds good on "Glorified G"? Dave Abbruzzese, whose smooth drum roll kicks the song off. Whenever I hear this song, I think about how Dave must have known that his singer was making fun of him in the lyrics. But he did his job anyway. And that's why I will always love him. I also understand why Eddie Vedder felt annoyed by his dopey drummer talking about guns in the studio. I believe everybody is justified in this scenario. And I think this hostile dynamic was absolutely crucial for Pearl Jam when they made one of their best records.

I refuse to pick sides in this conflict. I have love for both men. They needed each other. And then, one day, they didn't.

*

One of the many musical distinctions of my lifetime that used to seem important and now is completely forgotten is the difference between "alternative" and "indie" rock. People who were born in the late nineties or later tend to be utterly confused by this. For them, Nirvana and Pavement belong in the same bucket of rock music from a bygone era. It doesn't matter that the former was considered "alternative" and the latter was "indie" in 1992. This is what time does—art always outlasts the rhetorical baggage people attach to it in the moment. But if you were into Pavement in the early nineties, you likely saw indie rock as the alternative to alternative, just as alternative bands like Nirvana and Pearl Jam were positioned against the hair metal bands of the late eighties.

"Alternative" became part of the lexicon in the late eighties, after music magazines like *Billboard* and *Spin* used it to describe music played more often on college radio than on commercial radio stations. "Indie" bands meanwhile put out records on small, noncorporate-affiliated labels, though even that wasn't always true—Pavement's label Matador (also home to quintessential nineties indie acts such as Guided by Voices, Yo La Tengo, and Liz Phair) entered a partnership with Atlantic Records, the same label that put out Stone Temple Pilots albums, in 1993.

The distinction between indie and alternative was essentially philosophical. Indie bands carried themselves differently than alternative bands; "indie" was ironic, detached, and weary of careerism, and "alternative" was earnest, intense, and populist. I once saw an interview with the brilliant singer-songwriter David Berman of the Silver Jews in which he described early-nineties alt-rock bands as being composed of "all defensive lineman and offensive lineman." In this analogy, I suppose, indie rockers were the kids smoking cigarettes in the parking lot outside the football game.

The simplest way to define indie rock in the early nineties is that guys like David Berman did not sell one million albums in a week, like Pearl Jam did with *Vs.* But the massive success of *Vs.* also underscored how silly the term "alternative" seemed by the fall of 1993.

Clearly, Pearl Jam was no longer an "alternative" to mainstream rock by then; they *were* mainstream rock. This naturally made people cynical about whether the alternative movement was *really* an elaborate marketing scheme put on by record labels to trick kids into thinking that they were buying into a revolution. Sometimes, alt-rock's critics skewered the genre's pretentions with great wit. In 1994, the folk singer Todd Snider released a snarky rejoinder to Pearl Jam and their peers called "Talkin' Seattle Grunge Rock Blues," in which he posits music's truest alternative is . . . silence.

But most of the grumbling about alternative rock failed to reckon with why so many people were buying Pearl Jam records in the early nineties.

Let's assume that "alternative" *really* was just a marketing term without any greater, substantive importance. There's still the matter of *why* that marketing worked as well as it did.

Alternative music wasn't popular simply because it was promoted as being nonmainstream. It was embraced because it was alternative in the sense of being *oppositional*. If you were fourteen in 1993, buying a Pearl Jam CD felt like taking a stand against authority. Whether it was a *true* act of opposition is beside the point; in the minds of Pearl Jam fans, the band *signified* rebellion, and that projection fueled their massive popularity because being *oppositional* in this era was also *lucrative*.

There is an obvious parallel here with another dominant form of popular music in the early nineties, gangsta rap. Many of the same people buying Pearl Jam CDs in 1993 were also buying Dr. Dre, Snoop Dogg, Ice Cube, and Ice-T albums. (I know because I was one of those people.) Gangsta rap was even more oppositional than alternative rock in the sense that it seemed like a direct attack on the white suburbs where so many of the people who bought *The Chronic* that year—the sixth best-selling album of 1993, two spots above the still-popular *Ten* and nine spots above *Vs.*—lived. Whereas Eddie Vedder articulated the ennui of this audience, an artist like Ice Cube made this audience see how insignificant and even lame their ennui seemed compared to the horrors of systemic racism and police brutality. But gangsta rap was also an attack on the sort of traditional rock that Pearl Jam performed. In just a few years time, a generation who loved *The Chronic* and hard rock would embrace a new form of music that melded those genres—nü-metal—and in the process displace alt-rock permanently.

This "oppositional" idea was hardwired into all the significant alt-rock bands of the time, and it's another key difference between alternative and indie bands, who were averse to aping the political grandstanding of sixties boomer rock. Alt-rockers, however, had no such qualms. They strived To Be Important, without air-quotes. Pearl Jam wanted to change the world; more crucially, they felt that changing the world was possible.

The early nineties were a rare time in American pop culture when telling your audience about the corruption and stupidity of American pop culture was highly commercial. Prior to then, rock bands that pushed a subversive, anti-authority ideology were situated in niche scenes centered in large cities that felt exclusive and hip, like San Francisco in the sixties or New York City in the late seventies. When bands left those cities, they tended to tour to other large cities with their own exclusive and hip scenes. But alternative rock was popular *everywhere*, including vast swaths of Middle America where there were no cool record stores and MTV was the only decent radio station. Those bands mainstreamed being anti-mainstream.

While the bands of previous generations always pointed you back to the mainstream, the alt-rockers exposed the world that existed beyond what you saw right in front of you. It gestured, in a way, *toward* indie rock, as well as other forms of culture that were previously shut out of the era's dominant media. But more than anything, alternative rock made people who were otherwise isolated far outside the country's cool, clique-y urban enclaves feel, maybe for the first time, that they were not alone.

Remember that Generation X is the one demographic that straddles two different worlds almost equally: pre-internet and post-internet. Most millennials and all Zoomers only know the post-internet world, and boomers only leave the pre-internet world to post problematic memes on Facebook. But Gen Xers lived for a significant period of time in the pre-internet world, and we also know what it's like to spend huge portions of our lives online. This gives us a unique perspective on how the nature of authority has evolved over time.

The pre-internet world was a top-down society. Your view of the world was shaped by what you saw on television (which was run by huge corporations), what you heard on the radio (which was in the process of being consolidated and corporatized), and what you read in newspapers and magazines (which promoted a very narrow set of perspectives approved by the era's ruling political and business classes). If an article, an idea, or a song didn't appear in any of these media, it was very difficult for the average person to encounter it. An album or film deemed insufficiently commercial was literally *impossible* to be heard or seen by tens of millions of people living outside major urban areas. It was more likely that you didn't even know those things existed if you didn't happen to know someone who was familiar with underground culture or you lived in a nowhere town.

I'll give you an example: Today, anybody who is remotely interested in rock music has heard of the Pixies. But as a seventh grader living in Wisconsin in 1991, around the time that band was putting out their most acclaimed albums, I had never heard of them. I didn't know *Tromp le Monde* from *Reggata de Blanc*. They weren't played on the radio stations in my dinky, little town, and I didn't see their cassettes or CDs in the big-box record stores in my dinky, little town. I only learned about them after Krist Novoselic described "Smells Like Teen Spirit" as a Pixies rip-off. Back then, you didn't learn about rock bands on the internet; the internet *was* rock bands.

Now, the post-internet world is bottom-up. It no longer matters where you live—we all have access to the same news, music, films, and TV shows. And this has naturally eroded the power that authority figures have, to a degree that now seems scary and destabilizing. The writer Martin Gurri has called this "the revolt of the public," in which individuals react to online life by retreating to their own version of reality because "the mirror in which we used to find ourselves faithfully reflected in the world has shattered."

The exhilaration of coming of age in the late eighties and early nineties is that this "mirror-shattering" of reality was already happening in small but significant ways that weren't yet a threat to an underlying sense of reality. In March 1993, the same month that Pearl Jam began recording *Vs.*, the two biggest news stories posed a threat to the "top-down" dominance of elites. The first was the standoff in Waco, Texas, between a religious cult known as the Branch Davidians and the federal government. The second was the federal trial against the Los Angeles police officers charged with violating the civil rights of motorist Rodney King. In both cases, the public could see video evidence of government agents attacking American citizens with a brutality so obvious even a kid could understand it. And it was equally obvious that you were not *supposed* to see these things, which made you believe that these kinds of acts were far more common than any adult would ever tell you.

This "revolt" also occurred in softer, more benign ways. For millions of Gen Xers, it happened in pop culture most significantly with TV comedy, like *The Simpsons* and especially *Late Night with David Letterman*. By the time I entered junior high school, I had a strong suspicion that most of the people in charge of running my life—politicians, businessmen, teachers—were fools. But you never saw that perspective expressed anywhere. Television was wall-to-wall sitcoms like *Full House* and *Family Matters* and *Family Ties* and dozens of other shows about families living in houses full of ties that matter. But on *Late Night*, David Letterman routinely made fun of his own celebrity guests. He even mocked *his own bosses*, right on NBC's airwaves, just as the alt-rock bands would soon use their major-label platforms to talk about how much major-label platforms suck.

In the context of how tightly controlled the rest of culture was as the eighties became the nineties, David Letterman felt like a chaos agent, a disruption of the rigid order we all had drilled into us from watching so many hours of television. Generation X, after all, is a generation of latchkey kids *raised* by TV, so we needed someone like Letterman who was inside the box to finally lead us out.

On his show, he poked through the impenetrable façade of sterile politeness that permeated the shiny pop music and lovable rom-coms and cheery variety specials that you were routinely force-fed. He stared directly into the camera, flashed a crooked smile, and assured you that the skepticism that you felt about all this lameness that surrounded you was justified.

Somewhere, Eddie Vedder was also watching while working the night shift at a San Diego gas station. Dave made him feel like he was right, too.[2]

⚡

If we define "alternative" as oppositional to mainstream American culture, *Vs.* might very well be the most *alternative* alternative rock album ever made.

Released on October 19, 1993, *Vs.* has three distinct sections. The bulk of the album are "issues" tracks. They address (and stake positions against) authority in general ("Go"), sexual violence ("Animal"), parental control ("Daughter"), gun violence ("Glorified G"), political cowardice ("Dissident"), police brutality ("W.M.A."), the media ("Blood"), and human self-interest that comes at the expense of collective good ("Rats"). Then there are the "call to arms" songs, which attempt to rally the listener into transcending these problems ("Rearviewmirror" and "Leash"). Finally, there's the "existential" tunes, which turn inward to explore less dramatic but more profound realities about the passage of time and the limits of philosophical insight ("Elderly Woman Behind the Counter in a Small Town" and "Indifference").

On *Vs.*, even more than the lyrics, these ideas and themes are expressed most eloquently by the music. The most obvious improvement on *Vs.* over *Ten* concerns the aggressive physicality of Pearl Jam's instrumental attack. This was fostered by Brendan O'Brien pushing Pearl Jam to complete one track at a time, which facilitated the album's "live in a room" vitality. But most of the credit for the visceral punch of *Vs.* belongs to the band themselves, whose relentless touring in 1992 put them in peak fighting condition.

---

2 The mutual appreciation between Pearl Jam and David Letterman is well documented, culminating with Letterman inducting Pearl Jam into the Rock & Roll Hall of Fame in 2017.

Much of the musical power on *Vs.* derives from the rhythm section. Jeff Ament has said that Pearl Jam was essentially a new band when it started the record, as Abbruzzese didn't play on *Ten* and his style differed significantly from that album's timekeeper, Dave Krusen. A *Modern Drummer* cover story from December 1993 gives some insight into Abbruzzese's approach. In a sidebar listing his most influential albums, he mentions every Led Zeppelin LP, anchored by John Bonham, plus Peter Gabriel's *Shaking the Tree* and Robbie Robertson's 1987 self-titled solo debut, both of which feature the respected art-rock drummer Manu Katché. (Abbruzzese also picked *The Uplift Mofo Party Plan* by the Red Hot Chili Peppers, featuring his eventual replacement in Pearl Jam, Jack Irons.)

You can hear echoes of these musicians in Abbruzzese's playing on *Vs.*— he favors big, Bonham-esque beats delivered with the precision of a skilled technician, which suits the album's most explosive finger-pointing songs. Tellingly, Abbruzzese's presence is nonexistent on the "existential" tunes that signal where Vedder and the band were headed beyond this album.

Vs. is very much a young man's record, a "burn it all down" scream of disgust that resonated with a public that was just coming to grips with a national underbelly of fear, neglect, and violence signified by the Waco tragedy and the Rodney King case. As the nineties unfolded, this fury would evolve into the more overt surliness of nü-metal, which front-loaded the oppositional tendencies of bands like Pearl Jam and pumped them full of bile and self-absorption.

For all his anxiety upon Pearl Jam's first flashes of fame, Eddie Vedder was never a nihilist. His natural affinity for the underdog informs *Vs.* as well as much of Pearl Jam's greatest and most popular work. He is at heart a humanist; his empathy for the characters in his songs comes from a genuine love of people and concern for the prospects of humankind.[3]

---

3 Which is why "Rats" registers as the only truly false note on *Vs.* The song's caustic misanthropy feels like a put-on, a bad joke that Vedder likely regretted later on, given the song's relative scarcity in Pearl Jam's concert set lists.

This is especially true of the two most forward-looking and "existential" tracks on *Vs.*

On these songs, the most pressing problems aren't in the outside world but rather inside the human heart. "Elderly Woman" is about the regrets that accumulate over the course of a lifetime, and how growing older inevitably causes most people to lose interest in you. ("Hearts and thoughts they fade, fade away.") It's a remarkable song for any man in his midtwenties to write, much less the singer of a multiplatinum grunge band. But Vedder's humanist impulses compelled him to give voice to a senior citizen, the least likely character to show up in a rock song. (The most moving moment—the part when Eddie sings "I just want to scream *helloooo*"—evokes another famous tearjerker about the elderly, John Prine's "Hello in There.")

"Indifference" is a tougher and more enigmatic song, lacking the catharsis of Vedder's plaintive howl offered at the climax of "Elderly Woman." It's a gloomy soundscape in which a funeral organ and Jeff Ament's fretless bass glowers beneath Vedder's pained groaning. The scant trace of hope in "Indifference" comes courtesy of the protagonist's resolve to never quit pushing against life's daily grind, even as he wonders, "How much difference does it make?"

Whereas Vedder's writing on *Ten* is reminiscent of the teenaged melodrama of *Born to Run*, "Indifference" is him working in the mode of more grown-up Springsteen albums like *Darkness on the Edge of Town* and *The River*. The Springsteen song it most resembles is *The River*'s closer, "Wreck on the Highway." In the song, Bruce sings about climbing into bed with his partner after witnessing the aftermath of a fatal car accident, which causes him to ponder the fragility of human existence. In "Indifference," the main character climbs *out* of bed—it might as well be the morning after "Wreck on the Highway"—in order to "make my way / through one more day in hell."

The conundrum of modern life, Martin Gurri writes, is that we can't imagine a future that lies beyond "burn it all down." On *Vs.*, Pearl Jam struck out against the systemic failures that young Americans in the nineties were just starting to understand. And then Eddie Vedder found himself asking, *How much difference does it make?* This is the question that Generation X, and the generations that followed, is still trying to answer.

CHAPTER 7
"IMMORTALITY"

(4/12/94, Boston)

Kurt Cobain • Bill Clinton • Opera Man • A Lecture from Henry Rollins • The Chip on Jeff Ament's Shoulder • *Vitalogy* • The Vinyl Boom • Pearl Jam's Devil's Advocate

Has any band ever had a more tumultuous or surreal month than Pearl Jam in April 1994?

I'm not even talking about the whole month. It's really just about two weeks of extreme insanity, with historic highs and cataclysmic lows happening simultaneously. But for most bands, it would equal a decade worth of drama. Anyone who wonders why Pearl Jam checked out for a while in the mid-nineties and subsequently altered their career trajectory would be well advised to study this brief but momentous stretch of time closely.

Here's a timeline of events:

April 3: Pearl Jam plays the second night of a two-night stand in Atlanta. The concert is widely bootlegged and, in retrospect, many fans will regard it as one of the greatest shows in the band's history. The band sounds happy and also incredibly impassioned and impossibly tight and powerful. You could credibly argue that at least three Pearl Jam warhorses—"Release," "Porch," and the cover of the Dead Boys' "Sonic Reducer"—have never been played better. "Porch," especially, is inspired, stretching out to eleven minutes on a jam that includes a short segue into Sonic Youth's "Androgynous Mind," from the not-yet-released *Experimental Jet Set, Trash and No Star.* What you can't hear on the bootleg is the part during the jam when Eddie climbs the lighting rig while wearing a Cincinnati Bengals football helmet and gold bat wings. Then he throws a mannequin down to the stage, just to fuck with the (briefly horrified) audience. As usual, the band doesn't miss a beat.

Two and a half years of touring has led to this. Two weeks later, Pearl Jam plays its final show with Dave Abbruzzese. April 3 will be the pinnacle of this era of the band.

After the gig, Eddie hosts a DJ set from a van that is broadcast (like the concert) on scores of radio stations. At the end, he acknowledges that Kurt Cobain has been reported missing after sneaking out of a rehab facility in Los Angeles. "Hope he's all right," Eddie says. "Please be all right."

April 5: Kurt Cobain takes his own life.

April 8: Cobain's body is discovered by an electrician at his Seattle home. Pearl Jam is with Mudhoney on the opposite side of the country. When Vedder hears the news, he trashes his hotel room. That night, they play a show outside Washington, DC. Ian MacKaye of Fugazi is watching from the side of the stage. To Vedder's surprise,

MacKaye is complimentary about the gig. He then invites him to stay at the Dischord house.

April 9: Pearl Jam visits the White House and meets Bill Clinton. The president asks Eddie to help with messaging for the federal response to Cobain's death. But Eddie is too shell-shocked by the news to offer his assistance. Eddie, in turn, lobbies Clinton to let the band use abandoned military bases as concert venues that Pearl Jam can play as alternatives to Ticketmaster-affiliated spaces. Ultimately, the conversation turns to the Arkansas Razorbacks men's basketball team, who defeated Duke 76–72 five days prior in the NCAA National Championship.

April 12: They play a show at the twenty-seven-hundred-seat Orpheum Theatre in Boston, after two sold-out nights at the twelve-thousand-seat Boston Garden, their first gigs since Cobain's death.

April 16: Pearl Jam plays *Saturday Night Live* for the second time. Emilio Estevez is the host. While taping a promo for the episode, Vedder ignores Estevez and appears mildly amused by Adam Sandler as Opera Man. On that episode's *Weekend Update*, Opera Man sings a parody of "Even Flow." Nirvana was satirized by "Weird Al" Yankovic, and now it's Pearl Jam's turn.

In recognition of their status as the biggest act in rock, the show makes a rare concession and allows them to play three songs: the not-yet-released "Not for You," and two songs from *Vs.*, "Rearviewmirror" and "Daughter." Years later, Mike McCready admits that he is so intoxicated on the show that he blacked out during "Daughter." On top of everything else, McCready's substance abuse is also weighing heavily on the band—in an interview with the *Melody Maker*, Vedder rails about Pearl Jam's lead guitarist "getting fucked up way too much, doing stupid shit and I'm fuckin' worried for him." Later in the year, McCready will be in rehab.

While in New York City, Vedder gives an interview to the *Los Angeles Times* in which he casts doubt on Pearl Jam's future, as well as his own mental stability.

"People think you are this grand person who has all their shit together because you are able to put your feelings into some songs," he says. "They write letters and come to the shows and even to the house, hoping we can fix everything for them. But we can't . . . because we don't have all our shit together either. What they don't understand is that you can't save somebody from drowning if you're treading water yourself."

April 17: They play a "secret" show the night after *SNL* for hard-core fans. Before the concert, Vedder gives an emotional interview to Allan Jones of the *Melody Maker* that is even more charged than the *Los Angeles Times* interview.

"This could be our last show in fuckin' forever as far as I'm concerned. Kurt's death has changed everything. I don't know if I can do it anymore," Vedder tells Jones. "I don't know where we go from here. Maybe nowhere. I think this is going to be the last thing for a long time. I'm just gonna live in a fuckin' cave with my girlfriend. I don't think I'll be showing my face for a while. I don't think I'll be making any fuckin' videos. Maybe we'll eventually do some shows or something, I just don't know."

The concert is similarly fraught. After "Garden," someone yells "I love you!" at Vedder. "You don't love me," he says back wearily. He quotes a song by the Who that dates from one of Pete Townshend's most commercially successful and emotionally fragile periods, "I Don't Even Know Myself."

"If you really knew me, you wouldn't love me. You love who you *think* I am," Vedder spits.

This time, Henry Rollins is in attendance. After the show, he gently takes
Eddie aside and suggests that he should enjoy his fame more. Pearl Jam
won't play live again for another six months.

$$\lightning$$

I forgot to mention one more important event during this stretch. In
Atlanta, Eddie writes a song that will immediately change in meaning by
the time Pearl Jam plays it live for the first time at the second Boston Garden show April 11, and then the following night at the Orpheum Theatre.

The version of "Immortality" from those two nights is different from
how the world will come to know the song when it is released on *Vitalogy*
seven months later. The most significant change is to the lyrics, which to
my ears aren't actual lyrics, even though you can find transcriptions online
of what Eddie is supposedly saying. To me what Eddie is doing at this
stage—the best and most accessible take was eventually released on the
2011 concert album *Live at the Orpheum Theater*—is what I call "artic-
ulate mumbling," the sort of singing he also does on "Yellow Ledbetter"
and "Release," in which he expressively sings sounds that appear to be
words but aren't actually words.

Vedder is so adept at this that he doesn't *need* actual words because the
sounds themselves communicate the song's emotional truth. His pained
murmur on those early versions of "Immortality" might be vague if you're
a pedantic listener, but they are eloquent and profound if you locked into
an intuitive dialogue with the song. By the time Pearl Jam played it a
third time, at the Bridge School benefit concert in California that October, "Immortality" was more or less locked into its "final" version. (Only
the fiery, Who-like jam at the end of the early April performances, while
excised from the studio take, would remain in subsequent live versions of
"Immortality.")

When the press and the world at large heard *Vitalogy*, "Immortality"
immediately stood out. It's an excellent tune, with a minor-key folk-rock
melody that quickly insinuates itself with the listener even when the song

is played like a dirge. But "Immortality" also fit into a narrative about Pearl Jam's uneasy parallel with the rise and fall of their unwitting rival, Nirvana.

Presuming that "Immortality" was at least inspired by Cobain was hardly a stretch. Hearing the song in the wake of Kurt's suicide, it was hard *not* to think of him. There are lines that seem like they could have been written *by* Cobain: "As privileged as a whore / Victims in demand for public show / Swept out through the cracks beneath the door." And then there's the most famous lyric, which occurs at the end as an uneasy (and disturbing) epitaph: "Some die just to live."

Journalists inevitably asked Vedder if he wrote "Immortality" about Cobain. And Vedder, inevitably, denied it. In the *Los Angeles Times*, he pointed out that "Immortality" was written shortly before Cobain died. And then he implied that he was really writing about himself.

I can take Vedder at his word *and also* suggest that he certainly had Cobain on his mind (whether he was conscious of it or not) when he wrote it. The Atlanta stand coincided with Cobain going missing, but even before that, there was widespread concern about his well-being. Vedder dedicated "Go" to Cobain on March 15 in St. Louis, two weeks after Kurt was hospitalized in Rome from a drug overdose widely presumed to be a suicide attempt.

I don't want to delve too deeply into the troubled and sometimes painful dynamic between Eddie Vedder and Kurt Cobain, mainly because I've already written about it at length.[1] It's clear that Cobain was frequently (and unnecessarily) mean about Vedder and Pearl Jam in the press while Vedder just as obviously respected and admired Cobain. They were not close on a personal level, but they were linked—they *are* linked—by virtue of public perception and their shared moment in rock history. From Vedder's point of view, Cobain was as much a metaphor as a person, signifying a worst-case-scenario and cautionary tale for the pressures and anxieties that he was also experiencing. At his lowest, Cobain irrationally

---

1 I wrote a chapter about it in my first book, *Your Favorite Band Is Killing Me*.

believed that Nirvana was universally despised by the public as an overexposed fraud, and Vedder felt the same (with a small modicum of justification) about Pearl Jam.

As a writer, Vedder was naturally attracted to Cobain-as-metaphor as a way to get at his own feelings about being a "victim in demand for public show." The nature of art is that you take real life and exaggerate and heighten it. You do this to make reality more dramatic and cathartic, and also to remove that toxicity from your head so that it can finally exist outside you as a sovereign entity.

In this way, Vedder demonstrated an ability to compartmentalize that his grunge rock twin lacked. Kurt took the emotions that Eddie also felt to an untenable extreme. He was closer to the guy in the "Momma-Son" trilogy, a romantic nihilist destined to die young, than Eddie ever was. What Vedder viewed as a thought exercise, or an emotional and creative outlet that might keep him sane, was a lifestyle for Cobain that could not be sustained. In "Immortality," there is ultimately no difference whether it's about Eddie or Kurt, because it's really about Eddie *as* Kurt.

While Kurt turned himself into a martyr, Eddie put himself in the inherently problematic position of conflicted generational spokesman. Despite his constant protestations about the burdens of such a role, his willingness to attend a summit with no less than the president of the United States suggests that he wasn't entirely unwilling to accept the responsibility.

Pearl Jam's meeting with Bill Clinton, as much as anything else, signifies how powerful the band had become in just two and a half years. It also speaks to Clinton's savvy pandering—no matter how cynical or insincere it might seem now—to the alt-rock subculture of the early nineties. Critical to his election in 1992 was Rock the Vote, a nonprofit organization founded in 1990 by two record-label executives with a stated mission to encourage young voters to participate in elections. While ostensibly nonpartisan, the liberal leanings of Rock the Vote were impossible to miss, especially given the geriatric trappings of the previous two Republican presidents, Ronald Reagan and George Bush.

During the 1992 presidential campaign, Rock the Vote partnered with MTV to air PSAs starring some of the biggest rock stars of the period. Among them was Eddie Vedder, whose twenty-eight-second clip—in which the singer play-acts his mounting shock and disgust over poor turnout statistics for voters under the age of twenty-five between clips of skateboarders spinning through the air in slow motion—is now laughably anachronistic. But the campaign worked: Youth turnout in 1992 rose to its highest level since the mid-seventies. And this helped Clinton, at forty-six, to become the youngest person elected to the White House since John F. Kennedy thirty-two years prior.

MTV treated the end of the twelve-year Reagan–Bush administration unambiguously as glorious news, even hosting an inauguration party of their own for the first (and last) time in January 1993. The performance of the night (which also featured Don Henley, Boyz II Men, Soul Asylum, and 10,000 Maniacs) was the one-off supergroup Automatic Baby, which paired two members of R.E.M., Michael Stipe and Mike Mills, with two members of U2—the world's other leading progressive arena rock band—Adam Clayton and Larry Mullen, Jr.

It really did seem like change was in the air, though some of those musicians might have felt used after Clinton failed in ensuing years to follow through on the campaign's utopian "Don't Stop Thinking About Tomorrow" idealism. Calls for gay rights soon turned into the cop-out "Don't Ask, Don't Tell" policy for the military while promises of a more empathetic government gave way to the Personal Responsibility and Work Opportunity Act, a bill passed in 1996 that overhauled federal welfare programs with such an unsparing, bottom-line ruthlessness that it might as well have been enacted by a Republican president.

Six months after Pearl Jam's visit to the White House, President Clinton signed into law the Violent Crime Control and Law Enforcement Act, which provided billions of dollars for the hiring of one hundred thousand police officers and scores of new prisons while implementing a "three-strikes" policy guaranteeing life sentences for violent offenders, a policy that contributed to America's exploding incarcerated population. It was exactly the sort of thing that Vedder had taken a stand against in social justice anthems like "W.M.A.," only now the aggressive policing measures were being forwarded by Democrats instead of Republicans.

Not all rock bands were quick to jump on the Clinton bandwagon—Nirvana, for one, never made a Rock the Vote ad or espoused any sort of coherent political message. But Vedder, while also a sincere and prodigious activist, was something of a canny politician himself. His talent for ingratiating himself with childhood heroes like Pete Townshend and Neil Young was only exceeded by the charm and canniness he displayed in wooing potential critics from the underground, like Ian MacKaye and Henry Rollins, therefore mollifying the skepticism of those who revered Fugazi and Black Flag as the antithesis of Pearl Jam. Who was Bill Clinton compared to any of *those* dignitaries?

If allowing the president to use him for a photo-op made booking a tour without Ticketmaster venues more tenable, it was worth the field trip. Though, in the end, Bill Clinton failed to deliver on that count, too.

$$\notin$$

Another reason why I don't want to delve too much into the well-worn Eddie vs. Kurt conversation is because I'd rather explore the Jeff vs. Kurt dynamic.

This seems like the actual crux of the (mostly overblown but not entirely fabricated) Nirvana/Pearl Jam rivalry—Kurt Cobain apparently didn't like Jeff Ament and expressed that dislike by repeatedly calling Pearl Jam grunge careerists. He referred to Ament specifically as a careerist in Michael Azerrad's 1993 book *Come As You Are: The Story of Nirvana*, adding that he's "a person who will kiss ass to make sure his band gets popular so he can become rich." And Jeff Ament in turn resented this because he had roots in Seattle's punk scene that in fact went much deeper than Cobain's.

While Vedder either ignored Cobain's taunts or humbly deferred to them, Ament has consistently hit back against the narrative that Pearl Jam somehow had less credibility than Nirvana. Ament was the one who in the early eighties moved to Seattle from Montana with only forty bucks in his pocket. He was the one who lived on a diet of chicken pot pies while his punk band Deranged Diction opened for Hüsker Dü and D.O.A. And he (along with Stone Gossard) was in Green River, the first band to put out a record on Sub Pop. It irritated him—no, it *pissed him off*—to be accused of not paying his dues.

"Does he think we're riding his bandwagon?" Ament vented to *Rolling Stone* in 1992 for a Nirvana cover story also written by Azerrad. "We could turn around and say that Nirvana put out records on money we made for Sub Pop when we were in Green River—if we were that stupid about it."

Eight years later, he admitted that this "stuff never left my craw" in an interview with the *San Francisco Chronicle*. "The fact of the matter is, I was born in a pretty poor family and I've always had to have a day job up until 10 years ago," he said. "Maybe some of that drive that people see is maybe me not wanting to work in a restaurant for the rest of my life."

When Kurt Cobain comes up in Cameron Crowe's documentary *Pearl Jam Twenty*, the focus is on Vedder's feelings about their apparent reconciliation at the 1992 MTV Video Music Awards. There's that famous clip of them slow dancing backstage while Eric Clapton plays "Tears in Heaven," which might very well be the precise moment when the nineties peaked. Crowe also spends time on Vedder's solemn reaction to Cobain's death. But the book version of *Pearl Jam Twenty* is less sentimental, allowing for more biting reactions from Mike McCready ("I was pissed at him for a long time") and Ament.

"Stone has said something to the effect that when Kurt was judging us, it had an impact on us and how we did things. That might have been true for him, but not for me," Ament says. "I had a lot of musical peers at that time; people in my life that I really respected. Kurt wasn't one of them. I didn't even know him."

The split of Green River in 1988 was the original sin of the Seattle punk scene, dividing loyalists into camps for purists (Mudhoney) and hedonists (Mother Love Bone). A purist like Cobain was naturally pitted against Ament and Gossard's band, even if his own ambition and pop smarts were more in line with the Mother Love Bone side. Vedder, it seems, also couldn't help buying into that reductive dichotomy.

He might have genuinely appreciated Cobain from afar, but Cobain also exacerbated his acute imposter syndrome. These insecurities were especially raw for Vedder in 1994. He poured them out in that *Melody Maker* interview with uncommon vulnerability for a rock star of his stature.

"You'd think your ego would be massive, playing for all these people, having all these people sing your songs. The fact is, you never think you're that good," he told Allan Jones. "You don't feel like you deserve this kind of attention or adulation. And so what you end up feeling instead of this large ego is, you feel like you're worthless."

Whenever I listen to *Live at the Orpheum Theater*, I always wonder what's going through Ament and Gossard's heads when Vedder brings out Mudhoney's Mark Arm to sing "Sonic Reducer" and introduces him as "one of the forefathers of all the great music everybody listens to." Even if his tongue is slightly in cheek, it's still a weird thing to say considering his own band includes two guys who played with Arm in a pioneering band about a decade earlier.

Ament and Gossard had no reason to feel like imposters. They were Seattle rock "forefathers," too. That's why Ament could never stomach Cobain's criticisms—he was playing punk shows in Seattle back when Kurt Cobain was still hanging out under a bridge in Aberdeen. While Pearl Jam's rise was relatively rapid, the core of the band had done the whole "struggling musician" bit—sleeping on floors, living on pennies per day, eating bologna sandwiches for every meal—for years before *Ten* became the toast of MTV. But for whatever reason, not even Pearl Jam's singer could contextualize Pearl Jam in that way in 1994.

⚡

You can hear the chaos and confusion that reigned in April 1994 in the album that was released later that year, on November 22. *Vitalogy* is very much a record dominated by Vedder's diseased headspace. This is literalized by including an X-ray of his crooked teeth in the place of lyrics for "Corduroy" in the liner notes. But it's also plainly communicated by the tortured—sometimes surreal—lyrics and willfully shambolic music.

This unconventional approach even carried over to the format. The push to put *Vitalogy* out on vinyl two weeks before the usual CD and cassette releases was viewed in the moment as one of the band's eccentric indulgences. Vinyl was still years away from being fetishized as a collector's item by mainstream music fans. A 1988 article in the *Los Angeles Times* speculated that the vinyl format would probably be extinct by 1990. Maybe by 1992 if the stalwarts kept it on life support. The numbers seemed to bear this out: in 1973, 280 million vinyl records were sold, which represented 73 percent of total album sales in the United States, according to the Recording Industry Association of America. By 1987, vinyl's share had dropped to only 17.3 percent of total sales.

For a generation raised on CDs, which sold better than ever in the nineties, *Vitalogy* might very well have been the first vinyl record a Pearl Jam fan ever bought. In light of the so-called vinyl boom of the twenty-first century, Pearl Jam can take pride in being ahead of the curve. They likely inspired millions of kids to one day become middle-aged vinyl collectors.

Beyond stumping for the archaic format, it also makes artistic sense for *Vitalogy* to be divided into distinct halves. Side A of *Vitalogy* is the "songs" half, the part of the record that feels like an extension of the hits from *Vs.* "Last Exit" is pile-driving, existential bombast in the mold of "Go" and "Animal," and "Spin the Black Circle" and "Whipping" are hearty demonstrations of the band's pure, effortless physicality. From a mission-statement standpoint, the most crucial track on Side A is "Not for You," a lumbering slab of Crazy Horse–inspired crankiness in which Vedder once again aligns himself with the rebellious, oppositional teenage audience the band addressed on the first two albums.

But the most important track on this side is "Nothingman," a luminous ballad co-written by Vedder and Ament in the space of an hour. With its gently clanging guitar riff and Vedder's restrained vocals, it superficially feels like a moment of calm on an otherwise tumultuous record.

But it also lingers longer once the shock of the other tracks dissipates. Like "Indifference," "Nothingman" is a grown-up song about the very real emotional battles that sabotage adult relationships. I especially like the lyric where Vedder pinpoints the moment when a romantic partnership turns cold: "She once believed in every story he had to tell / One day she stiffened / took the other side." It's a moment as intimate and sensitive as the rest of *Vitalogy* is standoffish and pugilistic. On Pearl Jam's later albums, when Vedder became preoccupied with matters of family and mortality, the strongest material would frequently be pretty, thoughtful numbers that essentially follow the blueprint of this song.

Side B is where *Vitalogy* goes from an impressionistic album to an expressionistic one. It moves beyond telling you how fucked up it is inside Eddie Vedder's head to showing you. The process begins with the album's most literal song about corporate appropriation of grunge culture, "Corduroy."[2] In that *Los Angeles Times* interview, Vedder actually worried that the lyrics were "too obvious," hence the X-ray of his teeth. But "Corduroy" endures as one of the great Pearl Jam songs because of the tremendous ensemble playing by the band, which achieves an ecstatic transcendence during the raging instrumental bridge that recalls the brilliance of the 4/3/94 bootleg.

From there, the record's sense of equilibrium slowly, gleefully deteriorates. It's true that this side includes Pearl Jam's most straightforward pop song, "Better Man," though in the context of the album it's presented as a flashback to Vedder's past. Ultimately, the pervasive feelings of this side are grief ("Immortality"), fear (the demented and near-unlistenable "Stupid Mop"), and paranoia (the anti-groupie ode "Satan's Bed," which also debuted in April 1994). It's the *Melody Maker* interview in musical form.

And then there's "Bugs," Eddie's self-described "wank-off accordion piece" that he delighted in presenting to friends before *Vitalogy*'s release

---

2 "Corduroy" refers to a replica of Eddie Vedder's jacket being sold at the time; it's also a surfing term for a series of swells extending from the shore to the horizon.

as the album's first single. The best (and perhaps only) way to appreciate "Bugs" is as a meta performance art piece, as in "What if a song about eating bugs that's played on an accordion appeared as the ninth song on the biggest rock album of the year?" It's a prank—not on Pearl Jam's audience, exactly, but on the very concept of larger-than-life rock stardom. And it works, I think, if you listen to the album in sequence. Insert "Bugs" into a Pearl Jam playlist and it's an irritant. But on *Vitalogy*, it's part of a larger narrative about a man losing his damn mind in his art so that he doesn't do it in real life.

Vitalogy is ultimately such a personal and specific evocation of Vedder's headspace that it's understandable that the other members of Pearl Jam didn't really get it at first. Stone Gossard has been the most outspoken critic of *Vitalogy*, admitting that he checked out of the album before it was finished. "At the time, I thought, 'This isn't our best record.' I remember feeling kind of disappointed or feeling, like, not connected to it at the end, and I didn't help finish it," he says in *Pearl Jam Twenty*. "It was out of my hands for the first time."

For *Ten* and *Vs.*, Gossard was an idea generator, a riff machine who wrote the music that would forever keep Pearl Jam on the radio and in arenas. Like Ament, he had deep roots in the Seattle punk scene. But he was also, at heart, a metalhead whose first loves were Iron Maiden and Motörhead. He had a sense of decency for how a band should carry itself. But he also knew how to deliver the red meat that guitar-loving headbangers craved.

That "arena rock punk rock" idea that Pearl Jam was now carrying forward very much sprang from the way that Stone had long conceptualized his own music. He had every right to expect that he would be able to maintain that "master and commander" role on the third record. Particularly with *Vs.*, Gossard believed that he had figured out how Pearl Jam albums were supposed to work. Why not let him cook? But *Vitalogy* was "the first record where Ed was the guy making the final decisions," Gossard later recalled. "It was a real difficult record for me to make, because I was having to give up a lot of control."

This subtext is a big part of the lore on *Vitalogy*, and it's why it remains one of Pearl Jam's most interesting albums. It's the one where Gossard became a foil for Vedder. This dynamic was friendlier and more benign than the tension with Abbruzzese. But it was nonetheless a conflict.

"The song that you thought was going to be really great for the record wouldn't necessarily be the one he'd attach himself to," Gossard reminisced to *Spin* in 2001 about Vedder. "It would be some sort of third riff or silly little song: All of a sudden that would be the one he'd want to work on. Looking back on it, I can appreciate it, and I sort of resent it."

"I call Stone my archenemy in the band, mainly because he's the devil's advocate," Vedder countered. "You could have the best idea that was absolutely nonquestionable, and then he'd bring something up about why we can't just go do it. But it's really positive. Someone's gotta do it, and he does, unabashedly."

The jousting here is collegial. But there's no doubt that if Stone, despite his resentments, hadn't come to appreciate Eddie's stewardship of the band—or *Vitalogy*, which he came around on in a big way—it would have ended Pearl Jam right then and there. Stone had to accept that Eddie would take one of his precious chunky, mid-tempo riffs, "accidentally" speed it up several times, and turn it into the caustic "Spin the Black Circle." Stone and Jeff had already gotten that sort of music out of their system. But Eddie hadn't. And that alone made it a Pearl Jam song.

You can call that careerism. Or you can call it acceptable pragmatism. I lean toward the latter. People look at Kurt Cobain and see an example of punk purity because he would rather die than compromise. But in Pearl Jam, a background in punk prepared Stone and Jeff to see the wisdom in compromise, not least because it was a path toward a greater freedom that would enable their band to write their own ticket.

They ceded control because it was best for the band, and they had been in enough bands that crashed and burned to recognize the greater good. Ultimately, there's more freedom in surviving than not.

CHAPTER 8
"BETTER MAN"

(7/9/03, New York City)

Bad Radio (the Band) • Bad Radio (the Concept) • The English Beat
• Karen Vedder • Tom Petty's *Hard Promises* • The Indigo Girls
• Joni Mitchell's *Hejira*

Any conversation about Pearl Jam tends to focus on Eddie Vedder. Even this book so far has focused disproportionately on the lead singer. It's just how it goes with this band. He's the man at the top. And this fact is acknowledged by all involved parties. In the DVD extras for the 2017 concert film *Let's Play Two*, Vedder describes himself as the band's "player/coach." If I can abruptly change sports to fully land this analogy, he is to Pearl Jam what Bill Russell was to the late-sixties Boston Celtics.

But it would be a mistake to classify Pearl Jam as a one-man operation. This band absolutely would not have been able to function if Stone Gossard and Mike McCready had been fired and replaced by Dave Navarro and Buckethead. Or if Flea was subbed in the place of Jeff Ament had Jeff ever decided to permanently retire to his Montana compound. Those guys needed to be led to rock greatness by Eddie Vedder. But Eddie Vedder needed his bandmates to become *the* Eddie Vedder.

Anyone who doubts this needs to search for Bad Radio videos on YouTube.

Bad Radio was a punk-funk-metal hybrid band that existed in Southern California from 1986 to 1990. Like so many bands in that scene in the late eighties, Bad Radio was heavily indebted to the two most popular alt-rock bands from LA in that era, the Red Hot Chili Peppers and Jane's Addiction. What this means is that Bad Radio songs usually had at least one extremely wonky guitar solo, and way too many instances of the word "funk" being used as a replacement for the word "fuck."[1]

In 1988, Vedder was hired to be the lead singer. For the next two years, he pledged himself to making Bad Radio a success. But fame and fortune wasn't in the cards, and Vedder eventually realized that this was due to his uninspired bandmates. "We'd win 'battle of the bands' on intensity alone, but it was coming from *me*," he later recalled. "I couldn't get anybody else to give up their fucking bullshit. As far as songs and stuff, they weren't reading, they weren't living. They knew how big Tommy Lee's new drum kit was, but, you know, fuck that."

Lest you think he's being uncharitable, you can actually watch what is supposedly Vedder's final show with Bad Radio—which occurred on February 11, 1990, in San Diego—online. The timing of this concert is interesting for at least two reasons. First, it's just one month before the death of Andrew Wood, which signaled the immediate end of Mother Love Bone. Second, it's only about seven months before Eddie sends back the "Momma-Son" tape, which sets the formation of Pearl Jam into motion.

The Eddie Vedder you see with Bad Radio in the 2/11/90 video isn't all that far removed from the Eddie Vedder who will soon enter the world's stage. But what really slays you about the forty-minute clip is how

---

1 The funk-rock influence on Pearl Jam is happily minimal, showing up most clearly in the B-side "Dirty Frank" and the *Vs.* track "Rats."

impossibly far from rock stardom he seems. As he references a few times from the stage, the show is on a Sunday night and takes place in front of a scarce crowd. Vedder spends the first few songs gamely trying to get people to dance, and eventually about ten people comply. While it's impossible to tell for sure, this might very well be a majority of the audience.

It's very easy to make fun of Bad Radio based on this video, given how derivative they are of the most popular bands in their scene. (The bluesy "What," which resembles *Mother's Milk*–era Chili Peppers with the addition of some histrionic Stevie Ray Vaughan–style guitar, is particularly dreadful.) But Vedder already had most of the elements in place to be an A-list front man—his distinctive vocals are polished and strong, he exudes charisma, and he has the same combustible, go-for-broke energy that distinguished Pearl Jam's early shows. (At the end of the set-concluding "Waste My Days," he theatrically knocks down his mic stand.)

The guy clearly has talent. But he doesn't have a supporting cast to put him in a position to truly blossom. The video underscores an obvious truth: if not for some lucky breaks, Eddie Vedder might very well have never escaped the Sunday night slot at mostly empty San Diego bars.

Vedder himself acknowledged as much during a Pearl Jam concert at Madison Square Garden in 2003 while introducing a classic hit that originated from the Bad Radio era. "Without Jeff and Stone, I would certainly not get to play it here, or anywhere really," he says. "Or maybe somewhere that smelled like piss." (Vedder of course had to add: "That would have been all right.")

The song was "Better Man." Vedder has said he wrote it two decades before that Madison Square Garden concert, as a teenager living on his own in a cheap apartment in the early eighties. It was inspired partly by "Save It for Later," a song by the ska band the English Beat that was released as a single in April 1982, many years after it was written by the band's guitarist Dave Wakeling when *he* was a teenager.[2]

---

2 Pete Townshend also covered it on his 1986 live record, *Deep End Live!* PJ started occasionally tagging the song at the end of live renditions of "Better Man" in 1998.

Based on this timeline, it's likely that "Better Man" started coming together not long after Karen Vedder told her son the truth about his biological father, Edward Severson Jr., who died in 1981 and had been known to Eddie only as a friend of the family. This confrontation has been placed in the summer of 1982, after which Vedder moved into his own place while attending San Dieguito High School for his senior year. These events, and the successful chart run of "Save It for Later," seem to line up.

The most obvious interpretation of "Better Man" is that Vedder was writing about his mother's relationship with his stepfather, Peter Mueller, a man Vedder has never spoken of fondly. It is written from the perspective of a person who is close to the couple, presumably a child. The narrator can see the abusive dynamic at play but is powerless to stop it. The difference between "Better Man" and reality is that Karen Vedder *did* leave, a more uplifting ending than what Eddie offers in the song, where the woman wants to leave but appears resigned to stay out of a misguided sense of obligation. "She loved him, yeah / She don't want to leave this way / She feeds him, yeah / That's why she'll be back again."

"Better Man" didn't enter Pearl Jam's orbit until a full decade later, during the *Vs.* sessions. When producer Brendan O'Brien first heard it, he rightly recognized it as "a blatantly great pop song" and a potential smash, which was the exact wrong thing to say to Eddie Vedder in 1993. For a minute, the plan was to give the song away to a Greenpeace benefit album. But O'Brien claims that he went as far as sabotaging the *Vs.*-era version so that Pearl Jam would reconsider donating "Better Man" to charity, until which time he could convince them to record a proper take for a Pearl Jam album.

I'm sure that Vedder had some reservations about releasing a song as catchy and immediate as "Better Man" in the wake of *Ten*'s massive radio success. But I am skeptical that he would have followed through on burying "Better Man" on a benefit record. The song clearly meant something to him. If he didn't want the world to hear it, he could have just kept it to himself. But he held on to "Better Man" for years after he wrote it and spent considerable time refining it.

If you dig deeper into YouTube's Bad Radio archive, you'll find a video of Vedder singing "Better Man" with the band in 1989. The quality is poor, but the song is pretty much there—the melody and Vedder's vocals are unmistakable, even given the low-fidelity recording. What kills this version is the clumsy arrangement. To be fair, "Better Man" doesn't really fit with Bad Radio's usual meathead repertoire. Though there's evidence that Vedder chafed against that pretty early on, based on a faithful demo that he recorded of Bruce Springsteen's "One Step Up," from his 1987 "divorce" record *Tunnel of Love*, around this time. Like "Better Man" (and also "Nothingman"), "One Step Up" is a frank look at the failure of an adult romantic relationship, subject matter that doesn't really square with tunes about getting the "funk" out.

In the Bad Radio version of "Better Man," the band comes in early, right after the first verse. And then they ride the same groove for the next several minutes. This strips the song of the tension and drama of the Pearl Jam version, where the band doesn't enter until the 1:55 mark, nearly the song's midpoint. The result is that the Bad Radio rendition is awfully boring and repetitive, without the "quiet to loud" dynamics that made "Better Man" stand out on rock radio once it became *Vitalogy*'s breakout song.

When Pearl Jam first played "Better Man" in May 1993 during a benefit show at Slim's Café in San Francisco—a full eighteen months before it finally appeared on *Vitalogy*—they performed it the way Bad Radio had, albeit much better. The same goes for the handful of times they tried out "Better Man" in front of audiences in the spring of 1994. The performance from the iconic April 3, 1994, show in Atlanta eventually formed the basis of the track on *Vitalogy*, with one crucial difference. After Vedder once again demurred about putting "Better Man" on a Pearl Jam record, O'Brien suggested downplaying the first chorus by recutting the opening half of the song with just Eddie on guitar and vocal and O'Brien on organ.

This simple but important change to the arrangement of "Better Man" had two big benefits. One, it made the song Pearl Jam's most popular in-concert sing-along. This is ironic, considering that Vedder's original intention was to make that first chorus less poppy. In reality, this change did the opposite, giving "Better Man" a sense of communal uplift that it didn't have before. It now *invited* you to sing along with it.

This aspect of "Better Man" really came to a head on the 2003 tour. Before that, you can always hear on bootlegs from the nineties and the 2000 tour that the audience is singing *with* Vedder on the verses. But in 2003, he started handing them a line here and there. Gradually, he acquiesced and let the audience sing parts of the first verse and chorus in his place. By the Madison Square Garden gig, however, the collective strength of the fans' voices finally overwhelmed him, as they would for years afterward. "Better Man" was *their* song now.

The second benefit of the definitive "Better Man" arrangement is even more crucial—it actually changes the song's meaning. On the page, "Better Man" is downbeat. It's a song in which one person accepts abuse and neglect from a partner because a better alternative seems inconceivable. But the *sound* of "Better Man" tells a different story. We feel the protagonist's pain and isolation in the first half of the song because Vedder's voice is also anguished and isolated. But then the band comes in, and "Better Man" suddenly turns into a rousing, crowd-pleasing anthem.

Does this betray the heaviness of the lyric to hit the pop pleasure centers of the audience? I don't think so. I believe that the message of "Better Man" is that we all have daily struggles that seem insurmountable, but just because we feel defeated today doesn't necessarily mean we'll be defeated tomorrow. The arrangement supplies the hope that the lyric denies.

After all, what is a better example of hope than the story of this song? One day Eddie Vedder sang "Better Man" in a place that smelled like piss, and on another day he sang it at Madison Square Garden. For that to happen, "Better Man" needed better men.

$$\text{\Lightning}$$

About a year before "Save It for Later" entered his consciousness, young Eddie Vedder went into a record store in May 1981 and bought a copy of the fourth album by Tom Petty and the Heartbreakers, *Hard Promises*. Eddie purchased the LP the day it came out because, as the song goes, the waiting is the hardest part. In fact, as Vedder says in Peter Bogdanovich's 2007 documentary *Tom Petty and the Heartbreakers: Runnin' Down a Dream*, he learned how to play the album's iconic opening track, "The Waiting," that day.

At some point, Eddie surely got around to playing the second track on *Hard Promises*, "A Woman in Love (It's Not Me)." The song was also the second single released from the record, though it failed to reach the heights of "The Waiting." This was due in part to *another* Tom Petty and the Heartbreakers song rocketing up the charts in 1981, "Stop Draggin' My Heart Around," their duet with Stevie Nicks, which peaked at No. 3, higher than any Heartbreakers track without Stevie Nicks had charted at that time. The song was the product of a fruitful relationship with Nicks that also included one of the best *Hard Promises* deep cuts, "Insider."

I suspect that "A Woman in Love" and the Stevie Nicks songs might have had an osmosis effect on the sixteen-year-old Eddie Vedder as he obsessed over *Hard Promises*, especially as it pertains to "Better Man." In most instances, the influence of Petty's music on Pearl Jam is a little hard to place. Vedder has frequently proclaimed his love for Petty, both before and after Petty's death in 2017, and covered his songs with the band and during his solo shows. As Vedder is with so many classic rock heroes, he is a true Petty fan with a connoisseur's ear. His decision to play "Room at the Top"—one of Petty's most despairing songs about his own mental health—during the 2018 Oscars "In Memoriam" segment was astute if also pretty depressing.

But Pearl Jam's music doesn't sound all that much like Petty. His influence isn't as obvious as it is with the Who, Bruce Springsteen, and Neil Young. He's a little too laid-back, southern, and sunny to match up cleanly with these introspective gentlemen from the rainy Pacific Northwest. And you best believe that Petty—whose run of perfect car radio hits from the mid-seventies to the mid-nineties is unmatched in rock history—would've never balked at putting a sure-fire hit like "Better Man" on one of his own records.[3]

"Better Man" is the one Pearl Jam song that could have been on a Tom Petty record. The sing-along quality of the verses and chorus speak to that—every Tom Petty hit can easily turn into a massive, stadium-size sing-along. That's what makes a Tom Petty *song* a Tom Petty *classic*. Beyond that, "Better Man" is rootsier than most Pearl Jam songs. Sonically, it belongs in the same "live and cozy in the studio" lane as Petty's landmark 1994 album *Wildflowers*, which came out the same month as *Vitalogy*. But the most important connection to Petty is Vedder's empathy for the woman in the story, and his willingness to write from that point of view.

In the early nineties, Pearl Jam set themselves apart from the male-dominated (and male angst-centric) grunge scene by frequently centering women in their songs. This began with "Why Go" from *Ten*, in which a female mental patient rails against being institutionalized. But it really became a focus of Vedder's lyrics on *Vs.*, with the songs "Daughter," "Dissident," and "Elderly Woman Behind the Counter in a Small Town." ("Animal" also belongs in this discussion if you interpret it as a song about sexual assault.) Beyond the lyrics, "Elderly Woman Behind the Counter in a Small Town" has a strongly feminine musical feel as well—the robust, open-hearted folk strum is taken directly from the Indigo Girls songbook while Ament's fretless bass lines recall Joni Mitchell's work with the pioneering jazz bassist Jaco Pastorius on the 1976 album *Hejira*.

The only male singer-songwriter who has written more arena-rock songs about women than Vedder is Tom Petty. So many of his tunes are about female protagonists who—like the woman in "Better Man"—are straining toward imagining a happier life. This was subject matter that Petty returned to routinely throughout his career, starting with early hits like "American Girl," "Listen to Her Heart," and "Here Comes My Girl,"

---

3 Eddie Vedder's 2022 solo album *Earthling* is easily the most Petty-like music he's ever made.

on through mid-period smashes like "Free Fallin'," "Yer So Bad," and "Mary Jane's Last Dance," and finally with later tunes like "Turn This Car Around" and "Have Love Will Travel."

Petty's most famous song, "American Girl," pulls the same trick as "Better Man"—the music fools you into thinking the story is more triumphant than it really is. You think she's getting on 441 because she can't help thinking that there's a better life somewhere else. But if you pay close attention to the lyrics, she's only *thinking* about hitting the highway. It calls out to her on a cold night as she stands alone on a balcony. But like the woman in "Better Man," she's hamstrung by some guy. A change is so close but still so far out of reach.

"A Woman in Love" is not sung from the perspective of the woman in the story. It's about the guy that the woman leaves behind. It's the sequel to "Better Man"; rather, Vedder's song is the prequel to "A Woman in Love."

In his song, Petty sings in the first person, expressing the torment of being dumped for a better man. He says that "she laughed in my face" when she told him goodbye. She tells him "don't try to save me" but he won't listen. He warns that this guy is "gonna break her heart to pieces." But mostly he just feels sorry for himself. "She used to be the kind of woman / You have and you hold / She could understand the problems / She let the little things go."

Petty lays these pathetic details so thick in "A Woman in Love" that this poor schlub eventually comes off like an unreliable narrator. What exactly were "the little things" she let go? Did this guy understand her problems, too? Later, when Petty sings, "I don't understand what she needed," it's like a spontaneous confession. This guy is too needy and self-absorbed to understand the woman's needs.

Given the sensitivity and ample self-awareness Petty displays in other songs about relationships between men and women, I don't think any of this is accidental. And I'm willing to bet that a perceptive kid like Vedder would have picked up on this aspect of the song and even recognized how it seemed to line up with the circumstances of his own parents' relationship. I like to imagine this inspired him to write a backstory for "A Woman in Love," in order to explore the woman's experience and explain exactly the sort of "little things" that she had to put up with.

Just as Vedder was enlightened by listening to Tom Petty songs, I'm part of the generation of men who benefited from Vedder's impulse to step outside his own immediate frame of reference. So many teenaged guys heard songs like "Better Man," "Daughter," and "Elderly Woman Behind the Counter in a Small Town" and felt, if only temporarily, like it snapped them out of the profound myopia that's endemic to teenage guys.

Of course, framing those songs solely on the basis of how they "taught" men that "hey, women are people, too!" feels like an extension of that myopia. I think Petty and Vedder were both drawn to writing about women because they recognized that songs about women in existential distress are inherently more universal than songs about men.

Men singing about men tends to appeal mainly to men, which creates an energy that can easily curdle into something toxic and ugly. A song in which a man invites the audience to relate to a woman, whether you are a man or a woman, is a way of building a community. What "Better Man" is, even more than most PJ songs, is inclusive. People sing along because it's a great pop tune. But also because you've either been the woman in that song or you've loved that woman and wanted the best for her. The music makes you believe she'll finally get what she deserves.

CHAPTER 9
"I'M THE OCEAN"

(From the 1995 Neil Young album *Mirror Ball*)

Adam Curtis Documentaries • The Fight Against Ticketmaster • Live's *Throwing Copper* • Neil Young's "Ditch Era" • Jack Irons's Kickass Swing • "I Got Shit"

In 2005, a Russian professor named Alexei Yurchak published a book called *Everything Was Forever, Until It Was No More: The Last Soviet Generation*. It's about life in his home country as Communism fell apart in the seventies and eighties. At the time, there was a common understanding in the country that the system was corrupt and ineffectual, and yet everyone had to pretend it was working properly because there was simply no way of imagining a better system. Yurchak called this phenomenon "hypernormalization," a way of thinking that maintained a superficial (and artificial) sense of stability in a culture that was, in reality, rapidly disintegrating.

Lest you think I'm smarter than I am, allow me to make a confession: I haven't read Yurchak's book. I have never read a book by *any* Russian professor. (I am waiting for *any* Russian professor to write a book about grunge.) I learned about Yurchak from a three-hour documentary called *HyperNormalisation* that originally aired on the BBC in 2016. The film was directed by Adam Curtis, a British journalist who has made dozens of documentaries since the early eighties but didn't become widely known until he started focusing on how modern systems of power keep the public in the dark about how the world really works.

In *HyperNormalisation*, Curtis takes Yurchak's ideas about the Soviet Union and shows how this willful delusion took over in places throughout the world during the late twentieth century, as political power slowly was subsumed by international financial interests. For Yurchak, this idea explained why millions of people accepted that standing in line for hours for basic necessities was an unavoidable fact of life. For Americans, it can also explain why the wealth gap continues to expand. It's just a "law of nature" rather than the output of a system that human beings made and therefore can unmake if they so choose.

Again, because I am a huge dummy, I probably would not be interested in Curtis's films if he didn't have a talent for taking found news footage from the past and pairing it with evocative music by artists such as Brian Eno, Burial, and Suicide. Curtis—who doesn't consider himself a filmmaker—nonetheless has an incredible knack for taking material that would normally be reserved for a medium-interesting episode of PBS's *Frontline* and elevating it to a highly engaging cinematic experience. And that emotional connection is what makes his films embed themselves into your psyche, to the point where you see examples of hypernormalization everywhere.

Here's one example: Pearl Jam's failed battle against Ticketmaster.

In the mid-nineties, everybody knew that Ticketmaster was a monopoly. And everybody knew that the lack of competition for purchasing concert tickets was a disservice to fans. Therefore, everybody *should have known* that if the biggest artists and bands on the planet, with the full support of their fans, decided to do something to correct this, the

Ticketmaster situation would have changed because nothing about this system was inevitable.

But that's not what happened. Here's what *did* happen: Pearl Jam wanted Ticketmaster to charge no more than $1.80 on a proposed $18 ticket; Ticketmaster wanted to charge $4 to $6. Instead of caving, Pearl Jam canceled their 1994 summer tour. Also that year, Pearl Jam was called to testify before Congress in conjunction with a Justice Department investigation into Ticketmaster. Representatives for R.E.M. and Aerosmith also spoke out, but no other band took substantive steps to go against working with the company.

The following year, Pearl Jam attempted to tour using only venues not affiliated with Ticketmaster, and the hassles involved nearly wrecked the band as many fans publicly revolted. By the summer, the federal government quietly dropped its investigation into Ticketmaster. In response, the company issued this extremely Soviet-esque statement to *Rolling Stone*: "Getting attacked by a superstar rock band is a lot like being accused of kicking your dog: there's a general presumption of guilt until proven innocent. *Luckily the facts were on our side, and we prevailed.*"

Pearl Jam's attempt to hold Ticketmaster accountable remains the single most misunderstood aspect of their legacy. Over the years, it has been described with a dispiriting set of adjectives: "misguided," "ill-fated," "quixotic," "unwinnable." Basically, they've been regarded as dopes for even trying to change the system, even in a small way, because there was *never a chance* they would win.

In a sense, that's true, but only because people *chose* to believe it was true. This delusion was so profound that Pearl Jam's patchwork attempt to tour without Ticketmaster was taken as evidence that *they were wrong* rather than proof that this particular corporation was unfairly dominating the market. In the parlance of hypernormalization, Pearl Jam got crushed because their peers and even their fans, along with the federal government, lacked the resolve, energy, and imagination to come up with a better idea than simply allowing Ticketmaster do all the bad things they were obviously doing. Going along with the status quo was easier, and it was rationalized as a pragmatism.

In that infamous *Rolling Stone* hit piece from 1996, the Ticketmaster fight was at the center of the case for Eddie Vedder being an entitled prima donna. Though the magazine *also* argued that he was a fool for leaving millions of dollars on the table by not just keeping his mouth shut and playing ball. Insisting that Pearl Jam were somehow stuck up their own asses *because* they didn't make their own bottom line a priority truly is peak "hypernormalization" logic. But *Rolling Stone* favorably quoted an anonymous "manager of another multiplatinum rock act" making exactly that case. "Obviously, Eddie is attuned to the evils of the business. But how many of your fans really give a fuck? The majority of them don't. They don't care if it's in venue X, Y or Z, or what the ticket company is. They want to hear you play good music."

A common narrative about grunge is that the movement died when Kurt Cobain took his own life. There's a lot of truth to that. But the moment *when it was clear beyond a shadow of a doubt* that an era had ended was Pearl Jam's depressingly futile fight against Ticketmaster. Here was an example—the only example really—of an alt-rock band taking on the system in a very real and tangible way, and the campaign failed due entirely to a lack of any real conviction by the public to see the change through.

If Adam Curtis cared at all about Pearl Jam, I'm sure he would attribute this to the rise of individualism in the nineties at the expense of the selfless collective action that has driven any effective form of social change. This wasn't just apparent in the Ticketmaster controversy; it even filtered down to the music. Right as Pearl Jam was pulled away from the public eye in the mid-nineties, a new breed of alt-rock band rose to prominence that aped the sound and attitude of Pearl Jam but without any of the political baggage. These acts were *only* introspective, which reflected the preferences of listeners who were strictly interested in contemplating their own problems.

The most successful of these acts was Live, a band from Pennsylvania who briefly became one of America's biggest rock groups in the mid-nineties. Their rise was predicated largely on emulating Pearl Jam, with a dash of R.E.M.'s nineties records. Live's blockbuster 1994 LP *Throwing Copper* was significantly more guitar heavy and *Vs.*-like than their folk-rock debut, 1991's *Mental Jewelry*. Over the course of eighteen months, it sold millions and spawned multiple MTV hits like the melo-dramatic "Lightning Crashes"—the one with the lyric about a placenta falling to the floor, a stomach-turning image that could've only been com-mercial in 1995—and the heavier "I Alone." By the end of 1995, they were voted Artist of the Year in *Rolling Stone*'s year-end readers poll, capping their quick ascension.

"I Alone" doubled as a personal credo for a band resolutely commit-ted to *not* changing the world. "I've never identified with this I-wanna-be-a-hip-alternative-cool-guy thing," bassist Patrick Dahlheimer sniffed in their *Rolling Stone* cover story. "Live always wanted to be successful." This attitude also comes across on the dramatic climax of *Throwing Cop-per*, a thoroughly ridiculous rocker called "White, Discussion," in which lead singer Ed Kowalczyk claims to "talk of revolution" before decrying attempts at actual revolution, big or small, as self-indulgent: "All this discussion / Though politically correct / Is dead beyond destruction / Though it leaves me quite erect." Suffice it to say, Live did not join Pearl Jam in boycotting Ticketmaster.

Another band that rose to alt-rock prominence in the mid-nineties who took cues from Pearl Jam was Counting Crows. Their 1996 album *Recov-ering the Satellites* cranked the guitars in grunge-like fashion, instantly setting it apart from the gentle folk-rock of their multiplatinum 1993 debut, *August and Everything After*. Led by the fine singer-songwriter Adam Duritz, Counting Crows was a better band than Live and most of the other alt-rock also-rans dominating radio at the time. But like Live, they also set about stripping rock music of any activist baggage. In the early aughts, when Duritz's band opened for the Who, Eddie Vedder was moved to leave a book backstage on the negative effects of Coca-Cola on children. Counting Crows had recently appeared in a commercial for the soft drink company, a move that Vedder would forever find inconceivable for a rock band. But as Duritz later explained in an interview, taking the money was a "no-brainer" for him.

Pearl Jam's influence was so widespread that it finally filtered into the decade's most broadly appealing pop music in the form of Alanis Morissette's *Jagged Little Pill*, which came out in the summer of 1995 and later became the top-selling album of 1996. A former child star from Canada who once starred on Nickelodeon's variety show *You Can't Do That on Television*, Morissette had failed to make much of an impression outside her home country when she put out two mild dance-pop albums, 1991's *Alanis* and 1992's *Now Is the Time*, when she was still in high school. Her debut did produce one Canadian hit, "Too Hot," that led to a tour opening for Vanilla Ice. But a one-hit wonder opening for another one-hit wonder did not seem to portend the makings of a lasting career.

With *Jagged Little Pill*, she gave herself an appropriately angry make-over, singing venomously about performing fellatio on an ex-lover in her breakout hit, "You Oughta Know." The album's incredible success—it has sold over thirty-three million copies worldwide—led to a spate of "female rock renaissance" think pieces in the press, including an article in *New York* magazine in which Nirvana manager Danny Goldberg credited people like "Kurt Cobain, Eddie Vedder, Michael Stipe, and Billy Corgan" with breaking up "the macho hegemony over the rock part of the culture" and giving "oxygen for some of the women to find an audience."

Like Pearl Jam, Morissette was blamed by critics for inspiring a legion of lesser copycats (like Meredith Brooks, whose 1997 hit "Bitch" plays like an unwitting *Jagged Little Pill* parody) while overshadowing artistically superior colleagues like Liz Phair and PJ Harvey. But, as *New York*'s Kim France argued, she also deserved credit for, in effect, normalizing female rage, making it acceptable and even commercial in the same ways that male angst had already been embraced by audiences from the very beginning of rock music.

More than any other product of the alt-rock epoch, *Jagged Little Pill* showed that "alternative" as a concept had been fully assimilated by the same pop pros who had never fully abandoned their power positions in the music industry. Morissette's key collaborator, the producer and song-writer Glen Ballard, had overseen the ten-million-selling self-titled debut by the ultra-cheesy vocal trio Wilson Phillips just six years prior. He also co-wrote "Man in the Mirror" for Michael Jackson, the go-to symbol of pop hegemony that Nirvana had supposedly toppled when *Nevermind* replaced Jackson's 1991 LP *Dangerous* at the top of the *Billboard* chart in January 1992. Now that symbol of cultural supremacy was none other than . . . Pearl Jam.

While their imitators were happy to borrow from Pearl Jam's music and iconography, they did not, for the most part, emulate Eddie Vedder's skepticism about pop success. In a very short period of time, that sort of anti-professional behavior had fallen out of favor, as was made clear at the 1996 Grammys when Pearl Jam was handed a trophy for Best Hard Rock Performance, in recognition of "Spin the Black Circle." Dressed in a long black leather jacket and brown-green pants and acting like he just woke up from an especially annoying dream, Vedder famously muttered, "I don't know what this means. I don't think it means anything." This prompted a few scattered awkward laughs in the auditorium and a frozen rictus grin from Stone Gossard, who then proceeded with the rest of the band to express polite gratitude and humility over the award.

At the time—and perhaps even now—Vedder came off like an ingrate in his '96 Grammys speech. But this is a *Grammy* we're talking about. How many terrible songs and albums and artists have been "honored" at the Grammys? How many brilliant songs and albums and artists have been ignored? Vedder was rude, but he wasn't wrong: Winning a Grammy really doesn't mean anything, at least not anything important. Only now in this new era—the late nineties really are a separate era from the early nineties—being rude automatically made you wrong, no matter the con-tent or the justification. Just three years prior, Vedder's speech might've been viewed as another refreshing provocation against corporate banality. Now it was regarded as simply boorish. People suddenly didn't want the Grammys—a laughably terrible institution even relative to other award shows—to be *ruined*.

It's painful to admit this, but it rings true to me: As much as Gen Xers resented and mocked baby boomers, we ultimately shared our parents' self-centeredness. Pearl Jam was a brilliant live rock band, and their principled stands in the first half of the nineties made it inconvenient to see them. We were not interested in their *actual* opposition; we were already happy with their *performative* opposition on their albums and onstage. When *actual* opposition conflicted with *performative* opposition, we chose the latter.

And I get that, I really do. Back then I'm sure I was annoyed with Eddie Vedder. Even now, I wish it would have been easier to see Pearl Jam in the mid-nineties. But can we at least say that Pearl Jam wasn't wrong? That it was actually courageous that they tried to fight Ticketmaster? Looking back, I think we all could have taken "Here we are now, entertain us" a little less literally.

$$\notin$$

Pearl Jam's haphazard touring in 1994 and '95 dramatically scaled down their public profile at a time when their fame should have been peaking. But it's not the only reason why Eddie Vedder became an invisible man.

There was a woman who believed that he was Jesus Christ, and that he had raped her, and that he had subsequently fathered her two children. And this woman was stalking him, to the point of driving her car at fifty miles per hour into a wall protecting his house. "One of the reasons you're protecting yourself is because you've been forthcoming with your emotions," he later said. "So you have to build a wall. And now people are driving into the wall."

The intensity of Eddie Vedder's celebrity in the mid-nineties had reached that terrifying strata where it's very difficult to tell the difference between love and hate. It's that manic zone where the public becomes so obsessed with your every move that some fans come to believe that they can cure whatever is wrong in their heads by destroying the person who most dominates their thoughts. For anyone caught in that sort of titanic wave, staying out of the public eye suddenly becomes a matter of life or death.

Vedder's public appearances outside concerts in 1995 were minimal. In early January, he inducted Neil Young into the Rock & Roll Hall of Fame during a ceremony at New York City's Waldorf-Astoria Grand Ballroom. At one point, he implored the audience—jokingly, though perhaps not *that* jokingly—to gang up on the people seated at the table designated for Ticketmaster. But otherwise he was forced to lay low. He would later recall spending a lot of time in the laundry room of his house, "with an ashtray that I trusted." Anybody other than that ashtray was held at arm's length.

Pearl Jam was not inactive that year. They played thirty-nine shows in seven countries and started work on their fourth studio album, *No Code*. But 1995 does seem like something of a lost year. It was a time when they came very close to breaking up, and in some sense *kind of did* break up.

I would describe what happened to Pearl Jam that year as a transfiguration. They ceased being the band that they were on the first three albums and started the process of becoming the band they would be in the twenty-first century. I've already talked about the Red Rocks concert on June 20, 1995, being a turning point in that regard, but this was not a spontaneous change. It took a while for Pearl Jam to turn into the new version of themselves. On this journey, there were crucial way stations where they were able to take stock of themselves and accumulate invaluable experiences and insights that ultimately paid off in the future.

In 1995, one of those way stations was *Mirror Ball*.

Is *Mirror Ball*—the album where Neil Young is backed by the members of Pearl Jam, mostly without Vedder—underrated? In terms of Neil Young's discography, it tends to be overshadowed by the preceding LP, *Sleeps with Angels*. A bruised and battered update of *Tonight's the Night* for the nineties, *Sleeps with Angels* speaks to Young's unique status that decade as a boomer-era rocker who felt like he was part of the contemporary rock scene. (The only other person of Young's generation to pull this off was

Tom Petty.) While the era's most prominent Seattle bands reacted to Kurt Cobain's death by slowly imploding over the course of the next several years, Young was perhaps the only musician to really process the tragedy, using his album to grieve while also subtly refuting his own lyric—"It's better to burn out than to fade away"—that Cobain used as a sign off in his suicide note. On *Sleeps with Angels*, Young reasserted himself as a stalwart survivor, a man who could assess the damage around him, express what it meant, and then move forward. Miraculously, he seemed to neither burn out nor fade away.

Mirror Ball doesn't have that sort of thematic power. It's not an album *about* survival; it's an album that *shows* how one survives and remains vital despite the psychic damage inherent to a long, eventful life. The message is the sound of the record—aggressive, gnarled, energetic, boisterous, pissed off. Which is why it required a backing band with the indefatigable brawniness of mid-nineties Pearl Jam. Neil needed the band to express his ageless perseverance. The members of the band, meanwhile, very much needed to be needed.

The urgency of this union makes it easy for me to dismiss any potential cynicism about why these very different collaborators from seemingly opposing generations ended up making a record together. Certainly, not everyone agrees. Was Neil an opportunist looking to capitalize on Pearl Jam's popularity? Were Pearl Jam opportunists looking to use Neil's bulletproof credibility to bolster their own reputations? These questions haunt *Mirror Ball* even now.[1] There's certainly not much precedence for a band as significant as Pearl Jam sublimating themselves as backing musicians to another artist right in the prime of their career. The only parallel to Neil Young and Pearl Jam in the mid-nineties is Bob Dylan joining up

---

1 Eddie Vedder sometimes acknowledged this in concert while introducing "I Got Shit," like this sardonic quip from the August 4, 2000, show in Charlotte: "He figured he'd use us and steal our youth, and we'd use him and steal his wisdom, and I think it worked out. Though he's probably younger than we are wise."

with Tom Petty and the Heartbreakers in the mid-eighties,[2] though that comparison doesn't quite do justice to the enormity of Pearl Jam's fame at the time of *Mirror Ball*.

Also, unlike Dylan joining up with the Heartbreakers to "bring it all back home" to his classic *Highway 61 Revisited*–era sound, *Mirror Ball* feels more like an equal collaboration. Yes, Young wrote the songs. But the sound is pure grunge. For that reason, I consider *Mirror Ball* as much a Pearl Jam album as I do a Neil Young one. Though it's probably most appropriate to place it outside either act's work. As Young himself later said in an interview with *Guitar World*, "It sounds more like a band than it does Neil Young. I mixed it like it's a band, instead of having some big voice up front and a little band behind it."

Young admitted that he essentially gave himself over to the Pearl Jam operation, working with their producer Brendan O'Brien at a Seattle recording studio, Bad Animals, that was solidly on the band's home turf. Work began just three weeks after Vedder inducted Young into the Rock Hall, which shows that he wasted no time resting on his laurels.

There was no rest at all during *Mirror Ball*—it was recorded in just four days, during sessions in late January and early February. Predetermined arrangements appear to have been nonexistent. Neil brought in his songs, many of which were written right before he arrived. Then they all plugged and played. Neil apparently wanted Pearl Jam to sound like Pearl Jam with minimal thought or self-consciousness. Perhaps if the guys had more time to think, they would have instinctually emulated the loose, untrained sprawl of Crazy Horse. They had seen Young play with his regular backing band at the Rock Hall ceremony, where they played one of the tunes, "Act of Love," earmarked for the new record. They had even bootlegged the performance with a tape recorder they spirited past security.

But while the band learned "Act of Love" from that tape, they didn't copy Crazy Horse's lumbering, shaggy-dog style. Instead, they became a

---

2 Though *Mirror Ball* sounds more like Dylan's brief union with LA punk band the Plugz on *Late Night with David Letterman* in 1984.

leaner and even more intense version of themselves under Young's leadership, closing in on themselves musically like a fist. They had occasionally adopted this battle stance on *Vitalogy*, most memorably on that transcendent bridge from "Corduroy." But Pearl Jam's third album was in many ways their version of a "ditch era" Neil Young album, which refers to the music Young put out after 1972's *Harvest* made him one of the world's most popular singer-songwriters. The album's biggest hit "Heart of Gold"—his only no. 1 song in the United States—"put me in the middle of the road," Young famously said. "Traveling there soon became a bore so I headed for the ditch."

These "ditch" records include future classics like *On the Beach* and *Tonight's the Night*, in which the gaffes, stumbles, and chemically addled goofs are accentuated rather than excised. That was the style to which *Vitalogy* aspired. But now that Pearl Jam was making music with Young himself—and without Vedder—they reverted to a brutalist, zero-bullshit operation. This was Pearl Jam, once again, attacking the music like Mike Tyson, hitting out at the listener with nonstop body blows as a unified rhythm machine.

It proved to be an incredible entrée into the Pearl Jam world for Jack Irons, who had only joined the band the previous fall. And now he was suddenly tasked with providing the engine for Neil Young's twenty-first studio album. Anyone who expected the former Red Hot Chili Pepper to revert to the funk must have been shocked by his playing—on *Mirror Ball*, he immediately demonstrated his ability to hit with both power and finesse, making the band sound nimbler than it had with Dave Abbruzzese without sacrificing an iota of muscle.

Less obvious were Mike McCready's contributions. Pearl Jam's lead guitarist had to forfeit the solos to Young, which he seemed happy to do. McCready instead was drawn into the relentless riffing powered by Stone Gossard and Jeff Ament, putting Pearl Jam's veteran instrumentalists into a tight sonic space that made *Mirror Ball* sound all the more violent and exciting.

My favorite track on *Mirror Ball* is also the album's most unusual: "I'm the Ocean" has no chorus, no guitar solo, and no dramatic dynamic shifts.

It starts with the band throwing themselves into a mid-tempo groove and riding it for just over seven minutes, as Young spins a series of seemingly disconnected images over ten verses. These images evoke a mix of hope and dread. Neil describes himself as an accident moving way too fast. He brags about how people his age "don't do the things I do." He sees "a rider in the night" who might in fact be death. He notices homeless men who used to be sports stars. He expresses a desire for "random violence." He likens himself to an Oldsmobile Cutlass Supreme.

But Neil is not the ocean. Pearl Jam is the ocean. The band just keeps on relentlessly churning while he muses, acting as "the giant undertow" that eventually takes over the song.

The water metaphor brings to mind a song that Vedder wrote during the *Mirror Ball* sessions. Released as "I Got Id" along with "The Long Road" on the *Merkin Ball* EP in December 1995, "I Got Shit" functioned as an official Pearl Jam release despite only including Vedder and Irons, along with Neil Young on lead guitar and Brendan O'Brien on bass. That the Neil Young album included more members of Pearl Jam than the Pearl Jam EP reflects the upside-down nature of the band's world at the time.

In "I Got Shit," Vedder describes his state of mind as his world was reduced to a laundry room and a trusty ashtray. His lips are shaking and his nails are bit off. He hasn't heard himself talk in a month. He's got so many questions but nobody to ask. It's like the guy from "Footsteps" became a rock star instead of being executed. But he's not that much better off, all things considered: "Picture a cup in the middle of the sea." That was Eddie Vedder in 1995.

On his own, Vedder felt adrift in the surf. But with Neil Young, his bandmates were learning how to go with the tide. The challenge now was clear: How do we do this together? Are we capable of determining this ourselves? Or must we simply allow the great undertow to take us wherever it will?

CHAPTER 10
"GIVEN TO FLY"

(From *Yield*)

Mike McCready Walking in Circles Onstage • Ripping Off Led Zeppelin • Switching the Release Dates of *No Code* and *Yield* • The Fall of Alt-Rock in 1996 • Soundgarden's *Down on the Upside* • Bill Clinton's Impeachment • Jack Irons's Exit

Nobody remembers the 2016 TV series *Roadies*, but I do. I don't remember that it aired for one season on Showtime because I liked it. (I didn't.) And I don't remember it because I happen to be a fan of everything that Cameron Crowe does. (He created the show, but I'm sure he would rather you watch *Almost Famous* or *Say Anything . . .*) I remember *Roadies* precisely for a single scene in the pilot, in which one-time rapper and current pop-punk musician Machine Gun Kelly portrays a Pearl Jam guitar tech.

Actually, I don't remember the *entire* scene. I can only recall one particular line of dialogue, which is shouted by MGK during an apparent moment of distress. (I don't recall why he was upset; perhaps he has misplaced his import CD copy of the "Jeremy" single.)

Anyway, here's what he says: "I love fucking McCready!"

In the annals of Cameron Crowe scripted dialogue, "I love fucking McCready" isn't as universally quotable as, say, "You complete me" from *Jerry Maguire*. But for me it rings twice as true. Mike McCready completes *me*, and he completes Pearl Jam.

I'm not sure when I realized that Mike is my favorite member of Pearl Jam. But I appreciate the man's duality—he seems like the most chill guy in the band off-stage, and he's the wildest one onstage. In Pearl Jam's early days, Mike looked the most like a rock star. This was likely due to his background in the eighties metal band Shadow, which had done the whole "move to LA and try to become the next Guns N' Roses by doing pay-to-play gigs in crappy nightclubs" act before turning tail and returning to Seattle. The point is that he didn't come from punk. His roots were in music in which musical chops and showmanship weren't just celebrated but expected.

When the rest of the band favored baggy shorts and frayed T-shirts, Mike strode onstage in floppy hats and silk scarves. Eventually he got with the shorts-and-T-shirts program, but he still stalks stage right like a madman furiously looking for his car keys. Among Mike McCready's accomplishments as a big-time rock guitarist is the ability to walk ten miles by pacing the same ten-foot box onstage over the course of a two-and-a-half-hour concert.

In the decades since the nineties, as Pearl Jam's focus shifted from putting out new albums every two years to performing physically demanding shows all over the world, Mike's stature in the band has skyrocketed. The tension of a Pearl Jam show is that each song is played more or less the same, with a consistent level of energy, instrumental prowess, and emotional intensity. And yet at the same time each performance is also different, and the differences come primarily from McCready's solos.

On one hand you *need* to be consistent in order to keep yourself in arenas and stadiums; on some level, audiences expect "Even Flow" to sound a certain way, even if it's for the 250th time. On the other hand, nobody wants to be bored, so a flash of new inspiration must also be *consistently* present. And, more often than not, Mike is the one providing that inspiration. He paces in his corner of the stage like a penned-in pit bull who hasn't been fed for a week. And then some red meat appears, like the guitar solo in "Even Flow," and Mike will rip it to shreds with a violent, instinctual relish that can't help but come out in some novel way each and every time.

But I'm getting ahead of myself. In our timeline, we're still in the nineties, though just barely. Mike at this time already had that unlikely mix of wild musical instinct and personal pragmatism. In the time between *No Code* and *Yield*, he was spending a lot time with Eddie and encouraging him to, well, yield. "I remember telling him we need to be very cognizant of the powers that be, because it's critical to our survival," McCready later recalled. "We needed to go out and play music, and enjoy it, within this capitalist structure. To still support those causes, but to work through the established channels."

For Mike, surviving "within this capitalist structure" as a band inspired a good idea informed by both his practical and primal sides: he ripped off Led Zeppelin for one of the most accessible and radio-friendly singles of Pearl Jam's career.

It's just as well that Mike denies consciously lifting the riff for "Given to Fly" from Zeppelin's "Going to California." Robbing from Zeppelin is like stealing from John Dillinger; in rock 'n' roll, there's no such thing as honor among thieves, especially if you're taking from the guys who took from Willie Dixon and Bukka White.

Mike has said that the music for "Given to Fly" came out of a period in his life when he was just emerging from the haze of substance abuse, and you can imagine that the song's surging, anthemic feel resonated with a man who felt grateful just to be alive. But along with being a personal expression, "Given to Fly" was also aspirational in the commercial sense.

The song's quiet verse/loud chorus structure, believe it or not, was unique to Pearl Jam at the time. (The big hits off *Ten* start at eleven and pretty much stay there.) It can't help but draw you in and sweep you up.

"Given to Fly" is *engaging*, in other words, in a way that few previous Pearl Jam songs had ever been. (Not on purpose, anyway.) But was it now too late for a pop-friendly Pearl Jam single?

$$\lightning$$

Here's a thought experiment I've often played with Pearl Jam's late-nineties output: What if *Yield* came out before *No Code*? Imagine if "Given to Fly" entered the rock radio ecosystem two years after *Vitalogy* came and went with six million units shipped. How would *that* have affected Pearl Jam's career? Would they now be better or worse off, career-wise?

Before you answer—or before *I* answer, you can think what you want when you want—let's consider the facts. *No Code* was released on August 27, 1996, exactly five years after *Ten*. The first single was "Who You Are," an Eastern-tinged sorta . . . *ballad*? That doesn't seem like an apt classification, but it's not really a rocker, either. In the lyrics, Vedder gets extremely chin-stroke-y about the meaning of existence, landing on the Zen idea that each person's purpose in the world is to be exactly who they are. (Pete Townshend's various Meher Baba–inspired songs, including "Too Much of Anything" and "Let My Love Open the Door," profess a similar worldview.)

There was nothing remotely like "Who You Are" on rock radio in the early fall of 1996. The biggest mainstream rock hit of the year was Metallica's "Until It Sleeps," from their first post–"Black Album" release, *Load*, a track one could accurately describe as extremely un-Zen. The most distinctive aspect of "Who You Are" is Jack Irons's drum part, a complicated polyrhythm he claimed to have written when he was eight. I assume Lars Ulrich was too busy at that age playing tennis in Denmark to be thinking about his future band's rhythm section.

Part of the narrative of *No Code* is that "Who You Are" tanked the record commercially. The band themselves have forwarded this idea, both with pride and regret. In a 1997 *Spin* cover story, Eddie Vedder insisted it was a "conscious decision" to scale down the size of their enormous audience by putting out a philosophical single with an exotic backbeat. But later on, in the *Pearl Jam Twenty* book, Jeff Ament ruefully argued that there were "four or five songs" on *No Code* that would have served as a more appropriate introduction to the record.

It certainly seems like the latter view influenced the direction of *Yield*, which came out on February 3, 1998, just eighteen months after *No Code*, one of the shortest gaps between Pearl Jam albums. Brendan O'Brien has said that the animating idea of the album was to "put together the best, most accessible songs they possibly could." *Songs* is the operative word here—*No Code* is Pearl Jam at their loosest and most jam-oriented, which resulted in tracks like "Who You Are" where Irons's drum part inspired Stone Gossard to play a noisy guitar riff and Vedder to strum an electric sitar. But on *Yield*, the jamming was set aside in favor of fully realized songs that were already thought out by the time Pearl Jam entered the studio. Whereas *No Code* was described by Gossard as "semi-unprofessional," *Yield* is Pearl Jam's shave and suit up record.

You can imagine a scenario in which Pearl Jam follows up *Vitalogy*—the platonic ideal in terms of balancing the band's "hit" and "weird" sides—with an album that delivers tuneful, mid-tempo pop-rock songs situated squarely in the wheelhouse of radio as it existed in 1996. (Without question "Given to Fly" would have done better that year than "Who You Are.") It seems logical that *Yield* in this slot sells more than *No Code*, which "only" went platinum once. Let's say *Yield* goes double or even triple platinum. That might have provided a softer landing for the experimentation of *No Code* upon its new, hypothetical release date in early 1998. And if *that* happens, perhaps Pearl Jam's career has a completely different trajectory.

All this feels right to me on paper until I remember the rest of the rock world in 1996. That's when this silly thought experiment falls apart.

Pearl Jam wasn't the only superstar rock band experiencing profound changes that year. In 1996, there was a series of would-be blockbusters released by groups who only two or three years prior were at the peak of their careers. Along with *No Code*, there was R.E.M.'s *New Adventures in Hi-Fi*, Soundgarden's *Down on the Upside*, Counting Crows' *Recovering the Satellites*, and Weezer's *Pinkerton*. It speaks to the insane industry standards of the time that all these records were considered disappointments, even though most of them sold at least one million copies. Some of them even produced multiple radio hits.

But none of them did as well as the bands' previous albums from the early nineties. And this failure cemented the perception that the leading lights of the alternative rock revolution were now past their prime. Right when their commercial fortunes slightly lagged, there was a new generation of nü-metal bands and teen-pop singers who were about to put up some of the gaudiest sales figures in the history of the record business.

The contrast with the DIY spirit of the early nineties couldn't be any starker. The late nineties were all about excess and hedonism. Questioning the ethics of rock stardom suddenly seemed lame and tiresome. People were now into things that were stupidly, needlessly big. Popular music was fueled by a kind of celebrity steroids, a metaphorical version of the performance-enhancing drugs that made the homerun race between Mark McGwire and Sammy Sosa—in which both men sailed easily past Roger Maris's thirty-seven-year-old record—a national obsession in the summer of 1998. In music, superstars vacuously pumped themselves up into all sorts of bulky, grotesque shapes. It was decadence for the sake of decadence, and it made the alt-rock bands of the early nineties seem awfully old and stodgy before their time.

The first time I ever felt like an old man was when I was only nineteen, which coincided with the rise of bands like Korn and Limp Bizkit in late 1996 and throughout 1997. Whereas *No Code* barely went platinum upon its release in August 1996, Korn exploded upon American youth culture with their second album, *Life Is Peachy*, which came out two months later on October 15, 1996. The LP eventually went double platinum in the United States and moved more than six million units worldwide.

I despised nü-metal at the time; more than that, I didn't understand how *anyone* could love it. From my vantage point as a music fan weaned on classic and alternative rock, nü-metal seemed to be lacking all the qualities I sought from music. There was no melody, no power chords, no uplifting choruses, no idealism, no humanism, and no connection to the lineage of rock I had been taught to revere.

Over time, I came to appreciate nü-metal precisely for how it bucked those rock conventions. Whatever your opinion of Korn might be, there's no denying that they spearheaded a genuinely original and even innovative form of rock music that could have come to prominence only in the nineties. While it was easy to place Pearl Jam in the mold of a traditional rock band, Korn truly broke that mold, at the exact moment when rock was about to enter a period of commercial decline. And the pessimism of these bands—best typified by the Slipknot song "People = Shit," from their 2001 album *Iowa*—spoke to the times as much as *Vs.* had reflected the cultural mood of the early nineties.

Music really did change *that* quickly. Korn singer Jonathan Davis was never going to strum an acoustic guitar and sing a gentle folk ditty like "Elderly Woman Behind the Counter in a Small Town." Even "Spin the Black Circle" was not hard enough for an audience now primed to receive Davis's screamingly intense teen angst anthems, like the scathing anti-bullying confessional "Faget" from Korn's self-titled 1994 debut. The fact that someone like me in 1996—still a young man, but part of a different generation from the thirteen-year-old A. J. Soprano types gravitating to Korn—didn't get it was not a fault of nü-metal. It was, in fact, the entire point.

⚡

Given all that, the idea that *Yield*—or putting out a more commercial single from *No Code*—would have changed the tide for Pearl Jam is like arguing that picking up litter on the streets of New Orleans would have spared the city from Hurricane Katrina. There were simply larger forces at play that doomed alternative rock in a macro sense, and *No Code* in a micro sense.

Also, I must declare something for the record: I love *No Code*. On most days it's my favorite Pearl Jam LP. It's the sort of album that seems like an "interesting misfire" in the moment and then slowly ages into the "endlessly fresh-sounding" one decades later.[1] I am in the group of Pearl Jam fans—a minority, I'm sure—who wishes that subsequent albums were actually jammier. The path not taken for this band would have been a long, strange trip.

As it is, *No Code* is the most Beatles-esque Pearl Jam album. Sometimes this is literally true, like how the outro to "Red Mosquito" sounds like side two of *Abbey Road* or how "In My Tree" slyly references "Strawberry Fields Forever."[2] But *No Code* ultimately is the record where they retreated from public view just as the Beatles had thirty years earlier, in order to dig deep into big metaphysical questions while stretching out musically like never before.

The idea that *No Code* is some sour or inaccessible indulgence has never rung true for me. For a band that's hardly known for jokes, this is often a darkly funny record. Vedder's most pointed anti-stardom songs, "Off He Goes" and "Lukin," are mostly directed inward, less concerned with hitting out at the music business than figuring out how to cope with the surreal circumstances of his life. The songs in general are more bemused than angry, with sarcasm offering an unlikely refuge. I'm thinking of Vedder's droll aside about "speaking as a child of the nineties" in "Habit," as well as Gossard's takedown of grunge rip-off bands in "Mankind," which coincidentally sounds like Urge Overkill.

As much as I adore *No Code*, I don't think it really has a single that would have "saved" it. "Hail Hail" is the most obvious choice, but I prefer that song in the context of the album rather than as a stand-alone entity. It hits a lot harder coming after "Sometimes," the quietest (and in my mind greatest) Pearl Jam album opener. So much of this record feels like Pearl

---

1 Stone Gossard once likened *No Code* to *Emotional Rescue* by the Rolling Stones, a comparison that made no sense to me until I thought about it constantly for a few days afterward.

2 Like John Lennon, Eddie Vedder didn't want anyone else in his tree.

Jam in "White Album" mode, in which they throw everything against the wall to see what sticks because it's better than simply letting yourself fall apart. But "Sometimes" is Eddie's *Plastic Ono Band* track, the moment of clarity that comes after a zealous period of self-examination. "Seek my part, devote myself / My small self / Like a book amongst the many on a shelf" was his way of saying, "I don't believe in grunge, I just believe in me."

The most famous song from *No Code*, "Present Tense," might very well be the album's emotional center. The music (written by McCready) is like a slow-release capsule version of "Given to Fly," in which the anthemic catharsis doesn't come until the song's final third. But it's Vedder's lyric that registers as a mission statement for the next phase of Pearl Jam's career: "You can spend your time alone redigesting past regrets oh / Or you can come to terms and realize / You're the only one who can forgive yourself."

Millions of people rediscovered this song in 2020 when it was featured at the end of *The Last Dance*, the sprawling ESPN and Netflix documentary about Michael Jordan and the nineties Chicago Bulls. In the context of the multipart film, "Present Tense" was meant to convey MJ's relentlessly forward-facing posture after acting like a vindictive dick during his playing career toward everyone from Isiah Thomas to B. J. Armstrong.

For Pearl Jam, though, "Present Tense" was a statement about not being defined by their past, which was as a very real danger even as far back as 1996. *No Code* was an important step in wriggling free of those restrictions. If Pearl Jam was destined to have their commercial status diminished no matter what they did, then why not do exactly what you want to do?

$$\pmb{\it \star}$$

Imagining *No Code* coming out at a different time is a dead end because it could have come out *only* in 1996, just as those other albums by Pearl Jam's peer group—all of which I love—could have come out only that year. Those records are *about* what was happening in rock at the time. You put them on and you can hear the weariness, disappointment, and exhaustion that had settled in. But no album in that class sounds quite as weary, disappointed, and exhausted as Soundgarden's *Down on the Upside*.

It's possible that I'm projecting these attributes on what became Soundgarden's final LP before their breakup in 1997.[3] But even before they split up, *Down on the Upside* lived up (or down) to its title. Like every other multiplatinum alt-rock band of the era, Soundgarden attempted to reconcile their newfound status as hit makers with their punk-rock past by making a consciously "difficult" follow-up to 1994's massively successful instant classic, *Superunknown*. And in a sense they achieved that goal—*Down on the Upside* is definitely weirder than its predecessor, which definitely did not include songs about an unnamed dog or Ty Cobb. But it also produced some of their most popular songs. One of the album's best tracks, "Burden in My Hand," was no. 1 on the mainstream rock chart the week *No Code* was released.

The problem is that *Down on the Upside* was torture to make, though it wasn't necessarily a different or more arduous form of torture than what Pearl Jam underwent around the same time. Soundgarden's issues were remarkably similar to Pearl Jam's, just as all bands' problems tend to be remarkably similar. There was tension between the singer and the guitar player. There were conflicting feelings about "going commercial" versus "staying underground." Everybody was overworked. Nobody was talking to one another. Substance abuse filled the void.

The difference is that Soundgarden went on tour for several months in support of *Down on the Upside*, and then Chris Cornell decided to break up the band. Frankly, it's what most bands do in that situation. But it's not what Pearl Jam did. Instead, they made *Yield*.

I know *Yield* is supposed to be a "catchy return to form" record, but that's not how I hear it. Maybe I'm the *only* person who hears it this way, but I find it to be a deeply sad and even depressing record. This is not a

---

3 They reunited thirteen years later and released one more studio album, *King Animal*, in 2012.

criticism—if anything, I'm arguing that *Yield* is a deeper and more powerful album than it is given credit for. If it were just the record in which Pearl Jam returned to writing (in O'Brien's words) "the best, most accessible songs they possibly could," I think *Yield* would sound empty now. But I think it's as much a product of its (deeply fucked-up) time as *No Code*.

There are two ways of thinking about 1998. A nostalgist might look at that year and see a golden age, a time of relative peace when the United States hit the lowest level of unemployment in twenty-eight years and the biggest political scandal was Bill Clinton's impeachment over lying about a relatively inconsequential sexual dalliance with a White House intern.

But even the year's silliest stories have a dark, troubling undertow. Clinton was elected at the height of grunge in 1992, after a dozen years of Republican rule. His impeachment would eventually help usher in another Republican presidential administration in the early twenty-first century. The feeling of social and political progress that had once made alternative rock feel like a significant cultural force in the early nineties was now gone. The man that Pearl Jam had once visited in the White House at the height of their popularity was now viewed even by his supporters as a rank opportunist. When the US military launched missiles against terrorist camps in Afghanistan that August just three days after Clinton was impeached, there was widespread suspicion of a cynical "wag the dog" motive. And yet the cynicism of the time was so deep that few could muster up any real outrage.

Beyond the optimistic headlines about economic growth and low unemployment was the consolidation of political and economic power by a small number of elites, which would only grow worse in the twenty-first century. Pearl Jam's valiant but ill-fated battle against Ticketmaster feels like small potatoes when set against the massive corporate merger that produced Citigroup, then the world's largest financial-services conglomerate, which happened two months after *Yield*'s release. A decade later, Citigroup would play a key role in the housing crisis that leveled the American economy, as the scores of subprime loans they issued to millions of homebuyers—many of whom were Gen Xers entering the real estate market for the first time—went belly up.

And then there's the Telecommunications Act of 1996, a massive overhaul of established broadcasters and emerging internet networks signed into law by Bill Clinton that deregulated the industry and set the table for, among other things, the dominance of radio station chains like Clear Channel. Years after Pearl Jam fought against the monopolization of the concert business, the trend of fewer and fewer power players controlling more and more of the music industry would continue to be the norm. Meanwhile, the resolve to fight against this or even question it only weakened. A world with fewer options was simply the new normal.

I'm reminded of the indifferent, blasé mood of 1998 whenever I return to *Yield*. On that album, righteous anger and proactive activism give way to a pained resignation. Pearl Jam was now a long way from the finger-pointing of *Vs.* (Is it possible for an album title to be more diametrically opposed to *Vs.* than *Yield*?) But instead of giving up and packing it in like Soundgarden, they made a record about processing the profound hurt lurking beneath the era's happy-go-lucky facade.[4] *Yield* was their comeback album about defeat. A record of slick songs with poisoned hearts that sonically emulates the delusion of the era.

Even "Given to Fly" is a downer if you bother to parse the lyrics. It's one of the album's two Christ narratives, in which a savior comes to Earth, gets rejected, and then leaves. (The other one is "Pilate," where the man who sentenced Jesus to death tries to make himself feel better by hanging out with his dog.) Not that this is an album of faith; the song "Faithfull" criticizes pious people and questions the validity of their belief system. (The next track, "No Way," explicitly gives up on "trying to make a difference.")

Sometimes *Yield* makes me think about the indifferent, blasé mood of *now*. The conspiracy theorizing of "Brain of J" and the constant striving

---

4 A companion album to *No Code* and *Yield* is Modest Mouse's 1997 masterpiece *The Lonesome Crowded West*, which explicitly addresses the urban sprawl and faceless suburbia that began to take over the Pacific Northwest (and Seattle specifically) in the late nineties.

to be something that you're not of "Wishlist" are like commentaries on internet culture before internet culture became commonplace. And then there's the album's most sardonic (and, for Pearl Jam, uniquely satirical) song, "Do the Evolution," in which the misplaced faith put on technology and human superiority that is still endemic in our culture portends creeping doom.

It's no wonder that the most exhilarating songs on *Yield* are about escape—"MFC," in which Vedder once again sings about getting into a car and driving very fast toward an uncertain destination, and "In Hiding," which reads like a first-person account of his "laundry room and ashtray" period. ("I shut and locked the front door / No way in or out / I turned and walked the hallways / And pulled the curtains down.")

The album ends with "All Those Yesterdays," which in 1998 seemed like it could very well be the final song on the final Pearl Jam album. "Don't you think you ought to rest?" Vedder gently purrs, like he's singing his own band a lullaby. Toward the end, he softly pleads, "It's no crime to escape."

He's right. It's not. Soundgarden escaped. Almost all Pearl Jam's peers escaped. *This* version of Pearl Jam was also finished soon after *Yield* was released, with the departure of their fourth drummer, Jack Irons.

But this band would eventually take a new form—the *definitive* Pearl Jam that would carry them forward, out of the nineties and beyond.

SIDE B

"There's a lot of bands that get to a certain level, and it just stops. They scrap it. Compare this to, say, The Rolling Stones or The Who, where they just continued on forever and are still playing, or they quit after 20 years. But Talking Heads, or Jane's Addiction, or The Police, or even Nirvana you could say, got to a point and then that was just it. I was wondering what the difference was between the early bands and these bands . . ."

—Eddie Vedder to *Spin* in 1994

CHAPTER 11
"LONG ROAD"

(10/21/00, Phoenix, Arizona)

My First Pearl Jam Show (Which Was Not My Last) • A Snotty *Pitchfork* Review • "Workmanlike" As a Compliment and Not a Put-down • Seventy-Two Bootlegs from the Same Tour • "Gutter Punks and Whiskey" • The Meaning of Life (Really!)

I saw Pearl Jam in concert for the first time on June 30, 1998, at the Target Center in Minneapolis. Though at the time it felt more like an ending than a beginning.

I remember the show being pretty great. Actually, I *know* it's pretty great because I have the bootleg. They opened with "Sometimes," which I appreciated, because even then I felt like *No Code* was underrated. They played the B-side "Leatherman," which I did not recognize in the moment, because I hadn't purchased the "Given to Fly" single. They played a really cool version of "Porch" that was prefaced with the bluesy version of the

Who's "My Generation," which I loved, because like Eddie Vedder I am a fan of *The Kids Are Alright*.

On the bootleg, you can hear Eddie address the audience during the encore about how surprised he is that the Minneapolis show ended up being so raucous. He says he expected the concert the night before in Chicago to be the highlight of the run, but he claims that *this* gig gave *that* gig a run for its money. I remember being skeptical about this. I hadn't attended a ton of concerts at that point, but I knew enough to be aware that rock stars are like politicians when they're glad-handing concert audiences. *Of course* he would say that we were a good audience. And taking a dig at Chicago always plays well in Minneapolis.

But now that I've heard recordings of the Chicago and Minneapolis gigs, I have to say that Eddie was being truthful. The Minneapolis show really was that good. The audience—*we*—killed it.

There were eight songs from *Yield* in that night's set list, and I knew those songs because I bought the album the week it came out. But *Yield* would ultimately be, for many years, the last Pearl Jam album I bought immediately upon release. In the four months between the album's release in early '98 and the concert, *Yield* had quietly slipped out of my regular music rotation, which is saying a lot given that I was a cash-strapped college student who didn't buy many CDs. (Remember this was about a year before Napster made buying CDs irrelevant for a generation of music fans.) Even with limited options, I didn't choose *Yield*.

And yet, just as I liked seeing Pearl Jam play live, I also liked *Yield*. But for me and my buddy Erik, who had also grown up on Pearl Jam's records, seeing them on this tour already felt like nostalgia for a couple of ripe old men now in our early twenties. Which is crazy given that it wasn't even seven years since the release of *Ten*. But in 1998 it felt like 1991 was seventy years in the past. I was about to turn fourteen when Pearl Jam's debut dropped; now I was few months shy of my twenty-first birthday. That meant hanging out at bars and being a sort of grown-up. Pearl Jam meanwhile signified my childhood, and like all almost-twenty-one-year-olds, I was eager to get away from my childhood.

Eventually I would come to see the error in this. But in 1998, I really thought Pearl Jam was finished, along with every other remnant of early-nineties alternative rock culture. So, when I saw Pearl Jam for the first time, I truly believed it would also be the last time. I came to the Target Center to say goodbye to a band I thought I no longer loved, and a past I was trying to escape.

I mention all this because I don't think my situation is unique. It seems like so many rock fans of my generation went through the exact same change of heart with Pearl Jam at around the same time. This band was so central to the coming-of-age experiences of millions of people that once those people got older it suddenly became unbearable to listen to Pearl Jam.

This, of course, is unfair to Pearl Jam, whose only crime was making extremely popular rock music that defined the era in which it was made. But a certain stigma fell on them regardless.

What was that stigma, exactly? Here's an excerpt from *Pitchfork's* review of the career retrospective, *Rearviewmirror (Greatest Hits 1991–2003)*, published upon the album's release in 2004:

> After deftly turning their backs on fame just as much of the public seemed poised to turn on them, Pearl Jam cultivated the unwavering support of a cabal of devotees who followed the band across a string of studio albums that casual observers have likely forgotten—*No Code, Yield, Binaural,* and *Riot Act*—and the almost comical release of every live show from their 2000 tour, a move that, depending on your level of cynicism, was either a thank you or an unintentional fuck you to their lemmingesque fanbase. Musically, Pearl Jam slightly spiced up their sound over the course of a decade, adding a few Eastern-tinged delicacies and some garage-rock snackfood to their typical meat-and-potatoes diet. By the time Creed became a permanent fixture on late-90s rock radio, the Florida band sounded as much like Pearl Jam as, well, Pearl Jam themselves.

Is this take reductive and even a little mean-spirited? Certainly. But it also ruthlessly articulates what became the conventional wisdom for many music critics and casual listeners once Pearl Jam's commercial peak passed.

With the benefit of hindsight, detractors felt emboldened to blame Pearl Jam for all the terrible bands—the Creeds, the Nickelbacks, the Dayses of the New—that ripped them off. Their biggest songs were derided for being self-serious, histrionic, and earnest. Eddie Vedder was accused of being an unbearable, bombastic growler. They were mocked for their political activism. Above everything else, Pearl Jam was viewed as a nineties relic, like an old flannel shirt or a VHS tape loaded with episodes of *My So-Called Life*. They were a little . . . *embarrassing*.

This is bigger than Pearl Jam, however. The hostility with which the press and even many former fans treated this band feels inherent to the specific neuroses of Generation X. You don't typically hear baby boomers rushing to slam Bruce Springsteen, the Rolling Stones, or Bob Dylan, and they certainly wouldn't describe loyal fans of those acts as "lemmingesque." Even boomer acts who weren't critically well regarded in their time, like Queen or Kiss, tend to benefit from generous revisionism later.

Millennials and Zoomers are similarly loyal to their childhood favorites—whether it's Taylor Swift or Blink-182 or Limp Bizkit—even after they've stopped producing hit albums or even good music. Meanwhile they're quick to judge the favorites of previous generations against modern standards of political correctness, which inevitably makes *their* favorites look more virtuous in comparison.

But Gen Xers aren't nearly as protective of their turf. We were lightning quick to turn on Pearl Jam once we got a little older and started digging into our parents' record collections. This is anecdotal evidence, but again I suspect it is more common than just my experience: I know multiple friends who were introduced as teenagers to Neil Young by Pearl Jam, and these days they still listen to Neil Young but *not* Pearl Jam. Or maybe they're trying to talk themselves into liking the latest phenom that their children or younger coworkers are raving about. Anything but *their* music, which they swore they would leave behind after high school.

Now, there are other Gen Xers who *only* listen to music they liked in high school, which isn't great either. (This is the problem with speaking in generational generalities—it's easy to find exceptions to the rule.) And, personally speaking, I also love digging into music from different eras and cultures. Discovering new things should be a part of the evolutionary process of getting older. But I think it's generally true that my generation doesn't wave the flag for our homegrown heroes as much as other generations.

This is partly due to demographics—there are twelve million more boomers and eighteen million more millennials than Gen Xers. Because there are fewer of us, our generational markers are more susceptible to being marginalized by outsiders without any firsthand knowledge or intuitive understanding of why these things mattered so much once upon a time.

Few Gen X concepts have aged less gracefully than "selling out," a prospect that once haunted Eddie Vedder and now has virtually no relevance for musical artists in the modern world. It's now commonly understood that selling a song for an ad might be the only way for an artist to ever make any real money. And giving that artist a hard time for cashing in with a fast-food commercial is frowned upon as annoying scold behavior. So viewing a relatively pious band like Pearl Jam retrospectively via that lens will inevitably make them appear whiny or strident.

But in the nineties, an aversion to selling out meant that you wanted to stand apart from a mainstream culture that was frequently corrupt, stupid, and poisonous. It signaled a desire to exist in a space that cared about art, smart conversations, and empathy. It wasn't a joyless moral stand. It was an idealistic gesture made by those who otherwise struggled to find like-minded people in a stultifying world of network TV and corporate Top 40 radio stations. It was less about not selling out than not *buying in*.

That context is all but gone now because the gatekeepers who shepherd our cultural narratives never had any real affinity for the artists who moved so many of us in the nineties. Instead, bands like Pearl Jam have been reduced to passé generational caricatures.

A Pew Research poll once found that Gen Xers are less likely than boomers or millennials to define their age group as "special," which seems like a direct result of those imbalanced population numbers and the skewed historical discourse. Even though having fewer people should make your generation *more* special, you are less apt to hear your generation *described* as special in the media. To quote those famous Gen Xers in Radiohead, we're stuck *wishing* we were special.

But you don't need a poll to tell you that Gen Xers have a self-defeating tendency to view themselves as failures or retreads or nonentities in the larger view of history. This idea was drilled into us in the nineties by boomers who refused to abandon the levers of cultural power and instead crammed the sixties down our throats throughout our childhoods. (Never forget that there was only one Woodstock festival in the sixties, and two Woodstock festivals in the nineties.) And it was reiterated by younger generations who had none of our qualms about nostalgia because they never worshipped "kill your idols"–preaching punks and indie demigods. The kids simply didn't have that guilt-ridden and self-negating baggage, and because they also outnumbered us *and* the boomers, they could blot out preexisting cultural footprints and install their own figureheads. They succeeded where Generation X failed because failing is what we do best.

And many of us helped them do it! I went through my own period of forsaking my alt-rock heritage. For years, I felt little connection to the grunge rock that I grew up on. I sold off my old CDs and ditched my concert T-shirts. I pretended that the only nineties rock I ever cared about was made by unimpeachable indie-rockers like Pavement, Liz Phair, Sleater-Kinney, and Neutral Milk Hotel. And I tried to forget about the music that, in reality, I thought would change the world.

Where did this leave Pearl Jam, the rare nineties band to actually survive the decade and soldier on in the twenty-first century? At times, they seemed like a band without a country. Generation X had largely abandoned them, and the next group of young people were about to embrace a new wave of music stars.

The pathology of my generation is that we hate ourselves and anything we see ourselves in. And few things about the nineties seem more universally *us* than Pearl Jam.

$$\lightning$$

I want to go back to that *Pitchfork* excerpt, specifically this section: "the almost comical release of every live show from their 2000 tour, a move that, depending on your level of cynicism, was either a thank you or an unintentional fuck you to their lemmingesque fanbase."

This, again, sums up how many in the media viewed Pearl Jam's decision to self-bootleg seventy-two concerts from the tour in support of their sixth album, *Binaural*. It was depicted, with weird hostility, as both a foolish lark and a sneaky rip-off. In a 2000 interview with the *San Francisco Chronicle*, Jeff Ament was charged, with unapologetic rudeness, on both counts. "Do you think someone who listens to all these has to be kind of crazy?" went one question. "Just how many versions of 'Even Flow' does the average person need?" was the follow-up. Then came the kill shot: "A lot of people think you're just ripping off the kids," which isn't really a question, just a cheap dig.

Is it strange, craven, or exploitive to release seventy-two live albums from the same tour?[1] If this were still 1991, the answer would be "yes." But even in the year 2000, perspectives on this issue were already changing. It's disingenuous to ask whether the "average" person would want access to several dozen versions of the same song. In the new century, the media was hardly set up to accommodate only "average" listeners. If anything, technology has transformed even casual music listeners into obsessive consumers, constantly piping songs into every corner of our lives because it's so easy now to do just that.

What Pearl Jam did in 2000 is now commonplace online—if you follow a band with a rabid fan base, there's a very good chance that you can access

---

1 The one show from the *Binaural* tour that wasn't released was Roskilde, Denmark, for obvious reasons.

multiple live shows (if not *every single show they ever performed*) in exchange for a subscription fee. The only difference is that Pearl Jam was forced by existing technology to put that music on CDs rather than make it available on a streaming platform like Nugs.net (as Pearl Jam and many other bands presently do). Nevertheless, the *Binaural* tour bootlegs might still seem like an extreme indulgence rather than a prescient stroke of genius. Outside of fan blogs posted on obscure corners of the internet, they've never really been considered as a complete body of work . . . until now.

Here is my most contrarian Pearl Jam opinion (which might not seem contrarian depending on how obsessed with the band you happen to be): those seventy-two bootlegs from the year 2000, when you group them together, represent my very favorite Pearl Jam music. I like those recordings more than any studio album, and I feel they signify what's best about this band more than any of the hits they're known for. My case for Pearl Jam being one of the great American bands starts with those six dozen records.

If you like (but don't love) Pearl Jam, this probably sounds insane. (I won't even contemplate how PJ agnostics will react.) But I doubt I would have eventually returned to the fold as a Pearl Jam obsessive if the band hadn't decided to put out sparkling soundboard recordings of nearly everything they played live in that particular year. Hearing those records absolutely rewired my brain in terms of how I heard Pearl Jam and recalibrated what I appreciated about them. I would argue that the version of Pearl Jam you hear on those albums isn't even the same band from the nineties. They effectively remade themselves on that tour and became the band they have been ever since.

The journey that started that night at Red Rocks—when they flailed in public for an identity beyond the omnipresent angsty hard rock band on MTV—culminates here.

$$\lightning$$

Now, Pearl Jam was already a new band when I saw them in 1998. Matt Cameron entered Pearl Jam on the eve of the American leg of the *Yield* tour after Jack Irons flamed out from the pressure of playing in one of rock's most stressed-out bands. What was initially a quick fix that Cameron assumed was temporary—he was still holding out hope that Soundgarden would reunite—became a permanent solution to the turmoil of Pearl Jam's early years.

Cameron is by far the most tenured drummer in Pearl Jam history, even though I still think of him as the guy from Soundgarden. But there's no question at this point that the preternaturally level-headed Cameron belonged in Pearl Jam all along. There's a reason Pearl Jam manager Kelly Curtis called the *Yield* tour "the first non-drama tour in our life." The new drummer's consistency and calm instantly settled the band down. Cameron likewise appreciated what he called Pearl Jam's "workmanlike professionalism," which contrasted with the more volatile nature of his old band.

Cameron meant "workmanlike" as a compliment. But "workmanlike" has also been applied to Pearl Jam as a putdown. In their post-nineties career, they have been described (to quote *Pitchfork*'s unkind 4.6-scored review of 2009's *Backspacer*) as "the very definition of anonymously workmanlike, seemingly plugging along with their heads down from one colorlessly unimaginative album to the next." In this context, "workmanlike" is the antithesis of sexy, seductive, and thrilling rock music. It's a comparatively yeoman-like and rather dull alternative to everything this music is *supposed* to be.

But for Cameron—and I suspect the other members of Pearl Jam—making hard work their brand was a means of regaining control of their lives and careers. How easy it was to forget that when Pearl Jam was on top of the rock world, it was relatively difficult to see them live. Instead, their image was shaped by MTV, rock radio, and music magazines—all institutions that had their own agendas. For a person as wary of authority as Eddie Vedder, this simply wouldn't do. You can't trust any of those people. But you can put your faith in your own willingness to play for more than two hours with a different set list each night.

I started buying the *Binaural* tour boots in the early 2010s as my interest in Pearl Jam was revived. You could find them in used CD stores for a few bucks, so it was a cheap fix. What I heard on those discs intrigued me. The music didn't have the same "fighting with Mike Tyson" physicality of nineties Pearl Jam. Eddie Vedder wasn't swinging from the rafters and hurling himself into the audience; he was now chained to his guitar. Stone Gossard and Mike McCready weren't pogoing from one side of the stage to the other; they were interweaving riffs like wily veterans. With Cameron now firmly installed in the rhythm section, they didn't exhibit the reckless bombast of the Dave Abbruzzese era or the feral tribalism of the Jack Irons years. As he fused with Jeff Ament's limber bass, Cameron played drums like an assassin, hitting grace notes with cool, lethal precision.

Slowly, I collected more boots. This incarnation of the band had a large enough repertoire—covering six albums plus numerous left-field covers—to make surveying multiple shows interesting. And their nuanced playing sounded better and better the more time I put into listening. Pearl Jam's well-honed skill set came into sharper focus with each new show I absorbed, and I noticed that elements that seemed like minor indulgences at first were in fact critically important. One of my favorite tracks from *Binaural*, "Insignificance," seemed to be played with slightly greater intensity with each show. The jam in the middle of "Rearviewmirror" gradually got longer and spacier. McCready's guitar solos in "Even Flow" were wild in small but perceptively different ways each time.

Over time, I became obsessed with tracking how Pearl Jam changed and grew on this tour. It made them feel like an actual living and breathing entity in a way their overly familiar albums never could. That's how this specific kind of deep listening works. You feel like you're living with a band, as if you are following them on tour. It feels powerful and above all *intimate*.

Pearl Jam was never intimate in the nineties. Their ubiquity—whether it was Pearl Jam or the Pearl Jam copy-cats—eventually drove many casual listeners away. But digging into the bootlegs scaled them down in my mind and once again humanized Pearl Jam. They were no longer the grunge-rock troubadours who defined a specific moment in time. They now just seemed like an excellent working rock band that was capable of fresh reinventions, both big and small, at every gig.

I was used to doing this kind of listening with jam bands like the Grateful Dead and Phish, though my friends from that scene didn't understand how it worked with Pearl Jam, who improvise a little but not as much as those bands. Superficially, every version of "Rearviewmirror" sounds the same . . . unless you listen to *a lot* of them. When you play a Pearl Jam bootleg, you're hearing the atmosphere as much as the music. What goes on around the songs sometimes matters more. As I dug into the *Binaural* tour, certain moments stood out. Some of them were consistent through the tour, like how Eddie always pointed out how much he liked "Thin Air" and the fact that Stone Gossard wrote it whenever he introduced it. Or how he always mentioned before playing my favorite left-field cover of the tour, "Timeless Melody" by the La's,[2] that Matt Cameron introduced the song to him early in the tour before a show in Spain.

Other moments were specific to certain shows, like the fan who handed Eddie a harmonica in Paris. Or the shaky duet Eddie sang with a fan on the song "Smile" in Antioch, Tennessee. Or the part where Matt's drums broke down before "Last Kiss" in Barcelona. Or the barely attended show in Katowice, Poland, that sounds like it was played in some random Pole's backyard. Or the ice-cold gig the band powered through at Alpine Valley Music Theatre in Wisconsin.

With deep listening, everything becomes freighted with significance. A bit of stage patter or a seemingly miniscule change in a guitar solo feels special, like it's yours, a precious secret that only you and your fellow nerds are in on.

It's hard to pick a favorite from this year, but the show I most often go back to is 10/21/00 from Phoenix. For hard-core fans, it might seem

2 Pearl Jam debuted "Timeless Melody" at a concert in Manchester, England. The La's are most remembered for the lovely "There She Goes," later covered by Sixpence None the Richer. In introducing the song, Vedder dissed two very famous people from Manchester, Liam and Noel Gallagher of Oasis, who have counted the La's singer/songwriter Lee Mavers as one of their biggest influences.

like an undistinguished pick—it doesn't have the reputation of the second Katowice show or the third gig at Jones Beach in New York. But I think that's what I like about it. 10/21/00 feels like *my* show from the *Binaural* tour. (I suppose anyone who actually attended this concert can also claim it.)

I'm not sure I can adequately explain why I love this show so much, especially to the sort of person who would never consider listening to dozens of shows from the same tour. The distinctions will seem minor to the untrained ear. Nevertheless, I maintain that the version of "Insignificance" from this show is the most explosive from the whole tour. This show also has my favorite performance of "Timeless Melody," which seems even more surprising coming from Pearl Jam when played in the American southwest. And I love how Eddie introduces "Even Flow" with one of his best fake titles, "Gutter Punks and Whiskey."[3]

If the average Pearl Jam fan knows this show at all, it's from the excellent *Touring Band 2000* DVD, which opens with the performance of "Long Road" from this gig. If the band ever played this song more beautifully, I haven't heard it yet. As it is, I've played this version of "Long Road" so many times that I'd probably be hopelessly biased in its favor no matter the circumstance.

Unlike the shaky renditions they played back in 1995 when the song was still brand-new, this "Long Road" is thick with three churning guitars, which are mixed as loud as Vedder's vocal. Eddie in turn isn't trying to bellow over the band; he delivers it tenderly, almost like he's still backstage and sharing it as a heartfelt confession over a preshow cigarette. Only he's comfortable enough to be that real and vulnerable in front of fifteen thousand people.

"Long Road" has become one of the great Pearl Jam set openers because the song functions as a pledge from the band to its audience. "Will I walk

---

3 An ongoing Eddie bit from this tour was making up fake titles for "Even Flow," including "I Save Cigarette Butts for a Poor Girl" (5/25/00), "Don't Let the Sun Go Down on Your Grievance" (5/29/00), "Paralyzed Big Baby" (8/9/00), and "Buried Alive" (10/14/00).

the long road? Cannot stay / There's no need to say goodbye." In other words: What you are about to see is fleeting, as is everything good in life. Let's savor the moment while we can, and hope that there will be more good times tomorrow.

For a "workmanlike" band, this approximates a resolution to the great cosmic question: What are we here for? For Pearl Jam, the answer is this: We are here to live, and to appreciate living, and to help others appreciate their own lives. You do your job, you do it well, and then you do it again the next night.

CHAPTER 12
"CROWN OF THORNS"

(10/22/00, Las Vegas)

Roskilde • The Who's 1979 Tour • Andrew Wood • Why Staying Together Is Sometimes Better Than Stopping

My love of Pearl Jam's 2000 tour comes with a big, tragic asterisk: Roskilde.

For many people, one of the worst tragedies in rock history would automatically disqualify this tour from being a highlight of Pearl Jam's career. If you want to make the case that the band was in the midst of a rebirth, you also must reckon with the event that nearly ended them. These are not mutually exclusive ideas; they are intertwined and profoundly complicate each other.

Even after all these years, it's difficult to know what exactly to take from Roskilde. For Pearl Jam, the disaster that claimed the lives of nine people—all men between the ages of seventeen and twenty-six, who hailed from Germany, Holland, Sweden, Denmark, and Australia—had a silver lining of sorts, in that it ultimately caused the band members to reaffirm their commitment to one another and their fan base. After so many years in the nineties when Pearl Jam teetered on the brink of extinction, here was an actual life-or-death disaster that made the concerns about grunge commodification and MTV overexposure seem trivial. It fortified them for the long haul. In that way, you might even kid yourself into believing that some good came out of Roskilde.

As a rationalization for a senseless tragedy, this isn't all that satisfying, however. I suspect the band members themselves would admit this. The troubling truth about Roskilde is that the more you learn about it, the less understandable it becomes. Unlike the tragedy that occurred in 1979 at Cincinnati's Riverfront Coliseum before a Who concert—in which eleven people, mostly teenagers, were crushed to death as a large crowd bum-rushed the front doors—Roskilde offered no easy lessons or actionable solutions. In Cincinnati, the issue was festival seating, a general admission ticketing cash grab in which attendees jostled for the best spots on the arena floor in a "first come, first served" scenario. Festival seating was clearly a corrupt and unsafe business practice. Within three weeks of the Riverfront Coliseum disaster, the local government banned it at future concerts.

At Roskilde, though, there wasn't an obvious cause-and-effect course of action that could be taken to make people feel as though the deaths were rectified by a preventative response. In Cincinnati, there had been calls to reconsider festival seating as early as 1976; it had been an accident waiting to happen. Roskilde meanwhile had an excellent reputation as a safe and well-run music festival. Established in 1971 in a medium-sized city of the same name located about twenty miles west of Copenhagen in Denmark, Roskilde has been run as a nonprofit organization for most of its existence, with an emphasis on the same hippie idealism of the original founders. It's a place where most vendors sell organic food and measures are taken to encourage recycling and public transportation to and from the festival. It is, by most metrics, the antithesis of the crass, soulless, corporate-oriented scam peddling that defines most large-scale music festivals.

The year Pearl Jam played, attendance was voluntarily lowered from ninety thousand to seventy thousand to reduce the potential for over-crowding. In the field adjacent to the stage where Pearl Jam played, orga-nizers had installed metal barriers designed to prevent violent crowd surges. While they didn't often play festivals at this stage in their career—even if their albums were no longer selling in multiplatinum numbers, they remained an extremely popular concert draw—there was no reason to anticipate problems at Roskilde.

And yet a confluence of unlucky factors conspired against them on the night of June 30, 2000. Before Pearl Jam entered the stage at 10:30 p.m., torrents of rain made the grounds slick and unsteady. While there were fewer people overall at the festival, around fifty thousand bodies squeezed in to see Pearl Jam—about three-fourths of all the attendees on the grounds. And the sound was especially piss-poor for the audience farthest from the stage, which naturally caused many people to push forward for a better vantage point.

According to eyewitness accounts compiled in a harrowing *Rolling Stone* article, it seemed to many like a normal festival gig as Pearl Jam opened with a series of high-energy numbers: "Corduroy" into "Breaker-fall," then "Hail Hail" and "Animal." But the situation for audience mem-bers close to the stage was increasingly claustrophobic even before Pearl Jam went on. After about a half hour, some fans sensed that they had to push their way out of the crowd, for self-preservation.

People from the back kept pushing forward, sometimes putting their hands on the shoulders of strangers standing in their way to climb over. Gradually, Pearl Jam fans began literally walking over the bodies of other Pearl Jam fans. One eighteen-year-old concert attendee recalled to the Danish newspaper *Politiken* about seeing her friends close to the stage standing atop some crushed human beings because "they thought it was bags." But even when they realized their mistake they couldn't step off because they were too tightly packed in.

Another concertgoer identified only as "Charlotte" told *Politiken* a chilling story about seeing a man on the ground with five people standing on top of him. She implored the people to move but they couldn't. "I can't remember his face or anything, but I can remember that he was looking at me," she told the newspaper. "Then it was over. I think he died."

Security first attempted to alert the band to the growing chaos about forty-five minutes into the set. But it was another fifteen minutes before word was passed along to Vedder, who stopped the music after Pearl Jam wrapped the twelfth song of the night, "Daughter."

"What will happen in the next five minutes has nothing to do with music," he said to the audience. "But it is important. Imagine that I am your friend and that you must step back so as not to hurt me. You all have friends up front. I will now count to three, and you will all take three steps back. All who agree say 'Yes' now." Once they did as he asked, Vedder asked them to step back again.

As the mass of humanity receded, it revealed the worst possible nightmare for any band. But for Pearl Jam, it was especially painful. On this tour, they had successfully remade themselves, completing a process that began in the mid-nineties. They had willingly backed away from mainstream rock stardom, opting instead to cultivate a following of like-minded, passionate listeners who cared as much about Pearl Jam's music as anyone in the band. The individuals who had waited for hours to see Pearl Jam on this day had traveled hundreds, if not thousands, of miles to see this concert. They were willing to put themselves through the physical and mental discomfort of standing in a painfully crowded audience for the promise of transcendence at a rock show. They were true believers, the sort of fans that any band would be honored to play for. And now nine of them were dead.

Pearl Jam's statement—released a few hours later, shortly after 1 a.m., and apparently written by Vedder as the band sat in a daze in a Copenhagen hotel—was appropriately raw and wrenching:

> *"This is so painful . . . I think we are waiting for someone to wake us and say it was just a horrible nightmare . . . And there are absolutely no words to express our anguish in regard to the parents and loved ones of these precious lives that*

were lost. We have not yet been told what actually occurred, but it seemed random and sickeningly quick . . . it doesn't make sense. When you agree to play a festival of this size and reputation, it is impossible to imagine such a heart-wrenching scenario. Our lives will never be the same, but we know that is nothing compared to the grief of the families and friends of those involved. It is so tragic . . . there are no words.

It's ironic—if *ironic* is the right word—that Pearl Jam and the Who would be brought together in this very specific and uniquely awful way,[1] though the Who's disaster was arguably worse, at least in terms of media scrutiny. Pearl Jam was off in Europe and a few years past the peak of their fame; the Who was stranded in the heart of America and touring in the wake of one of their best-selling albums, *Who Are You.*

Cincinnati also occurred just one year after the death of Keith Moon, which did not prevent the Who from moving forward with a new drummer, Kenney Jones. The Who similarly trudged forward after the deaths at Riverfront Coliseum—incredibly, they played the very next night in Buffalo, where Roger Daltrey publicly dedicated the performance to the fallen in Cincinnati. And then they played nine more shows in fourteen days, before retreating back to England one week before Christmas.

In his critical biography of the Who, *Before I Get Old*, rock writer Dave Marsh takes the band to task for going along with the "greedy scheme" of festival seating, a stance that's easier to understand given their apparent coldness in response to the events in Cincinnati. It's not that the deaths didn't affect the band; decades later, Daltrey and Townshend still appeared haunted by that night when asked to recount the events. Townshend was particularly disturbed that the Who played while bodies were being carted away from the arena as the band's management had opted to not stop the show and inform the musicians about what had happened.

---

1 In 2021, a crowd surge at Houston's Astroworld music festival killed eight people and injured dozens more. That this occurred twenty-one years after Roskilde—which occurred twenty-one years after the Who's tragedy in Cincinnati—is a deeply strange and disturbing coincidence.

After Roskilde, Townshend swiftly stepped in to once again counsel Vedder. His message was simple: *Don't leave*. It was his eternal regret that the Who hadn't stayed in Cincinnati to mourn with the local community. Vedder of course was inclined to listen to his hero and then diverge from him, facing the horror of Roskilde head-on rather than running away from it.

Does Pearl Jam deserve any of the blame for what happened? Anyone who has listened to Pearl Jam bootlegs from the nineties will note the numerous instances of Eddie Vedder stopping the show to implore the audience to step back or tell the security guards to lay off the kids in the front row. They were not indifferent to the safety of fans.

After Roskilde, Vedder expressed regret about playing a rock festival and promised to not do it again. Pearl Jam eventually went back on that promise, but they redoubled their efforts on evaluating the safety procedures at any festival they played. They investigated the preparedness of on-site EMTs, the policies for selling alcohol, the types of barricades, and the communication channels in place between security and the band so that shows could be stopped promptly should an emergency arise. It was Pearl Jam's version of banning festival seating; these actions could make them feel they had done *something* to make the loss of life feel a little less meaningless.

But even if Pearl Jam had no legal or moral fault for Roskilde, the fact remained that nine people went to their show and didn't survive. Reckoning with this meant more than drawing up a better plan for playing festivals. It required asking some uncomfortable, existential questions:

Why are we still doing this?

And is it still worth it?

✦

Four months after Roskilde, Pearl Jam celebrated the tenth anniversary of their first show with a gig in Las Vegas. From the stage, Vedder thanked some of their most important benefactors, including producer Brendan O'Brien, who was on hand to play keyboards, as well as manager Kelly Curtis and label loyalists like Michael Goldstone and Michelle Anthony. He then paid tribute to each of his bandmates, culminating with Pearl Jam's original power couple, Stone Gossard and Jeff Ament.

Then Vedder introduced a song that Pearl Jam had never played live: Mother Love Bone's "Crown of Thorns."

In *Pearl Jam Twenty*, Ament directly links Roskilde to the death of Mother Love Bone's singer Andrew Wood. In both instances, he felt for a time that he might not play music again. In both instances, he eventually decided to carry on in rock 'n' roll. But how? Understanding how Pearl Jam coped with Andrew Wood's death is helpful in comprehending how they weathered Roskilde.

Wood has a curious place in Pearl Jam history—he is a footnote but also kind of a midwife, seemingly inessential and yet, in reality, inarguably crucial. Simply put, if he hadn't died of a drug overdose on March 19, 1990, at the age of twenty-four, Pearl Jam wouldn't exist. His death was a cruel, yet fortuitous, twist of fate for everybody involved in the band. Even as they faced tragedies in the years ahead, Pearl Jam would always be forged in this *original* tragedy.

As a front man, Wood was the antithesis of Eddie Vedder. A natural-born showman who worshipped Elton John, Freddie Mercury, and Kiss. In the few interviews with Wood that exist on grainy video, he openly craves the stardom that Vedder would come to shun. While Vedder used his brown hair and surly facial expressions to obscure his handsome features, Wood was a self-aware ditzy blond who donned makeup, glitter, and copious silk scarves in order to demand your attention.

In the 2005 documentary *Malfunkshun: The Andrew Wood Story*,[2] Wood is depicted as a larger-than-life character oozing with charisma and ambition. His most eloquent admirer is former roommate Chris

---

2 Malfunkshun was Andrew Wood's pre–Mother Love Bone band, formed with his brother Kevin Wood.

Cornell, who describes Wood as a prolific songwriter who was devoid of self-consciousness when it came to pursuing his grandiose and borderline ridiculous arena-rock muse. "He was the only rock star I ever met," Cornell insists.

The flip side of Wood's story is that he came from a highly dysfunctional family, and he dealt with the pain of that by taking heroin. He was also stuck in a band that wasn't aligned with his musical vision. In *Malfunkshun*, Gossard describes Mother Love Bone as "a difficult band for him to be in" because it was "filled with people trying to carve a niche out for themselves. There was a lot of competition, a lot of tension."

Frankly, it doesn't sound all that different from the early days of Pearl Jam. Only Vedder was the opposite of a junkie—his focus, resolve, and creative energy made him the confident band leader that Wood wasn't equipped to be, at least not in his early twenties. But Gossard and Ament were also probably more compatible with someone like Vedder, who favored a jeans-and-flannel approach to rock that's a stark contrast from Wood's overt glammy grandstanding.

Before Mother Love Bone, Gossard and Ament played together in Green River, the seminal eighties proto-grunge band that also featured eventual Mother Love Bone guitarist Bruce Fairweather and two future members of Mudhoney, Mark Arm and Steve Turner. Green River nodded to glam rock by covering David Bowie's "Queen Bitch," but they were essentially a fire-spitting garage band more suited to the back alley behind Madison Square Garden than the big stage inside the arena. The famous story explaining Green River's dissolution concerns the band opening for Jane's Addiction in Los Angeles near the end of their run. Ament and Gossard were blown away as they watched the bombastic neo-psychedelic rockers from the side of the stage; this was exactly the sort of "punk rock arena rock" to which they aspired. Arm meanwhile thought Jane's Addiction was a joke. At that moment, Ament knew that his musical future lay elsewhere.

In Wood, Ament and Gossard found a singer who was closer to the larger-than-life rock-god posturing of Jane's Addiction singer Perry

Farrell. As the front man of his previous band, Malfunkshun, Wood had affected the same poses with a knowing wink, simultaneously celebrating and mocking rock clichés. But with Mother Love Bone, he jettisoned the ironic distance and embodied those clichés with maximum earnestness.

On paper, this isn't radically different from what Eddie Vedder did with the same bassist and guitar player. But in practice, Mother Love Bone was a promising band with great individual parts that never totally gelled. When Eddie showed up in Seattle, his instant chemistry with the band precipitated their rapid creative and commercial rise. From the beginning, Pearl Jam was easy in a way that Mother Love Bone never was. As Soundgarden's Kim Thayil later said of Gossard and Ament's former band, "It seemed forced—like they were trying too hard."

Listening to Mother Love Bone's sole full-length LP *Apple*—released four months after Wood's death—you can hear traces of the iconic riffs that Gossard wrote for *Ten* in songs like the album opening "This Is Shangrila" and the nonsensical but nevertheless anthemic "Stardog Champion." But whereas Vedder's voice and lyrics give Pearl Jam a fresh "nineties" sensibility, Mother Love Bone with Wood at the helm resembles a thinking-man's hair metal band like Enuff Z'Nuff, or perhaps a more subversive Cinderella.

Wood's lyrics are directly lifted from the stoner "life on the road" fantasies endemic to Kiss's classic seventies albums. "Said, I've been around the world / Wrote a million songs, it's all a bore to me," he pouts in "This Is Shangrila," right before doing a delightfully snotty, mock-English pronunciation of *sleeping in the gut-ter.*

If Jane's Addiction was a model for Mother Love Bone, then *Apple* can be heard as a rather shallow emulation of that band's 1988 breakthrough *Nothing's Shocking.* It apes that record's thematic decadence and punk-metal hybrids, but it's never as exciting or substantive. Whereas Pearl Jam doesn't sound all that much like Jane's Addiction, but they were able to take the "punk rock arena rock" aesthetic of *Nothing's Shocking* and Jane's Addiction's masterpiece, 1990's *Ritual de lo Habitual,* much further.[3] Mother Love Bone captured Jane's Addiction façade, but Pearl Jam located their soul.

Let's say Wood hadn't died, and Mother Love Bone toured in support of *Apple* and proceeded to enter the studio in 1991 to record a follow-up. In this hypothetical, Pearl Jam does not make *Ten* because there is no such thing as Pearl Jam. But Nirvana still puts out *Nevermind*, Soundgarden still releases *Badmotorfinger*, the Red Hot Chili Peppers stay the course with *Blood Sugar Sex Magik*, and the nineties alt-rock revolution more or less moves forward as normal.

Did Mother Love Bone have the personality to keep pace with that revolution? Cornell once smartly remarked that MLB was like a bridge from the commercial hard rock of the eighties to *Nevermind*, and once Wood died that bridge disappeared. (Jane's Addiction was another bridge between those worlds that also fell apart around the same time.) But if he had lived, would Wood have evolved into an alt-rocker, or would he have looked and sounded like a remnant of an instantly bygone era?

It feels unfair to judge Wood's talents as a singer and songwriter since he was so young and unformed when he died. Assuming he would have conquered his addictions in this hypothetical, he surely would have improved his craft on subsequent records. But it's hard to imagine him writing angry grunge songs. It just doesn't seem like his personality to write a tune like "Alive" or "Black," even if Gossard had converted them to Mother Love Bone. Based on his small body of work, he seemed to be working toward writing an unapologetically grandiose masterwork like "November Rain."

The best song on *Apple* is "Crown of Thorns," an epic in a "November Rain" vein, especially when the piano-driven "Chloe Dancer" preamble from 1989's *Shine* EP is restored. (This is the version that millions first

---

3 Jane's Addiction broke up in 1991 at the end of a grueling thirteen-month tour in support of *Ritual de lo Habitual* marked by in-fighting and drug abuse. Pearl Jam was just about to get going at the time. They were able, in a sense, to take over the cultural momentum that Jane's Addiction had squandered.

heard on the *Singles* soundtrack.) It's telling that when Pearl Jam performed "Crown of Thorns" for the first time in Las Vegas—and most times afterward—they excised the "Chloe Dancer" section. It is out of Vedder's vocal range but also outside the band's acceptable bounds of grandiosity. It was Gossard and Ament finally reining in their prodigal former singer twenty years after the fact.

Ultimately "Crown of Thorns" is a fitting epitaph for Wood on aesthetic and thematic grounds—it's the greatest song he ever wrote, and also the most prescient. It's about becoming a martyr, starting with the crucifixion imagery of the title. In the lyric, Wood relates the story of Mr. Faded Glory, a man who "must someday fall." He speaks about how "death will rest your soul away." The chorus frames "my kind of love" as "the kind that moves on." Only by departing can he achieve his destiny.

On one hand, this is a frankly disturbing sentiment voiced by a man plagued by demons he could not shake. On the other hand, songs about martyrs are never really about the person who is martyred. They're about the people who are left behind and need something to believe in. It's these people who project meaning and even hope onto the lives of the departed. They do this because they are alive, and when you're alive you sometimes need to be convinced that life is worth it by thinking about death.

If Andrew Wood hadn't died, Pearl Jam wouldn't exist. But if Pearl Jam didn't exist, far fewer people would have heard of Andrew Wood or come to love "Crown of Thorns." Wood couldn't be more different than Vedder as an artist, but it's Vedder's voice that put Wood in the very arenas and stadiums he longed to perform in. This did not save his life, but it made his legacy more meaningful.

Pearl Jam's burden as a band of survivors is that they have had to reckon with tragedies throughout their existence. It's to their credit that they have never tried to bury their dead; rather, the dead walk with them as they have moved forward. Performing "Crown of Thorns" carries Andrew Wood forward. And they would carry the victims of Roskilde forward as well, like at a concert ten years later in Berlin, when Eddie stopped a show to tearfully ask for a moment of silence in remembrance of the worst day of the band's life.

"It's not like we're thinking about it any *more* today," Eddie told the audience a decade to the day after Roskilde, "because it's really something we've thought about *every* day."

Yes, people will die. And many of them will be far too young, whether it's Andrew Wood or the fallen at Roskilde. And the weight of this carnage will at times be more than you can bear. You might even feel like stopping. There is nothing wrong with stopping. We all must take care of ourselves.

But if you don't stop, the ones you've lost won't disappear. They will be conjured each night onstage in your songs and memories. They will walk with you again, as long you can manage to take the first step.

CHAPTER 13
"BU$HLEAGUER"

(4/30/03, Uniondale, New York)

Booing Fans • Darryl Worley's "Have You Forgotten?" • Tony Orlando and Dawn • Kenny G's Sax Solo on "Voices That Care" • *Binaural* • Tchad Blake's Tchad Blakeness • *Riot Act*

Nearly ten years after the release of their second album, Pearl Jam returned to *Vs.* mode at an arena in Long Island during one of the darkest and most delusional eras in modern American history.

That they did it with one of their least distinguished songs shouldn't diminish the overall power of the gesture. It's true that "Bu$hleaguer," the twelfth track on their seventh album, *Riot Act*, sounds like something Tom Waits would have written when he was still clearing out his throat before the morning's first cup of coffee. And I feel confident that Pearl Jam themselves probably know this, which would explain why "Bu$hleaguer" hasn't been played live since 2007.

As a piece of political-minded songwriting, "Bu$hleaguer" is Pearl Jam's equivalent to Neil Young's *Living with War*—it's their hyper-timely and musically suspect political broadside. Some protest songs remain timeless even after the circumstances that inspired them have faded into history. Neil hardly ever plays anything off *Living with War* anymore, but he will be expected to slip "Ohio" into his set lists for as long as there are Neil Young concerts. "Bu$hleaguer," to put it mildly, is not in the same class as "Ohio."

But on April 30, 2003, at Nassau Coliseum in Uniondale, New York, none of that matters. On this night, "Bu$hleaguer" is the biggest provocation yet in Pearl Jam's career. Actually, it's how "Bu$hleaguer" is executed that's the real provocation. They save it for the encore, when the audience expects to hear "Baba O'Riley," "Yellow Ledbetter," or "Rockin' in the Free World." Instead, Eddie Vedder struts out in a sparkly silver jacket with a champagne bottle in his hand and a rubber George W. Bush mask over his head. He removes the mask when it's time to sing, and what comes out is a torrent of drolly delivered comic venom.

This move is not unprecedented at this increasingly contentious show. During the proper set, Eddie plays Steven Van Zandt's "I Am a Patriot," an anti-anthem about rejecting ideology in favor of freedom. "And I ain't no Democrat so I ain't no Republican," goes one memorable line. The audience response is tepid. Is this because they object to the lyrical content, or because they don't know the song? Either way, Vedder's annoyance is obvious.

"Y'all all right?" he asks. The tension is rising. A few songs later, he spits out an apropos lyric from "Not for You"—"Where the fuck did they come from?"—with extra spite.

Now, during the encore, Eddie accuses the president of being a con man. He denounces his leadership skills. He says he was born on third and thinks he hit a triple. On paper, it's not really *that* scathing. It's not as direct or incendiary as simply saying "Let's Impeach the President" like Neil did on *Living with War*. But from the moment Eddie comes out in that mask, the hostility in the room is palpable. He's not merely criticizing George W. Bush. Eddie is belittling the president, cutting him down to size at the precise moment when he's historically popular among Americans. Which means he's *also* mocking the people who are foolish enough to support this confidence man who just one month prior led his country into war for the second time in eighteen months.

I'm not saying Eddie Vedder was *actually* mocking his own audience that night in Uniondale, but it appears that's how they took "Bu$hleaguer." And they respond by raining down boos and pissed-off expletives.

"You didn't like that one," Eddie drawls, not letting up on the sarcasm. "I don't understand. Maybe you like him 'cause he's gonna give you a tax cut. Maybe you like him because he is a real guy, that relates to you, because he is so down home."

At that, they start chanting "U.S.A.!" They're chanting "U.S.A!" over and over like we just beat the Russians at the 1980 Olympics all over again. Eddie knows he's losing them. Behind the kit, Matt Cameron wonders if they'll make it out alive.

Eddie decides to change course. Sarcastic Eddie disappears and is replaced by Earnest Eddie.

"I'm with you. U.S.A. I just think that all of us in this room should have a voice in how the U.S.A. is represented. And he didn't allow us our voice. That's all I'm saying. We love America. I am standing on a stage in front of a big crowd. I worked in a God damn drug store. I love America, right?"

Someone in the crowd yells, "Play some fucking rock 'n' roll!" This person clearly doesn't recognize a fucking rock 'n' roll moment even when it's right in front of his fucking face. Pissing off your fans is the most rock 'n' roll move there is.

"This is good, this is open, honest debate, and that's what it should be," Eddie continues. His voice is remarkably calm, but you suspect he's actually seething beneath the amiable rock front man exterior. "If you don't say anything, you don't know what will happen. 'Cause we are on a brink of forever. And if we don't participate on where this thing is going, when where we are the number one super power in the world, you want to have a part in it and make sure it is a good thing, yeah? Plus or minus, be active. This is a good thing."

After that, Pearl Jam plays two protest songs: The Clash's "Know Your Rights" and Neil Young's "Rockin' in the Free World." If you wish, you can choose to hear these songs as merely "fucking rock 'n' roll." But for the band, who are uptight and distraught after the "Bu$hleaguer" reaction, they are expressions of fury. This encore is not the usual "good time party" release. This feels charged.

This is not the first time during this tour that "Bu$hleaguer" pissed people off. There were also issues earlier in the month after it was played in Denver, though in that city people for the most part just quietly stormed out. Plus, that was the middle of the country. They expected the audience at Nassau to be on their side. But they were wrong. Pearl Jam came to speak out against a warmongering president, and their fans responded by chanting "U.S.A.!"

By the end of "Rockin' in the Free World," Eddie has had enough. "U.S.A.!" he chants back. "U.S.A.!" he screams again.

Later, he would reflect on this moment by ruminating over the utility of protest music, and whether it does any good to preach to the converted. But that was beside the point at Nassau. What was worse than preaching to the converted was realizing that people in their own tribe could love the music and simply tune out the message. Or, failing that, attempt to shout it down. For Pearl Jam, maybe this wasn't their choir after all.

$$\lightning$$

Pearl Jam obviously isn't the first band to deal with this problem. Many of their heroes—Bruce, Neil, the Who—also faced the same hard truth when they entered the arena-rock world. You can't put fifteen thousand people in a room and get them to agree politically just because they happen to like the same band. It's a peculiar exercise we all play at some point with the art we love—you locate the part that speaks to you, and you ignore (or at best tolerate) the rest. For many Pearl Jam fans in 2003, "Bu$hleaguer" had to either be tolerated or mentally edited out of the picture.

But even if the circumstances of this show weren't unprecedented, they certainly seem unique. The first leg of Pearl Jam's tour in support of *Riot Act*, which started on April 1 in Denver and ended in State College, Pennsylvania, on May 3, coincided almost exactly with the first leg of the disastrous US military campaign in Iraq. Airstrikes began on March 19, followed by twenty-six days of combat. This initial stage officially concluded on May 1, just one day after the Nassau concert, with President Bush's nationally televised "Mission Accomplished" speech aboard the USS *Abraham Lincoln*.

Looking back on this period, it's easy to take stock of all that went wrong and believe that the cumulative tragedy of all the poor and misguided decisions were already apparent to most sober-minded Americans. But that just wasn't so. Right after the invasion, a Gallup poll found 72 percent of Americans favored war against Iraq, and just 25 percent opposed. About the same number of people approved of President Bush.

This support was amplified and reinforced by popular culture. For seven weeks in April and May 2003, the number-one country song in the U.S. was Darryl Worley's "Have You Forgotten," the most despicable track to receive round-the-clock airplay on American radio during the early part of the twenty-first century. In the song, Worley links Sept. 11 to the need to wage war and scoffs at anyone who might be skeptical. "I hear people saying we don't need this war / I say there's some things worth fighting for," he sings.

A journeyman lunkhead who later posed nude for *Playgirl* magazine once his career pushing pro-war propaganda started flagging, Worley affected a guileless posture when pressed by reporters about putting out a song like "Have You Forgotten" during the run-up to the Iraq war. He wasn't promoting this *specific* war, he insisted. He only wanted Americans to stand up for the red, white, and blue. Anyone who heard "Have You Forgotten" as a call to *actual* arms was reading into it too much.

Corporate radio stations went along with that sort of blameless, responsibility-free thinking. As one DJ from a radio station in San Diego put it, "The audience is so wrapped up in the emotion of what it's about,

I don't think they're nitpicking at this point. I'm sure we'll get that as we play it more. I think, at this point, everybody's viewing all the bad guys in a big bucket."

This is the context that Pearl Jam was forced to contend with as they toured America in the shadow of war. Though it's worth taking a longer view of American culture and Pearl Jam's own generation to understand how things progressed to the extremely screwed-up junction of most US citizens "viewing all the bad guys in a big bucket."

As Generation X came of age in the eighties and nineties, they were prepped years in advance for the 2003 Iraq invasion by two factors. The first was a reactionary aversion to the hippie protest politics of baby boomers. Since I've already touched on that, I'd like to discuss the second factor: Vietnam movies.

If you were part of the latchkey kid generation who came to cinema via cable TV and Blockbuster Video, you were inevitably touched in some way by Vietnam movies. *Apocalypse Now, The Deer Hunter, Coming Home, Platoon, Full Metal Jacket, Born on the Fourth of July*—Vietnam as a genre was a bedrock of prestige cinema from the late seventies through the early nineties. These films were an extension of the same boomer/hippie protest politics that Nirvana laughed about at the start of "Territorial Pissings" from *Nevermind*.[1] But whereas boomer/hippie protest politics had a passive influence on Generation X, ultimately pushing us away from overt acts of resistance and toward cynical apathy, Vietnam movies had an aggressive influence.

Like Darryl Worley, filmmakers such as Francis Ford Coppola, Michael Cimino, and Oliver Stone used pop culture to make a sympathetic case for those who wage war. To be clear, I'm not equating those directors with Worley as artists; I love pretty much every movie I just listed. What I

---

1 The song famously opens with bassist Krist Novoselic mockingly singing the chorus of "Get Together" by the Youngbloods, a defining hit of the 1960s "flower power" era: "Come on people now, smile on your brother, everybody get together and try to love one another right now."

am saying is that Vietnam movies as a genre always make the same case for soldiers being victims who deserve our sympathy. These movies are never about *systems*; they're about the *people* who are *used* by systems. The audience isn't asked to confront the largely unseen forces that push governments into war, the middle management ghouls who serve up the PowerPoint presentations that justify murdering millions of people. Instead we see leading men put through hell—Robert De Niro mourning his damaged friends in *The Deer Hunter*, Jon Voight losing the use of his legs in *Coming Home*, Matthew Modine mourning his damaged friends in *Full Metal Jacket*, Tom Cruise losing the use of his legs in *Born on the Fourth of July*, and so on.

When I was growing up, all I really knew about Vietnam was that the people who fought there were treated badly by hippies when they returned home. And I learned that from Vietnam movies. My whole generation did. It even filtered down to the defining action franchise of the eighties, the *First Blood* movies, in which Sylvester Stallone's Vietnam vet John Rambo is triggered once again into becoming a war machine because his unfeeling countrymen won't welcome him home. In third grade, I had a lunchbox for *Rambo: First Blood Part II*, depicting a muscle-bound Stallone holding an absurdly large machine gun. It looked like he was lugging around a tank in his arms. That's what kids like me looked at every single day as we ate our snack-size bags of Doritos.

But even the serious Vietnam films of the era had a veneer of popcorn-movie excitement. They were rock 'n' roll movies at heart, and they were instantly embedded in pop culture. Watching jungles get napalmed into oblivion in *Apocalypse Now* made you love the song "The End" by the Doors. A scene in which American soldiers exploit a Vietnamese prostitute in *Full Metal Jacket* was turned into a comic sample in the chorus of "Me So Horny" by 2 Live Crew. It all boiled down to entertainment, not protest.

When the United States went to war with Iraq for the first time in 1990, there was a concerted effort to protect the feelings of soldiers while also delivering exciting images on CNN. "Support the Troops" became a ubiquitous phrase. An old hit from 1973 by Tony Orlando and Dawn, "Tie a Yellow Ribbon Round the Ole Oak Tree," was brought back and inspired Americans to wear yellow ribbons as a "promissory note" for combatants, to quote a *New York Times* article from 1991. "My brother was concerned that coming home would be bad, like Vietnam again," one yellow ribbon wearer told the *Times*. "I said, 'Under no circumstances.'"

In March 1991, a "We Are the World"–style soft-rock song called "Voices That Care" carried forward this conciliatory tone. Two of the song's writers, Peter Cetera and David Foster, were the creative forces behind a series of power-ballad smashes in the eighties performed by Chicago, including future cheeseball wedding classics like "You're the Inspiration" and "Hard for Me to Say I'm Sorry." They brought that same flair for heart-tugging sentimentality to "Voices That Care" and recruited a battalion of stars to perform it. The singers on "Voices That Care" included many of the era's most popular vocalists: Garth Brooks, Celine Dion, Will Smith, Michael Bolton, Bobby Brown, Matthew and Gunnar Nelson from the pop-metal band Nelson. Mark Knopfler played a guitar solo. Kenny G played a sax solo. Somehow, it only went to no. 11 on the pop charts, perhaps because the war had already ended by the time the single was released.[2]

Supporting friends, family members, and neighbors who go to war once they come home is such an obvious good and virtuous act that nobody could possibly oppose it. The problem was that "Support the Troops" was deftly used to shield the politicians and governments that put those soldiers in harm's way from criticism. It's a cheap, and extremely effective, PR ploy. Support for the first Iraq war in the nineties was even higher than the support for the second Iraq war in the aughts, topping out at 80 percent.

---

2 It's telling that two of the best anti-war songs of the era came from hard rock bands: Metallica's "One" and Guns N' Roses' "Civil War." The working-class audiences for those bands were made up of the same young people most likely to be sent to war.

In the nineties, the proper response to war was to wear a yellow ribbon and not become emotionally involved with the nitty-gritty of combat. That's what we were taught. So, when the most popular rock band of the nineties decided to push back against this, Pearl Jam's generation rebelled against them.

⚡

Of course, Pearl Jam didn't just alienate some fans with their politics in the early aughts. They also did it with their music.

I have a lot of affection for 2000's *Binaural* and 2002's *Riot Act*, the "ditch" portion of Pearl Jam's discography. But it's hardly surprising that these albums didn't connect with the larger public. I don't think they were wrongly overlooked, and I would never argue that they should have sold as well as Pearl Jam's nineties work. Rather, they were *made* to be in the ditch. Their "ditchiness," as it were, is what I like about them.

The standard complaint about *Binaural*—the first Pearl Jam album that did not go platinum upon its release on May 16, 2000—is that the production stinks. I'm not going to contradict the conventional wisdom. I only warmed to this album after I fell in love with the live versions from the 2000 tour bootlegs. While it's true with Pearl Jam that *all* their songs sound better live than on record, the transformation is most pronounced with *Binaural*, the most frustratingly muddled LP of their career.

I've tried for years to understand the point of binaural recording techniques. Perhaps I should hire Tchad Blake—the producer of *Binaural*, whose first name is a metaphor for his convoluted musical approach—to explain it to me. As I understand it, it's about using two microphones to create the impression sonically that you're surrounded by the music, a 3D effect that replicates the feeling of sitting in a room with the musicians. But that is not how it feels to listen to *Binaural*. It's somehow the *opposite* of how it feels to listen to *Binaural*. You feel like you're listening to the musicians play in a room above you. And there's a wet towel wrapped around your skull. And you have a bad head cold. That's what *Binaural* sounds like.

This is a criticism that many Pearl Jam fans have made. But I am not interested in once again blaming Tchad Blake for *Binaural*'s misgivings. Though Pearl Jam also blamed Blake (albeit implicitly) by running back to Brendan O'Brien at the eleventh hour and asking him to remix the harder rocking songs. But it's the band members themselves who must bear the brunt of the responsibility for making such a dull-sounding record out of otherwise strong material.

In the nineties, Pearl Jam made albums at a brisk pace because they had powerful gale-force winds of creative and cultural energy at their backs. But that incredible centrifugal force covered up their deficiencies as recording artists. Even at their best, Pearl Jam never conceptualized their records beyond simply going into the studio and recording their latest batch of songs. There was never a central idea animating their work beyond, "It's time to make another record."

With *Binaural*, those gale-force winds had slowed significantly. But Pearl Jam was still in the habit of making a new album every two years. Right about now, however, they needed a *reason* to make a record, and they didn't have one. The unrest in Seattle in late 1999 during the World Trade Organization protests that coincided with the *Binaural* sessions did not significantly inform the record beyond the musically spiky and lyrically vague "Grievance." Like most superstar bands tasked with making their sixth album, Pearl Jam was mostly consumed with themselves.

This was manifested by Eddie Vedder's writer's block, which was so stifling that a hidden track called "Writer's Block"—consisting only of the sounds of a typewriter, like Jack Nicholson hammering away impotently in *The Shining*—was added to the album. There was also the matter of Mike McCready, their musical sparkplug, returning to rehab for an addiction to prescription drugs. But even then, nobody stopped to ask, "What is *the point* of this record?" Maybe because asking that question would've prompted an uncomfortable follow-up: "If there's no point, does that means we should stop?"

Pearl Jam eventually found the point of *Binaural* on the road during the 2000 tour. But the fact that these songs flourished in a live setting makes the album seem, at best, like the means rather than the ends.

With the other ditch record, *Riot Act*, I am going to buck convention: I think it's their most underrated LP, and their last truly masterful one. Though at the time it was released on November 12, 2002, it was the record that caused all but the die-hards to write them off. The *New York Times* review seems the most apt in terms of capturing the consensus view of *Riot Act*, pointing out that "there's no catchy single, and not even the slightest echo of anything else happening in pop music now." In the end, the *Times* concluded, *Riot Act* "sounds as if it were made to slip quietly into the marketplace, connect with the faithful and leave everyone else alone." While that's not necessarily criticism—it strikes me as an accurate observation—it does paint an ambivalent portrait of a band that once conquered the world and is now working with much smaller stakes.

Riot Act sold even worse than *Binaural*, barely going gold. But I would argue that it's more sonically satisfying than *Binaural*—working with longtime Soundgarden associate Adam Kasper, *Riot Act* once again sounds like a muscular live band flexing in the studio. It might not solve Pearl Jam's usual conceptual issues, but recent trauma stepped in to give them the sense of purpose they didn't have on *Binaural*.

Whereas *Binaural* feels muted because of an unsuccessful approach in the studio, *Riot Act* comes by its numbness honestly. Like *Yield*, it's a record *about* numbness; specifically, the grief and PTSD wrought by Roskilde, 9/11, and the patina of disappointment and loss of innocence brought on by the end of the nineties and the return of the Bush dynasty Republican rule that had been vanquished at the start of Pearl Jam's career.

Pearl Jam was out of step with American culture for many reasons in the early aughts. But their insistence on confronting their grief, publicly and honestly, was by far the least fashionable thing about them. On *Riot Act*, they subscribe to the idea that the only way to get over pain is to go through it. "I Am Mine" and "Love Boat Captain" contain the most direct references to Roskilde—"Lost nine friends we'll never know . . . two years ago today," as he sings on the latter song—but the whole album has the vibe of a wake. When Eddie Vedder raises his voice, it's never a triumphant scream. It's a cry that sticks in the throat.

In the context of *Riot Act*, "Bu$hleaguer" is almost comic relief. A dirty joke that briefly alleviates the sorrow. Onstage, however, it was a renewal of Pearl Jam's uncool commitment to caring more than anyone else in their cohort.

CHAPTER 14
"GUARANTEED"

(From Eddie Vedder's *Into the Wild*)

Rearviewmirror: Greatest Hits (1991–2003) • Another Parallel to the Who • Chris McCandless • *Into the Wild* • Eddie Vedder Grows Up

It's been said, to quote my favorite *Kids in the Hall* sketch,[1] that greatest hits albums are for housewives and little girls. But this is just sexist hogwash. In actual fact, greatest hits albums are for fulfilling contractual obligations.

It's a mutually beneficial situation for all involved parties. For the record label, a greatest hits album is product that's cheap to produce and likely to yield high returns. For the artist, it can mean freedom from the demands of a piece of paper they signed many years prior. But as countless

---

1 I refer to the classic "Doors fan" sketch in which Bruce McCulloch plays a record store clerk who instructs Kevin McDonald on how to be a follower of the Lizard King.

jingoistic country songs in the aughts pointed out, freedom isn't free. A greatest hits album might require no work—if you're lucky enough to not get hoodwinked into shoehorning a newly recorded song into the tracklist to goad the hard-core fans into ponying up.[2] But the artistic implications of a compilation can be demoralizing, especially if most of the people in your band haven't even turned forty yet.

For Pearl Jam, the "greatest hits album" era commenced on November 16, 2004, with the release of *Rearviewmirror: Greatest Hits (1991–2003)*. Surveying the thirty-three-song tracklist, there aren't any real surprises: Pearl Jam really does have about three dozen songs that are recognizable enough to the average rock listener to register as "hits." They even leave some standards on the table: "Porch," "Release," "Blood," "Indifference," "Last Exit." Predictably, nineteen out of thirty-three songs originate from the first three years of Pearl Jam's recording career—five songs from *Ten*, both songs from *Singles*, six from *Vs.*, and six from *Vitalogy*.

Somewhat less predictably, there are just five songs released after 2000. Often with greatest hits albums, cuts from the later albums are over-represented to give a false impression that the act in question didn't seriously fall off, commercially and/or creatively, once the fame and glory of their early work faded. But *Rearviewmirror* doesn't bother with this. It's a straightforward presentation of Pearl Jam's best-known and most-loved work.

This ensures that, as a listening experience, *Rearviewmirror* is remarkably consistent and—if you don't know the albums—solidly satisfying. If all you knew about Pearl Jam was based on this record, you would assume that they were a crowd-pleasing radio band focused on producing durable earworms. A Tom Petty and the Heartbreakers for the nineties.

But that's not what Pearl Jam was. (The Tom Petty and the Heartbreakers of the nineties was still Tom Petty and the Heartbreakers.) What *Rearviewmirror* leaves out are songs like "Satan's Bed," "Sometimes," "Lukin," and "Push Me Pull Me"—the curveballs, the tangents, the provocations,

---

2 The only good example of this is Tom Petty and the Heartbreakers recording "Mary Jane's Last Dance" for their 1993 *Greatest Hits* album, which then became one of their *actual* greatest hits.

the temper tantrums, the willful weirdness that dot the band's albums from the era. As we've seen over and over so far, Pearl Jam's massive success in the first dozen years of their career is only part of the story. It's arguably the less interesting part, really. The more interesting part is how Pearl Jam reacted to that success by rebelling against the very image that *Rearviewmirror* promulgates.

So, yes, it's a dependable and pleasant lesson. But above all it's a convenient album for anyone who can't be bothered to dig deeper. And that ultimately makes *Rearviewmirror* a little boring, like a movie that's been re-edited to remove all the tension and eccentricity. When it comes to compilations of "early" Pearl Jam—I'm applying "early" here like I do with the Rolling Stones for their 1964 to 1972 period—I prefer the one that came out the year before *Rearviewmirror*. The album that's all curveballs, *Lost Dogs*.

If *Rearviewmirror* is about presenting the most accessible and radio-friendly version of Pearl Jam, *Lost Dogs* tips its cap to their outcast side. Now, Pearl Jam clearly weren't *actual* outcasts, at least not in the nineties. But they identified with outsiders, and *Lost Dogs* invites the listener to bask in the most obscure regions of their discography, gathering B-sides, outtakes, contributions for surfer-led charity compilations, and soundtrack spots for films about Chicago cab drivers and death row inmates. Of course, Pearl Jam can't avoid their hit-making ways even on *Lost Dogs*. Some of their most well-known songs were supposed to be buried and then became famous anyway: "Dirty Frank," "Footsteps," "Hard to Imagine," "Yellow Ledbetter," and "Last Kiss," the cover of the J. Frank Wilson and the Cavaliers 1964 hit that somehow became the highest charting single of their career in 1999. The last two songs are actually on both *Rearviewmirror* and *Lost Dogs*—those canines truly went from the doghouse to the penthouse and back again.[3]

Unlike *Rearviewmirror*, *Lost Dogs* is thick with tracks from the early twenty-first century years. There are six songs from the *Binaural* era,

---

3 Weirdly, the version of "Yellow Ledbetter" on *Lost Dogs* is three seconds shorter.

enough for an EP of leftovers from their most difficult record. I'm not sure I would trade anything on that album for what's on *Lost Dogs*—right or wrong, I think they picked the right material to convey that album's opaque and sullen mood. The *Binaural* outtakes meanwhile are loose and kind of wacky. The snaky "Sad" is the best of the bunch, but I'm also a fan of the goofy beach party rocker "Hitchhiker" and the *very* goofy Kareem Abdul-Jabbar tribute "Sweet Lew." I have not used the word "goofy" to describe Pearl Jam before now and I won't after. But it is appropriate for me to use the adjective twice in one sentence to describe the *Binaural* cast-offs collected on *Lost Dogs*.

While I am fine with the idea that these songs probably wouldn't have worked on *Binaural*, I must file a formal complaint with Pearl Jam HR about the decision not to include two B-sides from the "I Am Mine" single, "Down" and "Undone," on *Riot Act*. Both tracks are melodic mid-tempo rockers written by Eddie Vedder, and they are among the most tuneful and just plain likeable tracks to come out of this period. The jangly "Down" is the closest Pearl Jam has come to approximating *Lifes Rich Pageant*–era R.E.M. while "Undone" is zippy and catchy in a *Yield* sort of way. Not only would these songs have lightened up an otherwise dour record, they could have been forwarded as singles selling *Riot Act* to a bigger audience.

I'm not saying that *Riot Act* would have taken the world by storm in this scenario. But the decision to bury their most immediate songs at a time when immediate Pearl Jam songs weren't exactly plentiful registers as a different kind of perversity than relegating "Yellow Ledbetter" to B-side status in the early nineties. Back then, Pearl Jam had hits to burn. They had to *try* to not have hits. But in the early aughts, a song like "Undone" could have given them the boost they needed.

It doesn't seem like knowing self-sabotage. It points to a malady that would become more and more apparent as they waded deeper into their post–"greatest hits" years—Pearl Jam doesn't really know how to make albums.

I don't mean that Pearl Jam hasn't made great albums. (I hope it's obvi-ous by now that I am not arguing this.) What I mean is that the greatness of Pearl Jam albums is unrelated to their knowledge of how to make great Pearl Jam albums. They made great albums in the nineties because as songwriters they were producing top-notch material, and as musicians they were playing together extremely well. Great songs plus great musicianship will almost always overcome any deficiencies for how to creatively approach making records. Albums like *Vs.* and *Vitalogy* work because the tunes, the energy, and the playing are undeniable. Those aspects are so strong that it overcomes the overriding weakness of those early records—their monochromatic and unimaginative sound.

What's odd about this is that Pearl Jam used Brendan O'Brien at the same time as Stone Temple Pilots. But while Pearl Jam is a better band than Stone Temple Pilots, the albums they made with O'Brien aren't as dynamic as the ones O'Brien made with STP. Now, I think the Pearl Jam records are still better overall, but in terms of pure sonic ear candy, the STP records sound colorful and vibrant while the Pearl Jam records sound kind of gray.

It's yet another way in which Pearl Jam parallels the Who, a world-class rock 'n' roll band onstage who often struggled to sound as vital in the studio. Moving forward, this issue would become more pronounced for Pearl Jam as their songwriting slipped and their reticence to move quickly through the making of albums increased. They would come to rely more on craft, a significant evolution from the mid-nineties norm of chaotic jams haphazardly (and thrillingly) coalescing into compositions. And their albums would sound even flatter as a result.

In 1980, Pete Townshend was pressed by Greil Marcus about whether the Who was still "pushing their music forward" in an artistic sense. It's a classic rock-critic question: *What are you doing* [strokes chin thoughtfully] *to reckon with the profound changes to music and the greater world* [dramatic pause] *and the space that rock 'n' roll takes up in that world?*

This was his answer:

We've very much dropped our idealistic stance in terms of *our* weight of responsibility to rock's evolution. We haven't stopped caring about where it's going to go; I think we've realized that we're not capable of doing *that much*, in terms of actually pushing it forward. If we have got a chance of pushing it forward, I think we've got a better chance of doing it on the road than we do on record, to be quite honest.

At the time, Townshend would have been thirty-four or thirty-five—not very old for a rock star by modern standards, but in 1980 people had never seen thirty-something-year-old rock stars before. Greil Marcus was needling him because Pete was considered ancient in rock years. Plus, the Who was fifteen years into their recording career. Keith Moon had been dead since 1978. It's not a perfect analogy with the members of Pearl Jam, but it's fair to say that Townshend was roughly in the same position in 1980 as Eddie Vedder was in the early aughts.

I suppose it's possible to view Townshend's answer as cop-out. Maybe the venerable Greil Marcus—the most professorial and (I say this as a person who genuinely respects him) pretentious rock critic ever[4]—interpreted it as Townshend simply shrugging his shoulders and accepting his lot as an oldies act. But I think he's just being honest with himself. 1980 was not 1971. A new Who album was not going to change the world. More important, making Who albums at this point didn't seem especially pleasurable for him. But he still felt connected to his audience onstage. Playing Who songs for Who fans still had the potential to be transformational. And for Townshend in that moment, it's where the Who still had the chance to be their best.

This is also the attitude that Pearl Jam would adopt for the rest of their career. In that respect, *Rearviewmirror* was more than just a contractual obligation. It really does cap a discrete part of their career. The "greatest hits album" era was the time when they really did have hits. And after that they stopped having hits.

⚡

---

4 His 1975 book *Mystery Train* is the best book ever written about rock, full stop.

Lost Dogs and *Rearviewmirror* marked the end of Pearl Jam's deal with Epic Records. They were now free agents. And they responded to this as many bands in their position do: They slowed down. They slowed down *a lot*. Not as much as R.E.M., who broke up after closing out their contact with Warner Bros. in 2011. But they opted to work significantly less on being Pearl Jam and significantly more on being functional people outside a rock band.

The math is simple. There is a four-year gap between *Riot Act* and their next studio LP, *Pearl Jam*, their first and only release on Clive Davis's short-lived J Records. From the mid-aughts to the early twenties, there are only four Pearl Jam studio records, compared with seven released between 1991 and 2002. In the twenty-first century, the time between new albums grew so long and wide that each new release was inevitably billed as a grand "return" or "second coming," a continual reintroduction of the band to the general public that counterintuitively made them seem even more distant from the contemporary music world.

Even if Pearl Jam intends to course correct in their senior-citizen era and dramatically increase their recorded output, they probably won't ever approach their productivity from their first decade. And why should they? There is more to life than making albums. Every world-conquering rock band discovers this. You reach the mountaintop, and then there's nowhere else to go but back down the mountain. And then you return home to relax on the couch for a while because you just climbed a damn mountain and climbing a damn mountain is physically and mentally draining. This arc has been repeated time and again. And now it was Pearl Jam's turn. Marriages, children, side projects—these are the things that would now take up more time in their lives moving forward.

For Eddie Vedder, the aughts covered the full spectrum of loss, love, and redemption. In 2000, he divorced his first wife, Beth Liebling. Fortunately, he is a handsome and charming rock star, so he soon hooked up with a fashion model named Jill McCormick, with whom he had two daughters—Olivia in 2004 and Harper in 2008—before they were eventually married in 2010. At some point, he decamped to Maui, and have you ever tried to get any work done in Maui?

The net result of these life changes is that Vedder became a grown-up in the aughts. And this would affect his writing on subsequent Pearl Jam albums. His most famous songs have an adolescent point of view, in which young protagonists struggle to reconcile with profound life-changing developments freighted with the most intense emotions and the highest possible stakes. Contrary to popular perception, he didn't always write about himself; in fact his best songs were often about characters that he could empathize with. But the proximity from his own youth, the grimmest and most alienated part of his life, was growing more and more distant. And yet, in the right circumstances, he could still access that part of his creative self. It just seemed that "the right circumstances" in this case included "being outside of Pearl Jam."

My favorite Pearl Jam–related album from the post–"greatest hits" era is Eddie Vedder's soundtrack to Sean Penn's 2007 film *Into the Wild*. Based on Jon Krakauer's 1996 bestseller, *Into the Wild* tells the story of Chris McCandless, a brilliant and privileged twenty-four-year-old who took the radical step of dropping out of a promising post-collegiate life in order to bum around America anonymously under the name "Alexander Supertramp." McCandless's gambit was fueled by his dislike of materialism specifically and modern society in general; he exhibited this disdain by ditching his car in Arizona and burning the cash in his wallet.

Eventually, his odyssey takes him to Alaska, where he pledges to go "into the wild" and live off the land. A natural-born risk-taker, McCandless opted to do this without a map or any real knowledge of the area. His only resource was a book on edible plants. At first, he lives a charmed existence, finding an abandoned bus with a bed and a wood-burning stove within his first week. But eventually his luck runs out—one of the plants he eats daily for survival turns out to be poisonous. After 113 days on his own in the Alaskan wilderness, McCandless died from starvation.

Penn handed Vedder a copy of *Into the Wild*, and a few days later he showed him a rough cut of the film.[5] That Vedder connected strongly with

5 Penn originally approached Vedder about writing a song for 1995's *Dead Man Walking*. The song, "Dead Man," was ultimately rejected for the film and appeared instead on *Lost Dogs*.

the material is hardly a surprise. McCandless could have been one of the idealistic loners that Vedder wrote about on *Ten* and *Vs.* He most resembles the characters in "Porch" and "Rearviewmirror," who like McCandless sped away from their troubled lives in a swiftly accelerating car. But Chris went further than that. He also ditched the car and erased his old self from the world. And he did it in *real life* during the spring, summer, and fall of 1992, right when Pearl Jam was reaching the height of their fame.[6]

Speaking about McCandless later in interviews, Vedder's admiration was obvious, as was his instant empathy. "In the book, what I knew immediately was, I had some insight beyond the pages of what might explain the extreme actions and reactions of Chris McCandless," he said. "We had similar upbringings and similar events in our lives."

Some of those similarities were withheld from Krakauer's book at the request of his sister Carine, who finally divulged more of Chris's background in the 2014 PBS documentary, *Return to the Wild—the Chris McCandless Story.* According to the film, McCandless's affluent father, a rocket scientist for NASA, was an abusive tyrant who for several years carried on with two wives and families of children. As was the case for Vedder in his childhood, the sordid secrets of the McCandless family drove Chris to anger over adult hypocrisy, his sister believes. Also like Vedder, McCandless reacted to that duplicity in a manner that critics found melodramatic and self-indulgent while supporters viewed it as inspiring and relatable.

Because there are long dialogue-free stretches of *Into the Wild* in which McCandless (Emile Hirsch) wanders alone in the Alaskan wilderness, Penn hoped Vedder could act as the character's musical voice, communicating his essence through song. (Penn later admitted that he thought of Vedder because Hirsh looks like a younger version of him.) Getting into this kid's head proved to be very easy for Vedder to do, even though he was now

---

6 It's unclear if Chris McCandless—like many other twenty-four-year-olds in 1992—was a Pearl Jam fan. But he did appear to like the Who, as he dubbed his living quarters "The Magic Bus."

almost twice as old as McCandless when he passed away. "I found it to be uncomfortable how easy it was," Vedder said with a bemused laugh to *Billboard*, "because I thought I'd grown up. I think all this stuff was right under the surface for me, barely."

In another interview with Charlie Rose, Vedder described in near-metaphysical terms how quickly the *Into the Wild* songs came together. "I was just inside it," he said. "What happened was two weeks or three weeks went by and I kind of woke up and it was done. And I don't really remember a whole lot about it."

In practical terms, *Into the Wild* was very much in his wheelhouse. It allowed him to write from the point of view of a strong character who resembles the prototypical Eddie Vedder protagonist. The themes of the film synced with Vedder's own pet subjects: the desire for escape, a distrust of the craven corporate mainstream, the value of questioning authority, the yearning for spiritual transcendence, the lifelong battle to overcome childhood demons. Chris McCandless was the type of martyr that Vedder was inclined to romanticize. He sympathized with him instinctually. He might have even envied him on some level.

But *Into the Wild* also provided a musical solution to the common problems of the post–"greatest hits" era for Eddie Vedder. The project required that he work quickly, and that he write within set parameters. Sean Penn gave him a character to write for and a cinematic context in which he had to conform. And Vedder liked this. He *needed* this.

"In almost every aspect of this process, it simplified things," Vedder said. "There were fewer choices. The story was there and the scenes were there. If there was anything that I learned with my own writing process, maybe there's too many choices what to write about. Just the amount of subject matter in the world these days; maybe that feels chaotic for me. This took away all the choices."

As an album, *Into the Wild* is closer to the homey and unpolished outtakes on *Lost Dogs* than the hits of *Rearviewmirror*. I don't want to overstate the virtue of working quickly or dispute the value of taking ample time to finesse high craftsmanship. Certainly there are examples from

Pearl Jam's early career when more time would have fully baked their more half-baked experiments. (Or maybe they would have reconsidered putting a song like "Bugs" on an album at all.)

But when I put on *Into the Wild*, what hits me is the sense of urgency, which is stronger than it is on any Pearl Jam record post-*Yield*. It's the closest Vedder has come to making his own *Nebraska*, and I wish he had made three or four more albums in this vein. But the bittersweet fact is that *Into the Wild* sounds like a farewell from Vedder to the part of his career when he wrote very well from inside the minds of young, romantic dreamers like Chris McCandless.

The most moving song from *Into the Wild* for me is the final track, "Guaranteed." The melody is one of Vedder's finest, a luminous vehicle for delicate fingerpicking that could have been lifted from a Simon & Garfunkel record. The lyrics function as McCandless's goodbye to the world, and they are as wise and at peace as McCandless's actual departing words.[7] Vedder sings about feeling the wind in his hair and no road beneath his feet. Then comes one of his loveliest lyrics: "Late at night I hear the trees, they're singing with the dead."

Vedder isn't mourning McCandless in this song. He's letting him go. And with it, also a part of himself.

---

7 "I have had a happy life and thank the Lord. Goodbye and may God bless all!"

CHAPTER 15
"UNEMPLOYABLE"

(From *Pearl Jam*)

Pearl Jam Hires a Keyboardist • The Grateful Dead • Jammers vs. Jamily • That Foo Fighters Song About Being the Best • *Tattoo You* vs. *Voodoo Lounge*

They met on the beach. One guy was a native Hawaiian in his late forties who made his living playing keyboards in blues and reggae bands. The other guy was Eddie Vedder.

Only the first guy didn't know it. Or, at least, he didn't recognize the significance of this other guy being "Eddie Vedder." And this, of course, really appealed to Eddie Vedder. Like Neil Young in the song "On the Beach," Eddie needs a crowd of people but he can't face them day to day. But Eddie could face this guy because this guy had no clue who Eddie Vedder was.

The story as related by Boom Gaspar—Pearl Jam's unofficial sixth member who joined the band as a touring musician in 2002—about how he become acquainted with Vedder sounds like something out of a movie. Only this film would never get made because it's too implausible. Apparently, Boom knew Eddie because they frequented the same surf spot. For more than six months, they surfed in the same vicinity without interacting. Even after they were formally introduced by a mutual friend—Ed, this is Boom; Boom, this is Ed—they never discussed their careers.

Finally, after nearly a year of being surf buddies, Gaspar finally asked Vedder what band he was in.

"Just a Seattle band," Eddie said.

"OK, well, what's the name?" Boom pried.

"Pearl Jam."

"What? Who is that?"

Now, there's a part of me that has a hard time believing this. In fact, I sometimes wonder if Boom Gaspar did in fact know Eddie Vedder and Pearl Jam so well that he feigned ignorance because he figured that was precisely the way to get into Ed's good graces. Think about it: If you were a musician on the lower rungs of the Hawaiian music industry, and you were interested in possibly playing with one of the world's most successful arena rock bands, your best shot at securing employment would be *negging* your prospective patron. A Gen X institution would be especially vulnerable to this form of reverse psychology practiced by many of the world's most prodigious pickup artists. *If you act like you don't care, you will be treated with the utmost care.*

But this is rank speculation. All available evidence suggests that Boom Gaspar really was that guileless, and Eddie Vedder really was that charmed, and that's why Pearl Jam band photos now occasionally include a man who looks like the world's friendliest Hell's Angel hanging out on the periphery.

⚡

The reason I love this anecdote is that the Boom Gaspar origin story is the most Grateful Dead–like thing about Pearl Jam.

The Dead was well-known for having a battery of keyboardists during their thirty-year history, and nearly all of them died in horrible, depressing ways. Ron "Pigpen" McKernan perished at the age of twenty-seven after years of insane alcohol consumption. Keith Godchaux passed away after sustaining massive head injuries from a car accident on his thirty-second birthday. Brent Mydland departed after overdosing on a speedball of cocaine and morphine when he was thirty-seven. Vince Welnick took his own life at age fifty-five after a decade of declining mental health by slitting his own throat in his backyard. Tom Constanten and Bruce Hornsby are the only keyboardists to make it out of the Dead alive. (I pray I didn't just jinx them.)

But while Pearl Jam has had a checkered history with drummers, they've stuck with Boom since the early aughts. Every ten years or so, Eddie Vedder goes surfing and comes back with a revelatory musical discovery. In the nineties, it was "Momma-Son." In the 2000s, it was a keyboardist.

For the first sixteen years of their existence, almost nobody compared Pearl Jam to the Grateful Dead. They had the word "jam" right there in their name, but critics didn't contextualize them as a jam band. Occasionally, however, the band members themselves nodded to the Dead. In the summer of 1995, they played Soldier Field a few days after the Grateful Dead performed their last show ever with Jerry Garcia at the stadium. And this particular show ended up being the longest Pearl Jam gig ever up to that time—thirty songs for 155 minutes. But aside from Eddie making a joke about smoking the Dead's leftover joints, there didn't seem to be much kinship.[1]

That all changed in 2006, a year in which Pearl Jam courted the media more aggressively than they had since the early days of the *Ten* album cycle. The purpose of this was to promote their self-titled eighth LP (the "Avocado" record), their first with Clive Davis's newly established J Records. But most of the media attention wasn't focused on the album. Instead, it was about the devoted fan following that Pearl Jam had

---

1 Eddie also referenced the Dead at the Red Rocks show I wrote about in the first chapter, though again this seems more like a joke than an actual acknowledgment of the Dead being an influence.

cultivated in the years since their commercial prime in the nineties. Now, media outlets tripped over themselves to liken Pearl Jam to the most popular cult band in rock history.

For instance, here's the lede from an '06 feature by *Entertainment Weekly*:

> Admit it: You sort of thought Pearl Jam broke up. After 1998's *Yield*, the onetime alt-rock superstars slowly faded from public view, releasing two lackluster studio discs 2000's *Binaural* and 2002's *Riot Act*—that sold poorly compared with the band's early successes. But even as their mainstream profile diminished, Pearl Jam were quietly developing a fanatical cult following. The band now packs arenas for two, sometimes three nights in a row, thanks to thousands of intensely dedicated fans who call themselves the Jamily and travel hundreds of miles to sing along with every word. Sixteen years into their career, Pearl Jam have unexpectedly morphed into a modern Grateful Dead, and it just might be their saving grace. "You don't really set out for that to happen," says frontman Eddie Vedder. "But I think it's kind of the ultimate compliment."

Keep in mind that this was written for an audience that probably hadn't cared about a new Pearl Jam song since "Better Man." Which, to be fair, describes at least 80 percent of rock fans in 2006. A lot of those folks likely did think Pearl Jam had broken up. So, they surely were amazed that there were now people who supposedly referred to themselves as "The Jamily" and followed Pearl Jam around the country.[2]

This media blitz coincided with a small but significant sea change in how Pearl Jam conducted their career. In 2005, they toured for the first time without an album to support, an unusual practice for a rock band geared toward spinning radio hits but common for jam bands or legacy acts who can tour on the strength of their catalogs. For Pearl Jam, it was

---

2 As far as I can tell, "Jamily" is not a common name used among Pearl Jam fans. A *Relix* story from this period refers to PJ fans as "Jammers," which is not *as* dorky as "Jamily" but is still pretty damn dorky.

an early inkling for how their "mid to late" period would unfold, in which new tours came to greatly outnumber new albums.

The most interesting part of the *EW* article is the reporting on how Pearl Jam consciously studied the Grateful Dead business model as they transitioned from the tumultuous nineties to the steadier and saner twenty-first century. "We just went and hung out in their offices and looked at how they did things," band manager Kelly Curtis told the magazine. "It was so grassroots and so great."

The Dead was especially influential on Pearl Jam with the Ten Club, the fan club that went from a mail-based afterthought in the nineties to a central online hub for followers in the aughts. In 2003, Pearl Jam expanded their mail-order ticket system, allowing fans to buy two tickets to as many shows as they wished, another idea borrowed from the Dead.

Pearl Jam was now deliberate about cultivating and fortifying fan relationships and making the quality and variety of live shows the core of their brand. In 1993, the Grateful Dead started the archival *Dick's Picks* series, eventually releasing recordings of entire concerts in a format that mimicked the look and sound of the voluminous bootlegs that Dead fans had been trading for years. Seven years later, Pearl Jam went further than the Dead by releasing recordings of every concert on their 2000 tour.

But if Pearl Jam had truly "morphed into a modern Grateful Dead," as *Entertainment Weekly* proposed, you might expect them to actually *sound* like the Grateful Dead, or at least act more like a proper jam band. When you read media coverage of Pearl Jam from this period, it's fascinating how some writers seemed to really believe that Pearl Jam actually had evolved into that sort of group. Of course, because music critics tend to be anti–jam band, this didn't bode well for Pearl Jam.

"The group has even added a touch of jam band aesthetics to its signature sound," the *Washington Post* concluded in a concert review of Pearl Jam's D.C.-area show in 2006, which in the writer's estimation "meant a few too many noodling solos by guitarist Mike McCready, who is nearly as verbose with his playing as Pearl Jam's other guitarist, Stone Gossard, is economical with his."

I firmly believe that there is no such thing as "too many noodling solos" by Mike McCready, but otherwise the *Washington Post* critic was not entirely wrong. When it comes to jamming in Pearl Jam, McCready does most of the heavy lifting. Even in "Crazy Mary," the Victoria Williams cover that is traditionally Boom Gaspar's showcase for extended soloing on his B-3 organ, McCready eventually swoops in for some hotshot guitar-hero licks. Eddie Vedder might be the leader of Pearl Jam, but McCready is their closest musical equivalent to Jerry Garcia.[3]

But is Pearl Jam really a jam band? To answer this question, I'd like to borrow some terms from the jam world: Type I jams and Type II jams. Type I are jams in which a band plays over an established chord progression or key. Type II are jams that break away from the song and improvise the chord progression, key, and rhythms. Most of the time, Pearl Jam plays neither Type I nor Type II jams. They stick mostly with straightforward replications of their records, only played louder and more energetically. There are a number of Pearl Jam songs that I *wish* were extended onstage—imagine if the outro guitar jams on "Corduroy" or "MFC" were drawn out to "Down by the River" length, or if McCready was given even more space to explore in the middle of "Red Mosquito" or "Nothing As It Seems."

The most common Type I showcase for Pearl Jam is one of their sturdiest radio hits, "Even Flow." At practically every concert ever performed by Pearl Jam, this song is an excuse for McCready to hammer away for several minutes while Gossard dutifully plays the recognizable riff over and over. (Surely, this was the song that inspired the *Washington Post* critic to pout about all the glorious noodling.)

Type II jamming is much less likely to happen at a Pearl Jam concert. And when it occurs, it never goes on as long as it does at a Dead or Phish

---

3 It should be noted, however, that Eddie Vedder's middle name is Jerome, so technically speaking he is a "Jerry."

show. But if Pearl Jam is going to get *really* out there, it's probably going to happen during their "seize the day" anthem, "Porch." On the 2006 tour, they played some of the longest and most exploratory versions of the *Ten* classic yet, including a thrillingly wild version from Albany, New York, that raged for twelve minutes, most of which was McCready wailing away over a stormy musical bed powered by Matt Cameron's polyrhythms and Gossard's surly counter melodies.

When you listen to the Albany "Porch," Pearl Jam once again sounds like a bridge band, only this time they are connecting the worlds of punk and the spaced-out hippie music that punk allegedly is meant to oppose. For a Generation X band, this was a quietly revolutionary development. As a music fan coming of age in the nineties, it was drilled into me that you either liked indie/punk/alternative music or you liked the hippie stuff. There was no middle ground.

I feel like my experience here is fairly common—as a teenager, I hated the Grateful Dead, in spite of not really knowing their music, because alt-rock stars like Kurt Cobain made a point of telling me to hate the Dead. If I had done my homework, I would have learned that the Grateful Dead rose to fame by slowly building a grassroots following via live shows and bootleg tapes. Their philosophy was essentially DIY—precisely the ideology to which punk and indie rockers aspired. Somehow, this wasn't abundantly obvious to kids like me in the nineties. But a decade later, this punk vs. hippie binary—like practically all Gen X binaries—began to break down. And recovering teenaged alt-rockers like me started becoming Deadheads in their twenties and thirties.

When Pearl Jam bridges that "punk vs. hippie" gap in their live performances, it often results in their best and most exciting music. But for the most part Pearl Jam tends to stick mainly on the "punk-inspired rock" side. They're just jammy enough to make it interesting—that also goes for never playing the same set list twice—but they don't push it quite as far as some of us "Jammers" would like.

When the media reached for the Dead as a comparison to explain Pearl Jam's connection to their fan base, they overlooked a more appropriate point of reference: Bruce Springsteen. Like Deadheads, Springsteen fanatics follow him on tour and obsessively collect bootlegs. And this is maintained by various online fan groups and publications that cater specifically to the most committed Boss-heads. And, like Pearl Jam, Springsteen's draw as a live act has always been greater than his record sales, even when his record sales were astronomical.[4]

What all these acts share is a strong sense of self coupled with a lack of interest in keeping up with the passing trends of the pop world. When you go to see Pearl Jam or Bruce or whatever iteration of the Dead is on the road, you are going to experience what it is that these people do. You don't want it "updated" or modernized. Part of what people love about these acts is how *unlike* modern pop culture they are. So much of what we see and hear dissipates from our memory banks the moment we first encounter them. But some things, to quote the Grateful Dead, were built to last.

Why keep up with the times when you can step *outside* time? By the mid-aughts, this was the path forward for Pearl Jam.

$$\displaystyle \frac{}{} \quad \text{⚡}$$

The irony of all the Grateful Dead comparisons is that they came in the wake of Pearl Jam's most overt "rock" album in more than a decade. Released on May 2, 2006, *Pearl Jam* was pitched directly at the heart of modern rock radio like none of their albums since *Ten*. The songs were short, punchy, and riff-y. They could even be described as *grungy* in the classic sense. It was as if they made an album for the same audience of casual fans that they had chased away after *Vitalogy*.

It's not that this was a strange choice, exactly. Given that they were on a new label and therefore invested in a "fresh" career reboot, it even seems logical. But the strident rockiness of "Avocado" and the counterculture crunchiness of their live show did result in some cognitive dissonance.

---

4 There is also the storytelling aspect of Springsteen's stage patter, which Vedder has emulated from the start of Pearl Jam's career. The patter at a Grateful Dead gig, meanwhile, consists mainly of Bob Weir saying, "Take a step back!"

For Vedder, the point of reestablishing ties with the mainstream media was communicating the new album's political content to the widest possible audience. These were the dog days of the George W. Bush years, when the United States was locked into two costly, fruitless wars in Iraq and Afghanistan. Many of the songs have character-based narratives about people who either are fighting a war or struggling to come to terms with the war at home.

Many of those tunes were written by Vedder, who at one point considered structuring the playlist into a concept album that would have followed the trajectory of a soldier's life. He eventually decided the album worked better with a different playlist and without an overarching story, but one can still play the album and imagine the kid in "Severed Hand" turning into the solider in "Army Reserve," who then suffers the fate of the fighter in "World Wide Suicide."[5]

That is, if you're actually paying attention to the lyrics. But "Avocado" doesn't really put much emphasis on the words. It is first and foremost a record about presenting Pearl Jam's music at its most bludgeoning. At its best, the album conveys the power of Pearl Jam's live show more effectively than any album since *Vs.* The problem is that the subtlety they developed on the early aughts tours is mostly lost. *Pearl Jam* reduces their music down to its most basic and raw elements in ways that are both viscerally exciting and not terribly interesting. It's like a sonic whippet—you feel exhilarated for a moment, and then the sensation quickly passes.

But in terms of delivering a short-term rush, "Avocado" did do its job. The first single, "World Wide Suicide," was their first real radio success since the fluke-y "Last Kiss." It held the no. 1 spot for three weeks on the *Billboard* Alternative Songs chart, and it even did surprisingly well on the Hot 100, peaking at no. 41. But what's more striking than the song's chart performance is how "World Wide Suicide" sounds like a band *trying* to

---

5 "Avocado" is a distant musical cousin of *American Idiot*, the landmark 2004 Green Day album that stands as the era's defining concept record. Vedder said in the *Pearl Jam Twenty* book that he intentionally avoided listening to *American Idiot* during the writing of the *Pearl Jam* songs so he wouldn't be influenced.

have a hit, which certainly wasn't the case for "Last Kiss" or many of Pearl Jam's singles in the early aughts.

"I don't think two or three years ago you could even get a song called 'World Wide Suicide' with the word *soldier* in it played on the radio," Vedder remarked upon the song's release. But again this presupposes that most listeners paid attention to the words, or cared that they were inspired by the life and death of Pat Tillman, the former Arizona Cardinals safety who enlisted after Sept. 11 and was later killed by friendly fire.

Ultimately, the delivery of "World Wide Suicide" overwhelms the message. It has an aggressive, angry, and hectoring edge that was endemic to rock radio in 2006. Pearl Jam's producer at the time, Adam Kasper, also helmed early aughts albums by Foo Fighters and Queens of the Stone Age that defined the hyper-masculine, gonad-heavy rock of the era. Given Nirvana's position in the early nineties as the underground foil to Pearl Jam's world-conquering anthems, it was quite the reversal of fortune for Dave Grohl to now be one of the chief architects of ubiquitous and highly commercial meat-and-potatoes rock in the new century. "World Wide Suicide" was Pearl Jam's attempt to write the sort of lumbering rock hit that the Foo Fighters had taken repeatedly to the bank in the new century. Though it did have more lyrical substance than Grohl's big hit at the time, "Best of You," in which Grohl screams about how something is the best for what feels like 4,563 times. That's not necessarily a criticism, because I like the song.[6] If "Best of You" isn't the best song ever about how something is the best, it is undeniably the *most* song about how something is the best.

Reestablishing their radio bona fides with "World Wide Suicide" had an obvious upside. Pearl Jam in 2006 was about as old as the Who were when Eddie Vedder saw them for the first time in 1980. And, like Pearl Jam, the Who had reached a younger audience with a recent radio hit, "You Better You Bet." Introducing themselves to kids who had been born around the time that *Ten* came out was necessary for their long-term survival, as was reminding the public of Pearl Jam's place in the rock continuum.

---

6 Who am I to argue with Prince, who performed it at the 2007 Super Bowl?

Young Turks like the Strokes and My Morning Jacket talked in the mid-aughts about how foundational Pearl Jam, befitting their elder statesmen status, had been for them as teenagers. But these testimonials were sometimes treated with skepticism by the same music press who assumed most of their readers had already given up Pearl Jam for dead. Right or wrong, Pearl Jam was perceived to be a nineties band instead of a *current* band. The success of "World Wide Suicide" helped to temporarily rectify that but only for the "Avocado" album cycle.

Why did this happen? Because Pearl Jam in 2006 didn't have the same advantages that the Who had in 1980. Around the time that young Eddie Vedder saw his first Who show, the classic-rock format infiltrated American radio for the first time, ensuring that the boomer generation of stadium bands would have a permanent place on the airwaves. Moreover, the Who songs played most often on those stations—the hits from *Who's Next* and *Who Are You*—were less than a decade old. Even when they were "classic," the Who could still position themselves as "current."

By 2006, Pearl Jam songs were already appearing on classic rock radio, but they were mostly songs from *Ten*, by then already fifteen years old. This fixed the band forever in a nostalgic moment for millions of casual listeners, a dilemma compounded by Gen Xers being vastly outnumbered by graying boomers and insurgent millennials. In the end, "World Wide Suicide" couldn't solve this problem because it wasn't a great song. The same can be said of the overall album. My feelings about it haven't really changed over the years—it goes down pure and easy when it's on, but once it's over I have a hard time remembering it.

"Avocado" delineates the difference between a comeback album and a "we're back!" album. A comeback album genuinely reestablishes a legacy act by producing songs that can stand with their most famous hits. *Tattoo You* by the Rolling Stones is a comeback record—it features songs like "Start Me Up" and "Waiting on a Friend" that became commercial hits and lasting fan favorites. A "we're back!" album, meanwhile, seeks to remind listeners of what they liked about a legacy band, so that they're compelled to reinvestigate the old records or buy a concert ticket without ever fully committing to the new record. *Voodoo Lounge* by the Rolling Stones is a "we're back!" record—it has a lot of tunes that sound like classic Stones songs, but it doesn't top or match those songs. It just makes you excited about putting on *Sticky Fingers* or *Some Girls* again.

"Avocado" is a "we're back!" album. It does a good job of showing Pearl Jam's vitality and dexterity as a live band without ever actually delivering memorable songs.

Actually, there is one exception to this, my favorite song on "Avocado," the relatively low-key and amiable loser ode, "Unemployable." It's one of the few tracks on the album that doesn't beat you over the head with how hard Pearl Jam is rocking your face off. The way it goes from the herky-jerky verse to the soaring chorus is graceful and kind of gentle, though the song's low-stakes aimlessness has a quietly tense undercurrent that mirrors the lyrics.

The guy in the song is a working stiff who has just been fired from his job for smashing up his work locker. Now he's stuck smoking cigarettes on the couch at home with thirty unpaid bills weighing him down. The predicament in "Unemployable" is as heightened as the scenario in any Pearl Jam song; this guy is facing a life-or-death crossroads moment. But he's also a middle-aged person, not the disillusioned teens or idealistic twenty-somethings who populate the band's early tunes. He's the sort of person who grew up with Pearl Jam and now it's fifteen years later and he's suddenly psyched to hear a record like "Avocado" . . . if he can only survive this really bad day.

So much of "Avocado" seemed to be about erasing the years that occurred between *Ten* and 2006. But "Unemployable" is the kind of song that only an older and wiser Pearl Jam could have written, and that's why it sticks with me. "World Wide Suicide" was inspired by a real-life, larger-than-life American hero, but "Unemployable" is about an anonymous journeyman just trying to get by. And that seemed more in the spirit of this band as they embraced their own journeyman status.[7]

---

7 It's the one Pearl Jam song I would liken to a Pavement song.

I know the ending of "Unemployable" is bleak—the final lines are "near to death / here to die / scared of life"—but I like to imagine a more uplifting fate for the guy in the song. Maybe he makes a friend. Maybe they hang out at the beach. Maybe his problems are solved when the friend invites him to play in his rock band. It seems unlikely. But we all know it's not impossible.

CHAPTER 16
"SIRENS"

(From *Lightning Bolt*)

My Sister's Wedding • *Backspacer* • Pearl Jam Turns Twenty • Power Ballads That Make Me Cry

In the summer of 2014, my sister asked me to officiate her wedding. But instead of focusing on the task at hand, I was distracted by the soundtrack. As my sister and her husband-to-be walked down the aisle, a familiar yet surprising song played on a nearby speaker. It was the delicate tune the couple had picked for their procession, a fingerpicked acoustic ditty sung by a guy with a low voice who considers himself "a lucky man to count on both hands the ones I love." A humble ode about gratitude and devotion that was entirely appropriate for the occasion, but nevertheless I was taken aback.

Why in the world is my sister getting married to a Pearl Jam song?

The specific Pearl Jam song in question was "Just Breathe," the most popular track from their ninth album, 2009's *Backspacer*. It is also likely the most well-known Pearl Jam track of the twenty-first century. As of 2021, it has been streamed more times on Spotify than any Pearl Jam song released since 2000. To my astonishment, it's more popular on the platform than two other big ballads from the previous century, "Daughter" and "Better Man." It has even been covered by multiple artists, a rarity for a Pearl Jam tune, including Willie Nelson and Miley Cyrus.

And then there's the anecdotal evidence of my sister's wedding. She was born in 1990, about a year and a half before the release of *Ten*. (And exactly thirteen days before Andrew Wood's death.) I know for a fact that she knows next to nothing about Pearl Jam. I could play her "Alive" or "Jeremy" and elicit nothing but a blank stare. But she knew of "Just Breathe"—not necessarily as a Pearl Jam track, but as a *wedding song*.

The songwriter, Eddie Vedder, surely did not have this possibility in mind for "Just Breathe" when he brought it to the *Backspacer* sessions. Vedder came in with just one verse and a chorus, and he intended to put it at the end of the record as a brief postscript, like how Paul McCartney's charming but barely sketched out "Her Majesty" concludes the Beatles' *Abbey Road*. But Brendan O'Brien insisted on giving "Just Breathe" the full star treatment—gooey strings, a plush "Wichita Lineman"–style bass tone, and a tender arrangement that would dare listeners to not tear up. The goal was, in O'Brien's words, to make "the most beautiful Pearl Jam song ever."

Surely there were beautiful Pearl Jam songs before "Just Breathe"— "Release," "Nothingman," "Immortality," "Elderly Woman Behind the Counter in a Small Town," "Wishlist," "Thumbing My Way." But "Just Breathe" is beautiful in a *pop* sense. There's nothing remotely rock 'n' roll about it. It invites the sort of person without any connection to the band, like my sister, to integrate it into one of the most important occasions of their lives. It doesn't matter who Pearl Jam is in the context of "Just Breathe," just as a billion people love "Good Riddance (Time of Your Life)" without caring about any other Green Day song. "Just Breathe" has an identity that's entirely separate from the band.

It's also the kind of song you couldn't imagine Pearl Jam even considering putting on a record in the nineties. It's not merely a love ballad, or a slow number with some sensitive emoting. It is openly and unapologetically sentimental. It's about as cool as your great-aunt Ethel.

A decade before "Just Breathe," Pearl Jam fretted constantly about their credibility. Now they were *deliberately* making the most beautiful music in their catalog. You could take this as evidence that Pearl Jam—like practically every legacy rock band that has ever existed across several decades—got lamer as they grew older.

You could also, like me, not be bothered by this because you recognize that we all get lamer as we age. Getting lamer is a privilege.

⚡

As the aughts turned into the 2010s, and Pearl Jam celebrated their twentieth anniversary in 2011, it was clear that a new feeling of unselfconscious contentment had settled in for the band. The tumult of the nineties was a distant memory—the members of Pearl Jam lived great lives, and there (finally) appeared to be few qualms about openly enjoying it.

These are Pearl Jam's "dad rock" years, a period when they covered the kiddie hit "Let It Go" from the *Frozen* soundtrack live in concert to please Eddie Vedder's daughter.[1] They also started playing massive concerts in baseball stadiums every couple of years and even made the Chicago Cubs' 2016 World Series run the central narrative of their 2017 concert film, *Let's Play Two*, a true dad move. My favorite scene in the film is when the guys are hanging out on the rooftop of Murphy's Bleachers, the iconic Wrigleyville bar. And then they start jamming on Steely Dan's "Dirty Work," an appropriate choice for a group of middle-aged guys who now resemble extra-fit financial advisors who get together on the weekend for beers, mountain biking, and the occasional jam session.[2]

---

1 This occurred at a concert in Milan on June 20, 2014, as part of an extended version of "Daughter."

2 The biggest shock of this scene is that Eddie Vedder apparently doesn't know that "Dirty Work" is a Steely Dan song. I hope he picked up *Can't Buy a Thrill* after this embarrassing gaffe.

These developments inevitably made Pearl Jam seem less cool in their middle age, though it's debatable that "being less cool" is a status that any middle-aged rock band can avoid. If you study rock history, there are some obvious commonalities that occur once a band enters their second or third decade. You might notice that everyone's hair color is unnaturally dark, a sure sign that some dye has been applied to blot out gray hairs. Onstage, the tempos start to lag a bit. And the vocals sound a little haggard, as it's harder for the singer to catch his breath. At some point, a representative from the label will suggest hiring Don Was or Rick Rubin to produce your "comeback" album. The idea will be to either "update" your sound with drum machines and synthesizers, or to completely "strip back" to guitar and harmonica so it sounds as though you're performing on your deathbed. Or, if the situation is truly dire, writers-for-hire like Glen Ballard or Desmond Child will be brought in to help you make a hit. But the most important person on staff will be the personal trainer whose job it is to help your crew of weathered forty-eight-year-old rockers pass for relatively youthful thirty-seven-year-old whippersnappers.

Pearl Jam has avoided many of those pitfalls. But their trajectory isn't all that unusual for a band that sticks around as the members age into their fifties. This is what it means to "fade away," in the parlance of the Neil Young song "My, My, Hey, Hey (Into the Black)." Anyone still inclined to compare Pearl Jam unfavorably to Nirvana will point out that Kurt Cobain never wrote a wedding song. Kurt burned out. He has the street cred that only a dead person can have. Unfortunately for Kurt, this is the only advantage of being a dead person. Otherwise, being dead is a terrible way to live.

What separates Pearl Jam from other legacy rock bands is their apparent lack of vanity about growing older. Mick Jagger, Bono, and Dave Grohl are all deeply concerned with maintaining a certain profile in pop culture. Anytime the Rolling Stones, U2, or the Foo Fighters put out a record, the front men of those bands expend a lot of effort to make their albums actual hits among pop listeners. They are, in a sense, attempting to trick the public into forgetting that they are old white men who have virtually nothing in common with contemporary young people.

Pearl Jam has never done this. They are a middle-aged rock band that looks and acts like a middle-aged rock band.³ This is not to say that their tours in the 2010s lack vitality or energy. On the contrary, Pearl Jam works very hard to minimize the adverse effects of aging on their concerts. They play longer, and harder, than they ever have, and they make *a point* of doing it. This is part of the unspoken, Springsteen-esque contract that Pearl Jam has with its audience—if you still show up, we'll still present ourselves as the rock band you know and love.

But Pearl Jam doesn't pretend to care as much about teen angst as they did in the nineties, like Mick Jagger still obsesses about getting laid even as a man in his eighties who must in fact prefer the satisfaction of a good nap. The guys in Pearl Jam don't even seem to have much *middle-aged* angst. How angry can you be when it's your job to play songs you wrote thirty years ago for millions of dollars per gig?

Pearl Jam's situation is so comfortable at this point that it's not remotely relatable for the average person. But the average person can relate to "Just Breathe." It's a song about a person who has built a nice family life for himself, and he feels grateful that he was able to pull it off. When Pearl Jam made *Ten*, Eddie Vedder was a guy in his midtwenties who was still traumatized by having never really known his birth father. He was a broken man from a broken home. But by the time of *Backspacer*, he was a father himself, and it calmed him. It would have been a lie to claim otherwise.⁴ He was no longer railing against dads. He was making music *for* dads.

---

3 Perhaps the most middle-aged musical move of this period was Eddie Vedder releasing an album of songs played on a ukulele, appropriately titled *Ukulele Songs*, in 2011.

4 Vedder's father issues were apparently cured by none other than Bruce Springsteen during the 2004 Vote for Change tour, in which the two bonded. "He exposed me to some truths that he'd processed in a healthy way, that for me were still in a diseaselike state. He helped me cure some things I had been living with for a long time." Having

Calm can be dangerous for a rock band, especially one that once thrived on drama. But you need a little calm if you want to avoid self-immolating. For the audience, it might even provide a model for how to live.

$$\lightning$$

When *Backspacer* was released on September 20, 2009, the first single was not the album's eventual most popular track, "Just Breathe." It was a likeable, New-Wave-accented-rocker called "The Fixer." It's a pattern you can see recurring throughout Pearl Jam's career—release a "rock" single first, and then put out a "pretty" song that will eventually become the album's signature track. "Go" came out before "Daughter" on the *Vs.* album cycle, and "Spin the Black Circle" and "Not for You" preceded "Immortality" during the run of *Vitalogy*. When Pearl Jam's tenth LP, *Lightning Bolt*, came out on October 15, 2013, the pummeling quasi-punk of "Mind Your Matters" introduced the record to radio, and then the mid-tempo power ballad "Sirens" arrived as a thoughtful follow-up.

"It's an old way of thinking from back in the eighties and nineties that you want to come out and rock first," Stone Gossard admitted years later in an interview. "So I think we were still in that mindset of feeling like we wanted to come out hard."

As is the case with the "Avocado" record, the "hard" songs on *Backspacer* and *Lightning Bolt* are impressive displays of physicality that convey the excitement of seeing Pearl Jam even at an advanced age. As actual songs, however, they don't resonate all that much emotionally or musically. They kick up a lot of energy, and they're sung and played with considerable force and skill. But they also feel tossed off, acting more as demonstrations of the band's prowess than as genuine statements of purpose. They're just plain dull.

Bruce Springsteen act as your therapist is one of the many reasons why it's amazing to be Eddie Vedder.

On those albums, the slow songs are consistently more compelling and urgent, no matter the trappings of lightly strummed guitars and swelling string sections. In the nineties, Pearl Jam songs hinged on matters of life or death and were delivered with the maximum aggression of a person pleading for life with a gun to his head. Twenty years later, that intensity was now delivered in the hushed tones of men who have finally found homes in which they can "just breathe." Their early work was about fighting for your own place in the world; their later work was preoccupied with the fear of *losing* that hard-won place.

Songs like "Just Breathe," "Amongst the Waves," "Unthought Known," and "The End" from *Backspacer* and "Sirens," "Pendulum," and "Future Days" from *Lightning Bolt* address that fear head-on, either in the guise of philosophizing about mortality or reflecting on the peace that comes with sharing your life with people who love you unconditionally. In "Amongst the Waves," Vedder once again uses a surfing metaphor to describe how love has saved him from drowning. "Unthought Known" uses a hiking analogy to address the same subject matter ("Feel the path of every day / Which road you taking?). "Future Days" drops the sportsman symbolism to explicitly extol the virtues of family life: "If I ever were to lose you / I'd surely lose myself." But loss can't be avoided, as Vedder sings in "Pendulum": "We are here and then we go."

Like "Unemployable," these are songs that Pearl Jam could have performed at only *this* time of their career, after they had weathered so many trials and tribulations and come out stronger on the other side. That's why they register more powerfully than the "hard" songs, which sound like evocations of a version of themselves from when they were "young and less amazed," to quote "Amongst the Waves." Ultimately, they feel a little phony because that "young and less amazed" version of Pearl Jam no longer actually exists.

Of Pearl Jam's "mortality" songs, "The End" is the most startling. It shares a title with the 1967 classic by the Doors, in which Jim Morrison shares his Oedipal fantasies about killing his father and screwing his mother. Surely it was a song that influenced, knowingly or not, the similarly provocative "Momma-Son" songs. But in Pearl Jam's "The End," Eddie Vedder puts aside such childish outrageousness, singing with shocking directness, "I just want to grow old."

I just want to grow old. Really? Imagine Jim Morrison (or Kurt Cobain) ever singing *that.* He's talking about the comfort of a long-term relationship, and the knowledge that it will not last forever, so it must be affirmed and appreciated each day, a running theme that connects the song to "Just Breathe" and "Amongst the Waves." The song's final lines give *Backspacer* an unexpectedly jarring ending: "I'm here, but not much longer."

The most moving song from this era for me is also the most dad-centric. The first time I heard "Sirens," I thought it sounded like a contemporary country song. The twangy guitar hook and stately pacing was reminiscent of a Tim McGraw ballad about sharing a romantic dinner with your wife in the back of a pickup truck. I reflexively rolled my eyes at it. But over time, "Sirens" got under my skin. Now, I can't hear it without choking up.

Mike McCready, who wrote the music, was originally inspired not by Tim McGraw, but by seeing Roger Waters perform *The Wall* live in concert in the early '10s. While he didn't mention the song specifically as a reference, "Sirens" most resembles *The Wall*'s most ravishing track, "Comfortably Numb." The song's bridge features the greatest lyrics that Waters ever composed, in which he writes (from the perspective of the album's drugged-out rock star protagonist) about glimpsing his own innocence disappear. "The child is grown, the dream is gone," Pink Floyd guitarist David Gilmour sings before ripping another long, majestic solo.[5]

When Vedder penned lyrics to McCready's music, he wrote about his own loss of innocence, only through the lens of being a husband and father who worries at night when he hears sirens coming outside the comfortable

---

5 Pearl Jam debuted a live cover of "Comfortably Numb" on November 11, 2015, at a concert in Porto Alegre, Brazil, and played it more than two-dozen times in the late 2010s. Before that, Eddie Vedder performed the song with its cowriter, Roger Waters, at the 12-12-12 Hurricane Sandy benefit at Madison Square Garden in 2012, and then again with Waters at a concert in Chicago in 2017.

confines of his bedroom. In a distant time, the central character in a Pearl Jam song would have been the person *causing* those sirens. But in "Sirens," Eddie is merely listening to them, and it's making him think (what else?) about how death and loss walk hand in hand with the very best parts of being alive.

In the song, he confesses that thinking too much overwhelms him. But he can't help but be amazed by how people have the grace to carry on each day "with death over our shoulders." It's only when he turns to the person next to him, the one he loves, and "studies" her face that "the fear goes away."

The guy in the song—let's just call him "Eddie Vedder," who resembles the actual Eddie Vedder but is not necessarily the actual Eddie Vedder—might as well be the same guy in "Indifference," who might as well be the same guy in Bruce Springsteen's "Wreck on the Highway." The guy in "Indifference" has trouble getting out of bed because he can't see the point of it; he hasn't yet found a sense of meaning or purpose in his life. By the time of "Sirens," however, that same guy has found his meaning, and now his devotion to others has made him more concerned for their well-being than his own. Like the haunted character at the center of "Wreck on the Highway," he sits up at night and wonders how he will hold his blessed but fleeting life together, even as the universe conspires to pull it apart slowly but surely over time.

Songs like "Just Breathe" and "Sirens" are not "hard." They may in fact strike some as "soft." But they are actually "heavy" in the ways that matter most, dealing with the very essence of what it means to be alive when you reach the point when you have the most to lose. They also came along at an opportune time if you happened to grow up with Pearl Jam—Eddie Vedder is hardly the only person who felt like "Indifference" in his twenties and "Sirens" in his forties. For that listener, you might very well need a song like "Sirens" more than "Mind Your Manners." The latter is a fun and frivolous fantasy where you never have to grow old and you can stay a young punk forever. The former recognizes a shared reality in terms that couldn't be clearer.

If you're still in your twenties, the meaning of "Sirens" might be elusive. But trust me: It will hit home sooner than you think. And it will hit hard.

CHAPTER 17
"MAYBE IT'S TIME"

(9/29/19, Dana Point, California)

Bradley Cooper's Eddie Vedder Impression • The Death of Chris Cornell • *Walk Hard* • The Rock 'n' Roll Hall of Fame Induction • *Gigaton*

You either die a hero or you live long enough to become the villain. But there's also a third option. Sometimes, you can live long enough to see yourself become an archetype. And if that happens, there's a good chance that most of your contemporaries perished as young heroes.

This is what happened to Eddie Vedder by the end of the 2010s. He was the rock star that actors literally studied to learn how to pretend to be a rock star onscreen. Well, at least one actor did this: Bradley Cooper spent several days with Eddie before filming his debut directorial effort, the 2018 mega-hit *A Star Is Born*, in which he also stars as troubled Americana singer-songwriter Jackson Maine.

Cooper made sure to go the full method route as he prepared to steer the fourth version of *A Star Is Born*. While each film was updated to reflect the dominant trends in entertainment at the time they were released—the previous versions were released in 1937, 1954, and 1976—the story is always essentially the same: A man who is famous and successful but also stymied by alcoholism meets a woman who is not famous or successful but has the talent to become a star. Man and woman fall in love, and then the man starts to fall apart while the woman commences her rise to the top. Of course the story ends in tragedy for all involved parties. It's a formula for melodrama that truly applies to any and all eras.

It's not clear what rock star knowledge Vedder imparted on Cooper. "Make sure your guitar covers your balls at all times" was one piece of advice that Eddie said he gave the actor. Otherwise he was mum on what was shared. There must be a charter among rock singers that is similar to the code of silence followed by magicians—you don't reveal the tricks of the trade. (I'm sorry—*illusions* of the trade.) You must keep the public in the dark in order for the *illusions* to seem real. Otherwise, the audience will realize that the secret to pulling off a magical rock show comes down to merely keeping your ax in front of your testicles. And like that, the mystical spell will be broken.

Then again, when you watch *A Star Is Born*, it's clear that Cooper wasn't so much soliciting Vedder's advice as he was studying his mannerisms and speech patterns. He doesn't perform an Eddie Vedder impersonation in the film, but you can tell that he's riffing on an *idea* of Eddie Vedder, zeroing in on his soulful masculinity and wounded stoicism. As Jackson Maine, Cooper speaks a few octaves lower than normal, and draws out words like he's mentally inspecting each syllable with maximum thoughtfulness. His longish, walnut brown hair hangs just above his shoulders and is frequently tucked behind the ears, greasily framing his hangdog face. He exudes low-key charisma but never seems to go out of his way to get your attention. He simply commands it by being who he is. That's Jackson Maine in *A Star Is Born*. That's also Eddie Vedder in real life.

In the wake of the film's release, Vedder made a highly meta move: He covered one of his fictional doppelganger's signature songs, "Maybe

It's Time." He did this at least three times—first in Tempe, Arizona, in March 2019, one month after *A Star Is Born* won one Oscar (Best Original Song, for the instant karaoke classic "Shallow") out of eight nominations, including Best Picture; once in Berlin that June; and then again three months later in Dana Point, California, at the Ohana Festival with Lukas Nelson, Willie's son, who plays Jackson Maine's lead guitarist in the film.

Written by the great singer-songwriter Jason Isbell,[1] "Maybe It's Time" is about the struggle to change and the need to accept that some things will just happen whether we like it or not. The title is the first part of a Zen-like phrase that recurs throughout the song—it concludes with "to let the old ways die." In the movie, the song doubles as a comment on Maine's own professional predicament as his career starts to fade and his wife, Ally (played by Lady Gaga), ascends to pop superstardom. "The old ways" include the roughhewn country-rock that once put Jackson in stadiums and arenas and now seems antiquated next to the slick dance-pop songs about how asses look hot in tight jeans that Ally is singing.

I doubt that Vedder extended that read on "Maybe It's Time" to his own status as an alt-rock elder statesman in an age of social media insta-phenoms born around the time of the *Riot Act* tour. He certainly wasn't about to let *his* old ways die just yet. I also don't think he played "Maybe It's Time" simply as a self-referential joke. (Though I'm sure he also found it at least a little funny to dedicate it—as he did in California—to his "good friend Jack.")

"Maybe It's Time" just happens to sound a lot like a song that Vedder *could* have written for a late-period Pearl Jam album. It has a similar flavor to the mortality ballads on *Backspacer* and *Lightning Bolt*, the songs where Vedder takes stock of an uncertain world and expresses gratitude for the unconditional love and foundational stability provided by his family.

---

1 Jackson Maine in some ways also resembles Isbell, who has struggled with addiction but has thankfully been sober since the early 2010s.

Though in the end "Maybe It's Time" is more fatalistic and haunted than those Pearl Jam tunes.

"Nobody knows what awaits for the dead," the song goes. Eddie Vedder is not a believer, but he is a staunch humanist and enough of an optimist to give this line an ounce of hope. We may not be bound for heaven, but surely we are all connected by our shared humanity, and in that way we can achieve a measure of immortality through the lives and memories of those we leave behind. Think of it that way, and not knowing what awaits after we're gone no longer conjures existential fear. You can simply let the unanswerable question slip away with all the other unanswerable questions.

In that way, Eddie is unlike Jackson Maine. For Jackson, the question of what awaits for the dead does have an answer: nothing. Just as life also offers nothing. This leads to the ultimate act of self-negation.

⚡

Things do not end well for Jackson. (If you haven't seen *A Star Is Born*, you might want to skip ahead to later in this chapter. Or you could decide to not care about spoilers because the ending is telegraphed well in advance and knowing for sure what happens won't ruin the film.) For a while, he appears to be on the mend. He goes to rehab, takes up swimming, and reconciles with his majestically mustachioed brother (played by the frequently majestically mustachioed Sam Elliott). He returns to Ally and pledges his support of her career. It looks like he has his legs back.

Then Ally's conniving manager (Rafi Gavron) knocks out his legs. He calls him a liability to his wife. He says it's inevitable that he will fall off the wagon. And he all but declares that the world would be better off without him.

From there, it's no surprise when Jackson goes to his garage, backs out his truck, walks inside the garage, closes the door, and hangs himself.

Vedder has said that he was blown away by the film. On *The Howard Stern Show* in 2020, he said, "It really took me there. I'm getting chills right now." What he didn't remark upon was the obvious parallel to a real-life rock star who hung himself nearly seventeen months before the movie premiered.

While Bradley Cooper might have modeled his exterior after the look and sound of Eddie Vedder, the soul of the character is closer to Vedder's friend, Chris Cornell. Like Jackson Maine, Cornell had a history with addiction, but he seemed to have come out of that darkness. On the night of May 17, 2017, he played for five thousand people at the Fox Theater in Detroit with his longtime brothers in Soundgarden, including Matt Cameron, who joined the tour a month after he was inducted in the Rock & Roll Hall of Fame with Pearl Jam.

In light of what happened next, some fans felt that Cornell sounded off that night. His voice was a touch hoarse, and he was sluggish in comparison with the rest of the band. But videos posted online of the night's final song—"Slaves & Bulldozers" from 1991's *Badmotorfinger*, with an interpolation of Led Zeppelin's "In My Time of Dying"—hardly suggest a train wreck. It's a perfectly professional and reliably powerful rendition performed by a guy who appears to have every intention of making it to the next Soundgarden gig two days later in Columbus, Ohio.

But Cornell never made it to Columbus. Instead, he retired to his room at the MGM Grand Detroit. He phoned his wife, Vicky, who noticed he was slurring his words. Worried that he had taken an anxiety medication with a known side effect of prompting suicidal thoughts, she asked the band's security to check on him. After they broke down his door, they discovered Cornell in the bathroom with blood running from his mouth and a red exercise band wrapped around his neck. He was fifty-two.

In the days after Cornell's death, there was talk about Eddie Vedder being the "last" of the nineties rock stars. "Only Eddie Vedder is left," the *Washington Post* declared. "Let that sink in." Not that this was true, really. If Trent Reznor, Billy Corgan, Courtney Love, Liz Phair, PJ Harvey, or Thom Yorke read that *Washington Post* headline, they must have felt some mix of indignation and bemusement.

But it was accurate when it came to the class of superstar bands from Seattle that emerged in the early nineties. Out of the "big four" grunge bands, three of them now had dead lead singers. Kurt Cobain took his own life in 1994. Then Layne Staley committed a form of slow-motion suicide throughout the late nineties, eventually disappearing from Alice in Chains and public view in order to devote himself to heroin full-time. When he died in 2002, his body was left undiscovered for two weeks as it sat upright on a couch in front of a flickering television.

And then there was Cornell, who was especially important to Vedder. Back when Eddie was just a nobody from San Diego, Cornell was one of the few people in the Seattle music scene who didn't give the outsider a hard time. In fact, he made it a point to hang out with the shy new kid in town. They went hiking and mountain biking together. They drank crappy beer and goofed off. It was as if they had been friends for years, even though Chris was already something of a rock star. He surely *looked* like a rock star on the cover of 1989's *Louder Than Love*, with his long, impeccably tousled hair and strikingly shirtless torso distinguishing Soundgarden's major-label debut.

They came together publicly on "Hunger Strike," the big power ballad written by Cornell that helped to cement Eddie Vedder's rock star status. In *A Star Is Born*, Jackson Maine invites Ally onstage to perform an impromptu duet on the film's signature song, "Shallow." At that point, he's the star and she's the unknown. But from then on, their fates head in opposite directions. It's the first step toward her coronation and his dissolution. "Hunger Strike" proved to be a similar nexus moment for Eddie Vedder and Chris Cornell.

Does Eddie Vedder ever wonder why he made it and so many of his peers didn't? Was he lucky? Did he figure out some secret cheat code to rock star survival? As it is, Eddie is the only legendary Seattle singer from his generation who *isn't* Jackson Maine. He's more of an Ally—the person who loved Jackson Maine and now is forced to reckon with what he left behind.

$$\pmb{\prime}$$

Covering "Maybe It's Time" isn't the only, or the funniest, example of Eddie Vedder being self-referential. There is also his cameo in the 2007 film *Walk Hard: The Dewey Cox Story*, which immediately leap-frogged Vedder's appearance in *Singles* as the finest example of acting in the Pearl Jam canon. It helps that Eddie is playing himself, and he's performing a task he's pulled off admirably in his real life numerous times.

Walk Hard: The Dewey Cox Story stars John C. Reilly as Dewey Cox, a fifties rocker who goes through all the usual *Behind the Music* pitfalls— fame goes to his head, he turns to drugs, he dabbles in psychedelia, his career goes into the toilet, he repents, and he has an unlikely professional resurgence late in life. If that sounds like a collection of bad clichés, that's the point. *Walk Hard* is a brilliant parody of rock biopics, from *Walk the Line* to *Bohemian Rhapsody*, which was actually released eleven years after *Walk Hard* and yet commits all the narrative conventions that the film ruthlessly skewers.

Eddie comes in at the end, when Dewey is about to receive a lifetime achievement award. It's his job to give a speech honoring the man, and he admirably delivers the hilariously purple prose with nary a trace of a smile.

"We heard him sing about walking hard and we learned a little something about how we wanted to walk. What do we think about when we think about Cox?" he says in an impassioned deadpan, letting the double-entendre land without pushing it even a little bit. "He's been called the drifter, also the shape shifter, the master chef, the chameleon, the problem child, the hard one, the white Indian, the giant midget."

The speech is a pitch-perfect satire of award-show pomposity that's funny even if you haven't seen a million induction ceremonies for the Rock & Roll Hall of Fame.[2] But if you *have* seen a million induction ceremonies for the Rock & Roll Hall of Fame, then you know that Vedder has given four speeches over the years, honoring the Doors, Neil Young, the Ramones, and R.E.M. None of them are close to being as over-the-top as the speech in *Walk Hard*. The most memorable was his induction

---

2 My favorite Vedder bit from *Walk Hard* didn't make it in the movie. It wasn't seen until the special extended cut for home video. Vedder intones, "If Elvis and Buddy Holly are the Cain and Abel of rock and roll, Bruce Springsteen is Zachariah, Iggy Pop is Methuselah, of course Neil Young is the wise prophet Ezekiel, what does that make Dewey Cox?"

speech for the Ramones in 2002, when he appeared onstage in a shocking mohawk. Though the actual speech was meandering and, at times,
incoherent (everything about Pearl Jam was a little incoherent in the early
aughts). The R.E.M. speech in 2007 was much better, eloquently articu-
lating the band's greatness and importance with the same tender sensitivity he brings to Pearl Jam's most insightful songs.

It makes sense that Eddie was asked to do this so many times. He's
good at giving speeches about music he loves. And he's always been very
public—and generous—about being a fan and paying homage. But
there's also an element in which he and the other members of Pearl Jam
are students of rock band career arcs. They have examined these histories
closely—first as fans, and then as a means of self-preservation. Along with
learning from their own experiences, they applied their graduate-level
rock nerd knowledge to avoiding a lot of the old disasters, professional and
personal, that destroyed other bands. It can't be a coincidence that Eddie
has all this knowledge *while also* being one of the few rock stars of his peer
group to persevere.

When Pearl Jam themselves were inducted in 2017, they mostly avoided
platitudes and grandiosity. The five of them stood onstage with their first
drummer Dave Krusen, looking like the CEOs of a hip and hugely successful tech company. They wore dark jackets, dark shirts, and no ties. They
thanked their crew and management. They thanked their wives. (Matt
Cameron nervously mangled his own last name when mentioning his partner, April.) They naturally thanked the fans. Stone Gossard actually referred
to them as "one big happy Jamily," which was only slightly awkward.

Then it was Vedder's turn to speak. He was less polished than when he
inducted others in the Rock Hall. It must have been a heady experience
to finally be the one enshrined into semi-immortality. He was dutifully
humbled and awed. He even called Dave Abbruzzese "a great fucking
drummer," after Abbruzzese made a stink in the press ahead of time about
not being invited to the ceremony.

For Vedder, the speech boiled down to a theme that had become dominant on recent Pearl Jam albums. And this was one month before Chris

Cornell died. Which meant it would only loom larger as the members of Pearl Jam prepared to enter their senior years.

"Lucky and grateful are two things I am every day," he said. "I'm just grateful to be alive."

$$\lightning$$

During Eddie Vedder's induction speech for Neil Young in 1995, he made a salient point that probably bruised more than a few aging egos in the audience. "I don't know if there's been another artist that's been inducted into the Rock 'n' Roll Hall of Fame to commemorate a career that is still as vital as he is today," Vedder said. "Some of his best songs were on his last record."

Few would have said the same about Pearl Jam upon their induction. That's not a slight to their later work as much as it is an observation about how little "later" work there has been. The 2010s were by far their least active as a recording act, with only one album, *Lightning Bolt*. The follow-up to that record didn't arrive for another seven years, their longest gap between albums. It's the same length of time it took Pearl Jam to release their first four albums and record a fifth in the nineties.

When it finally came out on March 27, 2020, *Gigaton* felt minor and anticlimactic for reasons far bigger than any rock album. Earlier that month, much of the world went into shutdown mode to mitigate the spread of COVID-19. There would be no tour in support of the album, or much of a promotional campaign at all. There were a handful of interviews, and a strange PR gimmick in which Pearl Jam fans were encouraged to point their phones at the moon to trigger a snippet of the single "Superblood Wolfmoon." Otherwise, like pretty much every other album released at the time, *Gigaton* came and went as everyone grappled with a life-and-death pandemic.

Well, I shouldn't say "everyone." I reviewed *Gigaton* when it came out, so I was professionally obliged to care. I also felt personally invested as someone who had followed Pearl Jam now for two-thirds of my life.

Sequenced by Vedder out of a mountain of material they had amassed over the course of several years, *Gigaton* sounds like a survey of Pearl Jam's twenty-first century work, starting inevitably with rote, Who-like rockers like "Who Ever Said" and "Superblood Wolfmoon" that recall the similarly leaden headbangers from the previous three albums. The standout of this section is "Dance of the Clairvoyants," a rare nod to Vedder's love of David Byrne and Talking Heads that on paper absolutely should not work but in practice somehow does.

The middle part of the album is moodier and more experimental, recalling the band's early aughts work. "Take the Long Way" is mostly boilerplate rock leavened with some refreshing psychedelic passages while the odd "Buckle Up" resembles the whimsical prog-folk of Jethro Tull. If *Gigaton* had ended here, it would have landed in the same "solid if unspectacular" zone as the previous three albums. But the closing trio of tunes—in which the band returns to matters of mortality and existential, quasi-apocalyptic struggle—made *Gigaton* sound surprisingly relevant in the moment.

Two of these songs, "Retrograde" and "River Cross," nod to *Gigaton*'s overall theme of climate change.[3] The third track, "Comes Then Goes," is more personal, seemingly addressing the loss of a loved one. In the song, Vedder sings about searching in vain for his friend. But he knows this person is gone forever. Now he's just trying to understand why. "Evidence in the echoes of your mind / Leads to me to believe we missed the signs," he sings.

Is he singing about Cornell? Is he singing about all the Gen X rock stars who have died before their time? All that's clear is that "Comes Then Goes" is about an unresolvable feeling that's also universal. If "Maybe It's Time" is sung from the point of view of a person who ultimately chooses to let *himself* die, "Comes Then Goes" is a song for those who are left behind, the people whose time to die has not yet come.

---

3 The title and the album cover refer to the disappearing polar ice caps, which are losing between 92 and 159 gigatons—one gigaton is 1,000,000,000 tons—per year.

I don't think *Gigaton* is a great Pearl Jam album. But in March 2020, during a pandemic that was in the process of wreaking so much death and illness on millions of people, it felt like a salve. I liked how normal life felt when it was on. I appreciated that Eddie was struggling to process all this loss just like the rest of us.

After all this time and in the aftermath of so many disasters, Pearl Jam was still here. And simply being here was enough.

CHAPTER 18
"YELLOW LEDBETTER"

(4/29/16, Philadelphia)

The Ultimate Encore Closer As the Ultimate Book Closer

When Eddie Vedder awoke in Philadelphia on the morning of April 29, 2016, he did not plan on making Pearl Jam history. It wasn't until the venue they were playing that night reminded him that Pearl Jam history had already been made that he felt duly inspired.

As he would later explain to the audience gathered at the Wells Fargo Center for the second of two concerts, Vedder was moved by an "extremely kind" gesture on behalf of the city's multipurpose arena to hang a banner in the rafters commemorating Pearl Jam's tenth sold-out show in south Philadelphia. The band had been coming to the city for almost the entirety of their existence, dating all the way back to July 12, 1991, when they played J. C. Dobbs, an iconic south-side club that in its heyday hosted the cream of the nineties alt-rock generation—including Nirvana, Rage Against the Machine, and Green Day—before they achieved multiplatinum stardom. Pearl Jam played the venue six weeks before *Ten* even came out. The show would later be remembered by the band's fan-historians as marking the live debuts of "Oceans" and "State of Love and Trust." But, really, for anyone in the audience that night, *all* the songs would have been unfamiliar.

But that was all ancient history now. Just six months before Pearl Jam's two-show stand at the Wells Fargo Center, J. C. Dobbs closed its doors, ending a forty-one-year run. Pearl Jam had outlived another nineties rock institution.

For Vedder, the significance of the "10" banner set to be raised in the city's arena caused him to call a rather on-the-nose—but nonetheless sure to be popular—audible for that night's set list: Pearl Jam would open by playing all of *Ten* in its entirely, a near quarter-century after its release.

While this concert would go down as an instant classic from the moment that news of the set list hit the internet, playing an album in its entirety was hardly unprecedented for Pearl Jam. About two weeks before the so-called "*Ten* show" in Philadelphia, on April 16, they played their second album, *Vs.*, from front-to-back at Bon Secours Wellness Arena in Greenville, South Carolina. And then, about two weeks after Philadelphia, on May 10, they performed their sixth LP, *Binaural*, at the Air Canada Centre in Toronto.

This echoed a pattern of short-lived "full album" frenzy that occurred in 2014 during the *Lightning Bolt* tour when Pearl Jam was moved to play a set of the complete *No Code* on October 17 at the iWireless Center in Moline, Illinois, and then, on October 20, all of *Yield* at the BMO Harris Bradley Center in Milwaukee.[1]

Taking a broader perspective, "full album" concert tours became the norm among aging legacy rock bands in the 2010s. Around the time that Pearl Jam performed three of their records in their entirety in the spring of 2016, Bruce Springsteen and the E Street Band mounted a major international concert campaign in support of a new box set celebrating their

---

1 I was at this show!

thirty-six-year-old double album, 1980's *The River*, a gambit that resulted in that year's highest-grossing tour, ultimately netting just over $268 million.

Springsteen was following the lead of Roger Waters, who had similarly earned hundreds of millions of dollars on the road by reviving his own 1979 classic-rock landmark, *The Wall*, in arenas and stadiums all over the world. In 2017, U2 would be similarly moved to play their best-selling album, 1987's *The Joshua Tree*, for a thirtieth anniversary tour that grossed $317 million, which topped that year's highest concert earners and eventually spawned an additional leg in 2019 that made another $73.8 million.

The appeal of these tours for audiences was their absence of creative pretension. Fans would not be expected to humor the egos of rock stars by pretending to care about a new, late-period album that few wanted to hear. They would instead get precisely the songs they loved, and in the exact order they had always consumed them. What purists might describe as a mercenary ploy to exploit the audience's basest and most nostalgic impulses could also be viewed, from a more pragmatic perspective, as an acknowledgment that rock 'n' roll, before anything else, is a form of mass entertainment that loses its power when it fails to neither reach the masses nor entertain.

Even Pearl Jam's Gen X peers were getting in on the act—the Pixies, Public Enemy, Weezer, and Sugar's Bob Mould all did full album tours in the 2010s celebrating their most popular and enduing works. As for Pearl Jam themselves, they could never fully commit to being a full-on nineties nostalgia act. Their "full album" performances were all one-offs, an unannounced surprise for fans who had assembled for what they assumed was a "normal" Pearl Jam gig and instead were treated to a special event.

Jeff Ament, for one, claimed to not really enjoy "full album" performances, once telling *Rolling Stone* that he's "never been a fan" of the concert gimmick. But doing it as a spontaneous act, rather than as part of a heavily hyped and orchestrated tour, offered a different kind of appeal that played into Pearl Jam's inclination to switch up their live sets. "When we did those albums, we were on the plane going to the show and Ed said,

'Hey, what do you feel about doing *No Code* tonight?'" Ament told the magazine. "And then we basically scrambled and learned the five songs we hadn't played in 10 years right before the show. And it created, like, a good tension."

By choosing to play an album as popular as *Ten* just one time in a random city, as opposed to a proper *Ten* tour, Pearl Jam probably—and not for the first or even the hundredth time—left tens of millions of dollars on the table. But the band's strategy of forgoing short-term gain for long-term sanity and security likely served them well in this instance. Listening to the live Philadelphia 2016 tape, you can hear evidence that such a tour would be both incredible and . . . odd.

It could be argued that practically every concert Pearl Jam has ever performed has been a tribute to *Ten*. More than half the album consists of songs that have remained bedrocks of their live sets: "Alive," "Even Flow," "Jeremy," "Black," "Porch," "Release." While Pearl Jam doesn't have to play *all* those songs every night, they can't get away without doing *most* of them. But *Ten* also contains a significant number of tracks that they mostly left behind in the early nineties: "Once," "Why Go," "Deep." While it wasn't completely out of character for the older and grayer Pearl Jam to revisit those numbers, they didn't fit as comfortably with what the band had become. A frankly juvenile sentiment like "I got a sixteen gauge buried under my clothes" sounded strange coming out of Eddie Vedder's mouth now that he was a man in his fifties.

While Pearl Jam could still capably pull off the biggest hits from *Ten* in their middle-aged years, there was something about hearing those songs played in order by *this iteration* that affected their impact. In the early nineties, Pearl Jam's live ferocity had been likened to Mike Tyson, the combustible heavyweight champion who was more troubled by his inner demons than anyone he faced in the ring. Pearl Jam had their own demons early on, and the tension over whether they would ever be able to overcome them gave their early music a powerful edge. You hear that push-pull anxiety between survival and self-destruction on the albums and the bootlegs, peaking with that June 20, 1995, gig at Red Rocks. Are they going make it or are they going to destroy themselves? In those years, the odds for either outcome were, at best, even.

Hearing *Ten* onstage in Philadelphia twenty-five years later effectively changes the album's meaning. That original "life or death" tension was gone. The chorus of "Alive"—which in the early nineties seemed ambivalent, as if Eddie Vedder didn't care either way about his declaration of survival—was now solidly triumphant. It was also now clear that the guy in "Porch" did safely escape his circumstances, just as Eddie's bandmates were long past worrying about their singer falling to his death after swinging from the rafters during the song's jammed-out instrumental section. In the audience, the generation of troubled kids signified by "Jeremy" were now parents themselves. So was Eddie, which changed the context for the album's final track, the paternal mourning ode "Release." *Ten* was made by a band with an uncertain future—success, or even stability, were far from assured. But Pearl Jam now lived in the best possible version of their own future. They had made it. They were safe now.

What replaced the old tension was a new kind of tension: *Can they still do this?*

The band that had once acted out the rebellion of a generation was now here to provide solace, reassurance, and ballast to those same people as they aged, settled into family lives, and faced the prospect of inevitable loss. The feral energy of Pearl Jam's early-nineties stage show had long since been supplanted by a more reliable and less exhausting form of craftsmanship built for traversing an unknowably long road.

In musical terms, each man played a role. Jeff Ament kept them nimble while also propelling them forward. Matt Cameron locked into Ament with mathematically precise rhythms. Mike McCready played against that exactness with jolts of improvisatory genius. And Stone Gossard held it all together with his battery of red-meat riffs.

As for Vedder, his job remained more or less the same: He anticipated what his audience needed to hear and articulated it back to them better than they were capable of themselves. In that regard, his most crucial moment during the 4/29/16 show occurs between songs, during a speech that takes place before "Release."

Describing his aching tribute to his late birth father, Edward Louis Severson Jr., as a "healing song," he mentioned all the fans who throughout the tour made song requests in honor of loved ones who were lost, an acknowledgment that Pearl Jam's music now was a way for fans to cope with their personal tragedies. In this specific instance, he dedicated "Release" to the brothers of Colin McGovern, a twenty-four-year-old Pennsylvanian who had been stabbed to death just two months prior.

"It's not going to lessen the blow of any kind of tragedy," he says, "but in loud volumes or alone or with a lot of other people sometimes it just helps to get through, because you can't get around it, you don't get under it, you can't get over it . . . you got to get through it."

But this was about more than just one song, or one show, or one shattered family. For Pearl Jam, the tension of *can they still do this?* was now their central animating agent. If you love rock 'n' roll, your favorite bands give your life continuity. They keep your memories alive and accessible. They bond you to your friends. They link who you are to who you were. They endure even as the rest of your life fades into the past.

You see a band you have loved for most of your life, and if they can still move you, then time manages to stand still. But only for a while. And only if they can still do this. Because one day, they won't.

⚡

The song that ended the concert in Philadelphia on 4/29/16 derived from the *Ten* sessions but didn't make the album. It was eventually released on the "Jeremy" single, along with the outtake "Footsteps." But "Yellow Ledbetter" didn't stay obscure for long. The most popular and celebrated B-side of the nineties by *any* rock band, it would also become Pearl Jam's greatest concert closer.

In the liner notes for *Lost Dogs*, Mike McCready cryptically notes that the soaring, bluesy guitar riff is "loosely based on something." That "something" is obviously Jimi Hendrix's "Little Wing," which is so clearly the model for "Yellow Ledbetter" that I wonder if the fear of a potential lawsuit might at least partly explain why the song was kept off *Ten*. Though "Yellow Ledbetter" is also looser and less crafted than the rest of the album. While McCready estimated that the band ran through "Even Flow" thirty times before achieving a useable take, the master of "Yellow Ledbetter" was "probably the second take," he said.

"Eddie started making up words on the spot and we kept them," McCready writes in the *Lost Dogs* liners. "I still don't know what it's about and I don't want to! I love it. Fans like it, too!"

On early tours, a "Yellow Ledbetter" sighting was a rarity. In 1992, Pearl Jam started the year by often playing "Leash" or a jammed-out version of the Beatles' "I've Got a Feeling" as an encore. By the second half of '92, they were frequently closing with Neil Young's "Rockin' in the Free World." In subsequent years, they would also end with the Who's "Baba O'Riley" or the Dead Boys' napalm-spitting 1977 punk anthem "Sonic Reducer." "Yellow Ledbetter" didn't become a regular staple of Pearl Jam shows until the late nineties, though it wasn't always included in the encore. Not until the *Binaural* tour in 2000—when it was played at more than half the shows, and almost always last or close to last—did it finally achieve the status of definitive Pearl Jam concert closer.

While versions of "Yellow Ledbetter" don't vary radically from one show to the next, or even from era to era, it is possible to get a read on where Pearl Jam is at depending on when you hear it. The performance of "Yellow Ledbetter" from 4/12/94 in Boston—culled from the single most tumultuous month in their history, when Vedder was talking openly in the media about breaking the band up in the wake of Kurt Cobain's suicide—sounds raw, slow, and ravaged. The uniquely stripped down take from the 1997 Tibetan Freedom Concert, featuring just Eddie and Mike, is appropriately stark for the spartan *No Code* period. Meanwhile, the poignant and guardedly hopeful version of the song played in Virginia Beach, Virginia, from 8/3/00—their first concert after the disaster at Roskilde—captures Pearl Jam at another crucial nexus point, as does the fiery performance at the close of the 5/3/03 show in State College, Pennsylvania, the capper of their contentious tour paralleling the invasion of Iraq. Vedder marked this occasion by improvising the lyric, "I'd like to wish this war away, and I tried, but it just, just don't happen, don't happen that way / And my brother . . . they sent him off to fight for the flag. I just, I don't hope he comes home in a box or a bag."

Three years later, they played my all-time favorite "Yellow Ledbetter" on July 22, 2006, at the Gorge Amphitheatre in George, Washington, distinguished by McCready explicitly nodding to Hendrix by including snippets of "Little Wing" and "The Star Spangled Banner," the latter of which was a common tag for "Yellow Ledbetter" at the time.

All the while, "Yellow Ledbetter" remained mysterious. What exactly is Eddie bellowing about anyway? During a solo performance on August 7, 2008, at the New Jersey Performing Arts Center in Newark, Vedder finally tried to explain the meaning of "Yellow Ledbetter."

Prompted by a question from the audience, Vedder laid out a backstory that more or less jibed with interpretations of the lyrics by fans over the course of almost three decades. "Yellow Ledbetter" was based on a friend, Eddie confirmed, who received a "yellow letter" from the government telling him his brother had died in the first Gulf War. Eddie and his friend went for a walk, and at one point the "alternative-looking" friend stopped to salute an American flag perched on a nearby house, prompting disapproval from some misunderstanding bystanders seated on the porch.

Taken at face value, this explication of the mush-mouthed and constantly shifting lyrics of "Yellow Ledbetter" does seem to fit with the general tenor of Vedder's songwriting at the time of *Ten*. A young man is dead, and in the process the hypocrisy and ignorance of the adult world is exposed. It is resigned yet accusatory, melodramatic but also incisive, melancholy though with an angry edge.

And yet Vedder's impromptu answer reads suspiciously like an explanation laid down after the fact. By all accounts "Yellow Ledbetter" just came out of them, like all the early songs, before Pearl Jam could ever know or even hope to understand what they were doing. Explaining would always come later.

⚡

Fans love to "solve" the music they love. We dig through lyrics, read and reread interviews, and demand clarity from the sonic murk of records we can't stop playing even after we've long since evolved beyond our teenaged selves.

This book could be construed as an attempt to "solve" Pearl Jam, or to at least explain their popularity and perseverance. Though even I know that there is no pat answer. This band is tenacious. They are talented. They make good decisions, including the ones that looked like bad decisions at the time. At pivotal moments, they have put their mental and physical health above rock stardom. And they have made classic albums, though ultimately they have cared more about putting on great rock shows, which is why playing live remains their most important calling card. Somehow, they're all still alive, even the guys who are no longer in the band. Surely, they are lucky. But they have made a lot of their luck.

Above all, Pearl Jam remains a work in progress. Which is why "Yellow Ledbetter" comes at the end of this book as it does at the conclusion of so many of this band's concerts. If all you had was McCready's bravura musicianship and Vedder's passionate vocals, "Yellow Ledbetter" would simply be Pearl Jam's "Free Bird"—a big ballad with a blazing guitar solo that the most belligerently intoxicated guys in the audience start screaming for as soon as the band hits the stage. But "Yellow Ledbetter" is only 75 percent bravura guitar playing and passionate vocals. The remaining 25 percent comes from the raw material of the moment in which it is played. It's this part of the song that expresses pain over the loss of Kurt Cobain or the fallen at Roskilde, fury at the Iraq War, or wonderment over the sheer beauty of the landscape of central Washington.

It's a song that remains fundamentally unformed. And that's why people still want to hear it because "Yellow Ledbetter" will always sound new, so long as Pearl Jam keeps surviving, thriving, exploring, and living.

The tension of *can they still do this?* is what keeps them alive. But do they deserve to be? There is no question.

ACKNOWLEDGMENTS

Thanks as always to my agent Anthony Mattero and my editor Ben Schafer. Kudos to Corinne Cummings for making sure that everything is factually correct.

I am indebted to the invaluable Pearl Jam fan site Five Horizons and the people who kept it updated with concert information, including Caryn Rose, Jean Burns, Andrew Burns, and Carl Sylvester. I am also grateful for the input from Jessica Letkemann and the brain trust of the Live on 4 Legs podcast: Chris Everett, John Farrar, and Randy Sobel.

I appreciate the work of the following journalists and critics who informed this book: Kim Neely, Cameron Crowe, Jonathan Cohen, David Fricke, Brian Hiatt, Craig Marks, Robert Hilburn, Allan Jones, Greg Prato, Mark Yarm, Eric Weisbard, Whitney Pastorek, and Dave Marsh.

I am also grateful for the following friends and colleagues for their advice and inspiration: Rob Mitchum, Ian Cohen, Derek Madden, Steve Gorman, John Hendrick, and Mark Rackow.

Thank you to Pearl Jam for the music.

Thank you most of all to my family.

INDEX